BUDDHIST PRACTICE ON WESTERN GROUND

Buddhist Practice on Western Ground

RECONCILING EASTERN IDEALS
AND WESTERN PSYCHOLOGY

Harvey B. Aronson, Ph.D.

SHAMBHALA
BOSTON & LONDON
2004

Shambhala Publications, Inc.
Horticultural Hall
300 Massachusetts Avenue
Boston, Massachusetts 02115
www.shambhala.com

9   8   7   6   5   4   3   2   1

First Edition
Printed in the United States of America

⊛ This edition is printed on acid-free paper that meets the
American National Standards Institute Z39.48 Standard.
Distributed in the United States by Random House, Inc.,
and in Canada by Random House of Canada Ltd

Library of Congress Cataloging-in-Publication Data

Aronson, Harvey B.
Buddhist practice on Western ground: reconciling Eastern
ideals and Western psychology/Harvey B. Aronson.—1st ed.
p.   cm.
Includes index.
ISBN 1-59030-093-9 (pbk. : alk. paper)
1. Buddhism—Psychology.   2. Psychotherapy—Religious
aspects—Buddhism.   3. Psychology and religion.
4. Meditation—Buddhism.   5. East and West.   I. Title.
BQ4570.P76A76   2004
294.3′31615—dc22
2003027755

In homage to all the male and female teachers, beginning with Gautama Buddha, down to this very day, who have tirelessly dedicated themselves to understanding the nature of reality and compassionately communicated this to others.

In gratitude to all the psychoanalysts and therapists, beginning with Sigmund Freud, who have fearlessly sought to understand the nature of human subjectivity and the ways in which we obstruct ourselves from living life fully.

This book is not offered as an alternative to psychotherapy, which is called for when individuals are suffering from symptoms that interfere with their social, vocational, or spiritual life. The vignettes presented here have been altered to maintain the anonymity of those discussed and in several instances are fictional composites.

Contents

Acknowledgments

I T IS WITH A SENSE OF WARMTH and gratitude that I recognize all the key individuals who have contributed to the emergence of this work.

My quest began in earnest in 1964 after Richard Alpert came and talked to the psychology club of Brooklyn College about his recent research relating to altered states of consciousness, cognitive psychology, and Oriental mysticism. This was followed two years later by formal study in Buddhism at the University of Wisconsin under Richard Robinson, Geshe Sopa, Min Kiyota, Frances Wilson, and Khensur Ngawang Lekden. There a fateful encounter with Sonam Kazi opened my eyes to the particular riches of Tibetan Buddhist practice.

Beyond my formal academic training, for over three decades I have received ongoing instruction from a variety of Buddhist scholars and meditation teachers. In the Theravadin tradition, I practiced with S. N. Goenka, Robert Hover, Jack Kornfield, Joseph Goldstein, Jacqueline Mandell, Sharon Salzberg, and Nina Van Gorkom.

In the Tibetan traditions, I have studied and practiced with Geshe Wangyal, Khenpo Palden Sherab, Khetsun Sangpo Rinpoche, Geshe Gedun Lodro, Tenzin Drakpa, Denma Locho Rinpoche, Lati Rinpoche, Ga Rinpoche, Khensur Yeshe Thubten, His Holiness the Dalai Lama, Dudjom Rinpoche, Namkhai Norbu Rinpoche, Lama Gonpo Topgyal, Lama Gonpo Tseden Rinpoche, Tenzin Wangyal Rinpoche, Lopon Tenzin Namdak, Tulku Thondup, Khenpo Orgyen Trinley,

Tulku Thubten, Lama Tharchin Rinpoche, Adzom Paylo Rinpoche, Jetsunma Sherab Chontso, and Tulku Gyurmey Tsering.

Much of this collaboration with Tibetans was facilitated by groundwork study at the University of Virginia (1974–1982) with my colleague Jeffrey Hopkins, who served as a portal for my deep exposure to the Nyingma and Gelukpa traditions.

My appreciation of psychotherapy has been nurtured by the therapists with whom I have worked, who consistently encouraged me to look ever more deeply and in new ways into my own psyche and behavior. Professionally, there are all of my teachers, too numerous to mention, in courses, workshops, and seminars, beginning at the Boston University School of Social Work, who have instructed me in a variety of ways to both understand and conceptualize the workings of the human mind as well as to assist individuals, couples, and families as they make their way through life.

Friends and colleagues who have supported and furthered my explorations of Buddhism and psychotherapy include Paul Fulton, Stephanie Morgan, Dan Brown, Steve Joseph, Jack Engler, Larry Spiro, Frances Vaughan, Jacques Rutzky, John Welwood, Tsultrim Allione, David Petit, Dennis Portnoy, Phillip Hauptman, Helen Palmer, Mushim Ikeda-Nash, Nina Egert, Dick Anthony, Steve Flynn, Phyllis Pay, Natalie Maxwell Hauptman, Gregory Graham, Gerry McKinney, Bill Parsons, Jeff Kripal, Mary Rees, and Richard Shweder.

The last three years of intensive work on this book were made possible by a generous grant from the Ford Foundation to Dawn Mountain Research Institute in Houston. Constance Buchanan at Ford, with her deep commitment to cross-cultural understanding, offered particular support for this project.

I want to thank all of my colleagues in Houston, in particular Linda Bell, Barbara Ellman, Newton Hightower, Denise Weinberg, and Rosalie Hyde, for their support. Morton Letofsky and Debbie Ussery of Boulder, Colorado, offered guidance during the latter part of this project and introduced me to the work of A. H. Almaas. Joshua Cutler and Diana Marks of the Tibetan Buddhist Learning Center in Washington,

New Jersey, allowed me to publicly birth many of the ideas in this work at their center in 1995 and have offered their openhearted support on numerous occasions. Steven Goodman was helpful in making suggestions on an early version of the chapter on ego.

Michele Martin and Marianne Dresser contributed substantially through their careful editing of the manuscript in preparation for finding an agent. Robert Forman, Jack Kornfield, Katy Butler, Canyon Sam, Lila Kate Wheeler, Chuck Prebish, and China Galland all offered significant assistance in my search for an agent. Lama Surya Das introduced me to Susan Lee Cohen, who became my agent, and I have so appreciated Susan's heartfelt support for this project. David Bolduc and Jules Levinson guided me to Emily Bower, who was so helpful in getting this work on the Shambhala list and has patiently and skillfully guided me in preparing it for publication. The final version of this work benefited greatly from meticulous editing by Tracy Davis.

I am particularly appreciative of my clients and my students, whose concerns have led me ever to question my own presuppositions and never to rest content with simple answers. They have offered me references relevant to my research and led me to humility in the face of the pain, mystery, and grace of human life.

Finally, my wife, Anne C. Klein, has encouraged me from the start, been a willing listener to my ideas, a stimulating conversation partner, and a sustaining fellow traveler through the ups and downs in the journey of this book. Words cannot convey my gratitude and heartfelt affection.

Introduction

I N THE PAST FIFTY YEARS, a significant number of Westerners have adopted Buddhist practice as a spiritual path. We have learned much from contact with inspiring Asian Buddhist teachers about opening our hearts to others, easing our pain, and getting in touch with our most fundamental nature. Yet there is a dark side to the transplantation of this ancient spiritual tradition to American soil. Buddhist philosophy and meditation practice offer many tools for profound spiritual development, but they do not address all the psychological concerns of Westerners. Without more culturally appropriate interventions such as psychotherapy, even some advanced meditators continue to suffer from anxiety, depression, isolating narcissism, or numbed disengagement.

In the 1970s, when meditation was first taught widely, there was much hope for its therapeutic potential. New evidence showed that meditation contributed positively to reducing the physical correlates of stress such as high blood pressure. In our initial enthusiasm, many of us hoped that traditional meditation would help prevent the emotional turmoil that occurs in our relationships and work lives. When it did not, we often blamed ourselves first, assuming there was something wrong with the way we were practicing. But gradually we also came to ask, Were our expectations of traditional practice out of line with what it could actually deliver? Was something missing from the practices we were doing?

As a therapist and a teacher of meditation, I have seen these scenarios play out repeatedly over the years. Some meditators, overwhelmed by psychological problems, dropped their Buddhist practice altogether, seeing it as irrelevant. Others remained committed to practice and grappled with their problems without seeking professional assistance, sometimes struggling with repeated disappointments in relationships and career, believing that they needed to "practice harder." Still others, like me, sought professional help while continuing their involvement in traditional practice.

But a new series of issues arose for Western Buddhists who entered psychotherapy. Buddhist teachers counsel us to abandon anger, develop patience, give up attachment, and understand the absence of self; this is taught in a context of disciplined communal practice—the sangha. Therapists, conversely, encourage those who are emotionally shut down to experience feelings of anger, and they facilitate the quest for relationship and intimacy; this is done in a context that supports self-assertion and individuality. How are we to follow both approaches? How can we productively understand these inconsistencies? Can they be reconciled?

Answers have not come easily or quickly. Resources for considering these questions in depth were initially lacking. During the last decades of the twentieth century, not much attention was paid to the substantial differences in culture and psychology between traditional Buddhism and modern Western culture. Many of us initially wanted to ignore such issues, preferring what I would now call the culturally innocent position, that the "superficial" differences represented by culture do not matter. Indeed, such discrepancies and their import often do not become clear right away. However, over time they can affect our relationships with teachers, the tradition, and our practice itself. On the other hand, the sensitive exploration of these contrasts can bring to light the unique and valuable contributions that we can cull from both Asian and Western cultures. Such investigation can clarify in a respectful way the manner in which teachings and teachers may not address our particular emotional needs or cultural expectations. For example, a monk who has never had an intimate sexual relationship and comes from a culture where sharing personal feelings is not emphasized may find it difficult to respond adequately to the relationship questions of a Western student who has a deep interest in having a romantic partner and communicating effectively in an intimate relationship. For such students, other resources may be much more productive.

There is no end to the possible misunderstandings that can arise when students from our therapy-oriented culture wish to share their thoughts and emotions with a teacher who comes from a culture that honors restraint and humility. Teachers who explicitly or implicitly encourage such values may seem to be encouraging passivity and self-denial, and this can be particularly onerous to women, people of color, and other oppressed minorities who need to be appropriately self-assertive in their quest for social justice. When unacknowledged, such cultural gaps can cause teachers to misunderstand their students, who in turn suffer feelings of alienation and emotional injury and, in extreme instances, choose to leave. If we lack a clear understanding of our differences, opportunities for benefiting from the profound spiritual insights offered by the tradition can be lost.

In light of the experience of numerous Western Buddhist students in a variety of traditions, it has become clear that integrating Buddhist practice in a meaningful way requires us to move out from under the protective canopy of Buddhism to seek additional perspectives. Combining the skills of nuanced awareness cultivated through meditation with the reflectiveness that comes from sensitive cultural and psychological exploration provides a new opening on the process of adopting traditional practices in a modern venue. Few teachers and authors, however, acknowledge that given our values there will of necessity be enormous cultural and psychological pressure on us when we seek guidance from teachers who value tradition, communal support, discipline, and liberation from this world. Yet it is not a simple matter to discard the habitual inclinations of our personality and culture, and this can prove to be quite an obstacle in practice. For example, many of us, through direct experience with therapy or under its ubiquitous influence in our culture, will use time on the cushion to immerse ourselves in the contents of our mind, rather than observe its process as traditional teachers would instruct. Through engaging in the former, we may indeed further our psychological understanding of ourselves, but we prevent contact with a specific path to deeper reaches of freedom. It is through the mindful experience of such inclinations and a detailed emotional understanding of their workings that we can begin to have some control over the pervasive cultural influences that limit our lives.

This process is incremental. The longer I study and practice Buddhism, the better I understand its traditional context in relation to the psychological emphasis found in modern Western culture. Once we acknowledge our differences, it becomes possible for us to consider if there is something we wish to alter in our orientation. The more differences we can discern, the more opportunities we have to reflect on who we are and what we may wish to become.

Along with these cultural differences, certain predominant psychological propensities and vulnerabilities lend themselves to particular interpretations of Buddhist teachings. Individuals who find difficulty with commitment and motivation often find refuge in Buddhist language that counsels renunciation and nonattachment. Such students see only what they psychologically need to see rather than what is actually there, and consequently they limit what they can absorb from the tradition. Such an approach involves a similitude of spiritual life but prevents real personal change. Are we willing to look patiently at the obscuring emotional issues that we bring to our practice? Can we carefully discard our psychological distortion while leaving the nurturing kernel of Buddhist guidance? I believe we can take a curious, reflective, and wholeheartedly engaged approach to this process.

Buddhist Practice on Western Ground presents traditional teachings that illustrate the fundamental vision of Buddhism—a path to free our minds of limitation and open our hearts—along with cross-cultural and psychological reflections on approaching these teachings in a way that is respectful and appreciative of their—and our—cultural context. Choosing depth over breadth in this work, I have limited my focus to four central themes in Buddhist teachings that have significant yet often confusing psychological correlates: self, anger, love, and attachment. Considering the Buddhist and psychological teachings on these subjects has brought to the surface my deepest questions and led to the deepest positive change I have experienced.

I have felt tremendous appreciation for the breakthroughs provided by my experience of Buddhist practice and psychotherapy and my inquiries into their differences and convergences. Through the various reflections, instructions, teachings, and contemplations offered here, I hope to provide opportunities for Western students to look anew at the meaning and quality of their lives and to enhance and deepen their spiritual experience. In considering our emotional life from both a Buddhist and a therapeutic perspective, I look at ways in which both disciplines can be used to reduce harm to others as well as ourselves, while promoting sensitivity, enhancing autonomy, and opening paths to honest and intimate relationships.

It is my hope that those who are new to Buddhist practice can bring greater clarity to their spiritual endeavors from the start. For those already immersed, this book offers a new way of working with the traditional teachings that can multiply the rewards of practice.

Light and Shadow 1

MEDITATION CAN LEAD US to deep meaningful states beyond the confines of language and personality, yet in the earlier stages this is rare. Rather, our experience is molded by culture and personal background. The following story of diverse individuals at a Buddhist retreat points out how subtly culture insinuates itself into our spiritual lives.

Two years ago, I participated in a weeklong Chinese Ch'an (Zen) retreat attended by both white Americans and ethnic Chinese. At the end of the retreat, the master asked each participant to express what benefit he or she had derived from the retreat. The white Americans spoke uniformly of how the long hours of meditation helped them get in touch with themselves, gave them strength and sanity to cope with the pressures of society, and assisted them in the process of self-realization. The Chinese contributions were very different. The first Chinese woman broke down in tears as she spoke. The week of meditation had made her realize how selfish she usually was; she wanted, right then and there, to bow down and apologize before her family; she wanted to perform some act of deep repentance. The statements from the other Chinese people similarly revolved around feelings of shame and repentance. When the master asked the Americans if they felt repentance, one person replied, with a touch of impatience in his voice, "You always ask me that and I always reply, 'No.'"[1]

Will the "white Americans" be forever consigned to heightening their sense of individuality and thereby miss a different kind of spiritual experience? Is there some way in which the "white Americans" at the end of the retreat feel disconnected from their teacher's line of inquiry yet clearer about themselves and how to be successful within their own culture? Does the Chinese student feel closer to both her culture and her teacher? Is there some way that the teacher, whose culture emphasizes duty, respect for family, and repentance, finds his American students isolated, individualized, and perhaps even proud?

When we assimilate Buddhist practice into preexisting patterns, we merely introduce new content into old forms. This can occur with teachers and students and can show up in adherence to cultural norms or in more particularized reinforcement of psychological patterns. Without knowing anything about the individuals in this story, we can minimally see that the Chinese cultural emphasis on repentance and the American emphasis on strength, mental health, and self-realization both emerge more forcefully in response to the retreat. It isn't possible to say if these experiences will be beneficial or problematic in the long run for the individuals concerned, but we certainly see how the strengthening of particular cultural orientations could lead to a feeling of friction between the teacher and his "white American" students.

On the cultural side, it is helpful to clarify differences between Buddhist cultures and our own in order to make explicit the differences in cultural values and how deeply they insinuate themselves into our experience, including the spiritual. When teachers and students share cultural norms, this can lead to feelings of belonging and attunement; when they do not, it can lead to alienation, a subtle sense of disconnection, and in the worst cases, shame. When we make our cultural values explicit, we can consider how our responses to Buddhist instruction are informed by our own background, reflect on how we may or may not be in tune with traditional teachers' values, and consciously consider choices with respect to differences.

In addition to the enhancement of certain cultural trends—such as repentance and self-realization in the above story—that can occur during the course of involvement with Buddhist practice, there can also be an intensification of emotional issues, some of which may be contrary to our own reigning cultural values but seemingly in tune with certain Asian ones. If we are not thoughtful, we can end up mistakenly reinforcing our less than optimal habits, such as underexpression, feeling pressed to take care of others, defensively withdrawing from others, being puffed up about our spiritual accomplishments, or feeling driven to humility. Due to explicit and implicit values articulated by teachers, we might find support for strengthening our emotional habits. Without considering the variance in our cultural values, we might take admonitions to give up anger, calls for altruistic behavior, encouragement to renunciation, tales of extraordinary efforts by prior practitioners, and instructions to abandon pride as support for any and all of the emotional patterns enumerated above. Of course, none of these patterns is necessarily a major problem in small doses, but when fed by the fertilizer of religious enthusiasm, lit by the sun of misunderstood religious ideals, watered by unconscious fears and drives, and nurtured in the hothouse of communal spiritual life, they can blossom into significant difficulties.

My aim is to prevent such untoward development and to provide a context of understanding that supports balanced growth. First we need to recognize the subtle differences between the intent of Buddhist guidelines on the one hand and psychologically driven behavior that masquerades as Buddhism on the other. With this more finely tuned comprehension, we can make much better use of the tradition to effect spiritual change.

It is unrealistic to imagine that meditation, even when properly contextualized and understood, will free individuals from all their cultural predisposition and psychological patterns. We can, however, expect that optimally we will embody such predispositions and patterns with a greater sense of spaciousness and ease. My experience of accomplished teachers and advanced practitioners has shown me that balanced, relaxed, freshly present, open behavior characterizes Buddhist practice at its finest.

This cultural and psychological perspective was not the way I viewed things initially. What brought me to it?

INSPIRATION

In 1964, when I was a nineteen-year-old junior at Brooklyn College in New York, I attended a lecture by Richard Alpert, then a researcher at Harvard University. Alpert, who later became widely known as Ram Dass, was presenting a discussion of Eastern philosophy, cognitive psychology, and his recent research on altered states of consciousness. As he spoke, he was calm and centered and conveyed a sense of joy. Alpert claimed we can become free of our painful psychological patterns and experience deep love for others.

Everything Alpert said that day spoke to a longing in me that I had never before articulated. I felt I'd been waiting my whole life for this. At the time, I was a star chemistry student, but over the next few months I decided to give up my academic career in science and dedicate myself to learning all I could about the Asian traditions.

Six years later, I was in India doing research on Buddhist materials for my Ph.D. Though I had been studying Buddhism academically for years, it was here that I attended my first meditation course, under the direction of the Theravadin Buddhist master S. N. Goenka.

We were initially taught how to observe our breath, which we did for the first four days. After that we shifted to a careful observation of everything that was going on in our bodies and minds. This was mindfulness meditation, applying focused attention to physical and mental processes in order to understand their true nature. Most challenging were the vow sittings. For this hour, we were instructed to make a firm commitment to sit without moving and carefully observe what went on within.

After practicing in this way for two and a half days, I felt wonderful. My mind was focused. I felt calmer. I believed I had already become a skilled meditator. The very next day, I felt miserable, distracted and uncomfortable in my body. My mind was filled with doubt and frustration. What was I doing at a meditation retreat?

The abrupt shift in my mental state was startling. Though there had been no change in my circumstances, one day I was in heaven and the next in hell. The experience made clear to me the mind's power to shape our experience, whether good or bad. This revelation flew in the face of a belief system I'd inherited unconsciously from our culture, which holds that happiness depends on external circumstances—and particularly material possessions. At the end of that first ten-day retreat, I noticed less internal pressure as I reentered my everyday world. I felt noticeably more at peace, less frenetic.

My commitment to Theravadin mindfulness meditation continued for the next several years. Gradually in the early 1970s my practice turned toward Dzogchen under the guidance of Khetsun Sangpo Rinpoche. The initial stages of Dzogchen meditation integrate mindfulness with visualization, recitation of mantras, and quiet sitting practice. But my forward movement was to face an unanticipated obstacle.

Shadow

In the spring of 1978 I was living communally with several other Buddhist practitioners and working hard to finish enough publications to qualify for tenure as a professor of Buddhist studies. One day, while sitting at tea with one of our visiting lamas, I became very uncomfortable—sharp pains in my chest, pins and needles in my arms. I was breathing very rapidly. I felt as if I were going to die.

A medical examination showed no physiological cause for these symptoms. The internist identified what I was experiencing as a panic attack and offered me three choices: take a prescribed medication to physiologically temper my anxiety, train in biofeedback, or get involved in psychotherapy. I pondered these options. The medication would offer only temporary relief if my internal habits, the root cause of my anxiety, continued as before. Psychotherapy seemed as though it would just stir up more thoughts—and here I was engaged in meditation practice, trying to achieve mental focus with fewer thoughts. Biofeedback, which sounded like it might be closest to meditation, seemed the best choice.

Of course, I was aware that Buddhist meditation is also generally effective in reducing stress. But the short periods of visualization, recitation, and quiet sitting I practiced did not work to counteract the deeply rooted sources of my anxiety and panic. In addition to facing significant pressure to publish or lose my academic position, I also felt a lot of pressure in my relationships with friends and colleagues, though I didn't let myself acknowledge it. For a few months, my ongoing practice was strongly tinged with uncomfortable feelings of anxiety that were difficult to overcome. My anxiety was overpowering my meditation practice.

At the time of my panic attacks, I found it difficult to work and difficult to access spiritual sustenance. I was desperate and could only hope that perhaps Western biofeedback would reduce my anxiety and stress. Yet I experienced another setback. Though I had been successful at the training in biofeedback stress reduction and could create a physiological relaxation response under lab control, I failed the final exam. In the face of an emotionally charged question, I could not quiet down.

My hopes for a simple cure were dashed. Feeling defeated, I decided I had no choice but to try psychotherapy. Perhaps it would give me a handle on what now seemed beyond my control. The potential proliferation of thoughts that I feared was outweighed by the need for relief from my distress.

I began psychotherapy humbled by my biofeedback failure and confused by the inexplicable waves of anxiety I was experiencing. Yet I believed that generally things in my life really were "fine," and I did not think that I was working hard to keep them that way. During our sessions, the therapist would ask me questions about different areas of my life, and I always answered that everything was going well. However, a few days after our sessions, I would notice that I was irritable. Gradually this irritability began to arise closer to the therapist's questions, and I realized that not everything was fine.

My emotional stance in the world was clearly not working. Behind my overall personal restraint was anxiety punctuated by intermittent panic—not a picture of a healthy psychological life. Underneath the altruistic love and compassion I was working to cultivate in my meditation practice were other feelings that I was avoiding, particularly those involving disapproval, disagreement, or conflict.

My restricted awareness of my emotions had obvious physical effects. It also limited my effectiveness at work. My ability to engage in personal relationships was hampered as well because I was unwilling to let myself be fully seen. Over time, I realized that my spiritual development was being adversely affected because of these psychological blockages to direct experience and empathy.

As I continued working with the therapist, I became aware that as I experienced and exposed my feelings in therapy, there was a subtle shift away from the panic attacks. I did not experience a particular moment of breakthrough, but rather a gradual process of uncovering my emotions and a concomitant lessening of anxiety.

The process was revelatory. If my exposure to Buddhist meditation and mindfulness was a first awakening, my exposure to psychotherapy was a second one. I became aware not only of current emotions but also of feelings rooted in much earlier personal history. I recognized that I had been keeping my emotional life at bay, much like a song playing on Muzak—muted, without challenge, not clearly differentiated, and barely noticeable. Through the psychotherapeutic process, I discovered that there was available a complete symphony of feelings— vibrant, alive, and rich with meaning.

Over time, I began to recognize on a visceral level the ways in which I automatically restricted my feelings. I also recognized that meditating amid this restriction led to an experience of calmness, but there was still a subtle controlled holding with a concomitant subliminal sense of disquiet. If, on the other hand, I meditated with my body and energy open, which was increasingly possible thanks to psychotherapy, a broad range of feelings was accessible and I had a more fully embodied experience of presence.

WALKING IN TWO WORLDS

My initial psychological work, though astounding in its efficacy, presented many problems as I struggled to reconcile my Buddhist practice with what I was learning in therapy. Crucially, on day-to-day matters of human emotion, these disciplines seemed to be in direct conflict.

The conflict became apparent during a therapy session. Many Buddhist teachings present injunctions against expressing or even feeling "anger," and I was earnestly trying to adhere to these teachings. However, in this particular session, I began to feel irritated disagreement with something the therapist said, and I was about to voice this when I stopped myself. When my therapist asked me why I was holding my feelings back, I was faced with what felt like a terrible choice—fidelity to Buddhist practice as I then understood it or to the emotional expression of negativity. My therapist, with a clear sense of support, encouraged my self-assertion—which he called "anger."

In stark contrast, a few years earlier I had had a very different experience with a Theravadin Buddhist meditation instructor. I described negative feelings I had toward someone, and, true to his tradition, the teacher said to me gravely, "I'm not going to sit here and condone anger"—by which he meant harmfulness.

It has taken me over twenty years to be able to add some meaningful qualifiers to the different instructions I have received on anger. What I heard in the middle 1970s was a spiritual mentor unequivocally discouraging anger and my therapist encouraging it. I faced what felt like two contradictory approaches to an emotion that was becoming increasingly important for me to understand. Psychotherapy made it possible for me to breathe without anxiety. Buddhism gave me depth of vision and profoundly meaningful experiences. Because of these rewards, I was highly motivated to take both traditions' guidance seriously. How was I to reconcile their approaches to anger, a troubling feeling that I had to contend with every day?

During this period, I found myself facing two divergent life tasks. Inspired by my teachers and my experiences in meditation, I wanted to better understand the whole framework for Buddhist practice. At the same time, due to my anxiety and the difficulties in my personal and professional life, I realized I needed to resolve the issues that were left untouched by following Buddhist practice exclusively.

I now understand that when I began traditional Buddhist meditation, I was expecting too much. I believed it would allow me not only to develop spiritually but also to transcend my emotional and psychological problems. This hope is not uncommon among individuals initially hearing of the potential benefits of meditation.

I have now arrived at a both/and approach: Traditional meditation is beneficial, *and* it may not solve one's psychological issues. Psychotherapy is helpful, *and* it does not necessarily address spiritual concerns. For a balanced psychological and spiritual life, we in the West can benefit from both meditation and psychological assistance. One approach does not preclude the other. At their best, they can mutually inform and enrich each other. In the end, there are also some differences between the traditional and modern visions, and these can be respectfully acknowledged. Engaging in meditation and therapy has led me to a more sensitive appreciation of the Buddhist tradition and a better understanding of myself. My goal is to facilitate a similar process for others, a process that leads to heightened awareness and more nuanced spiritual choice.

Eastern Ideals 2

OST POPULAR BOOKS on Buddhist practice are
ahistorical. They assume that teachings from 2,500
years ago can simply be abstracted from their historical context and directly applied in the present. This makes me
think of the Ladakhi lady I met in India who asked me for a Band-
Aid, which she promptly applied to her forehead to cure her headache.
Hadn't she seen Band-Aids applied where there is pain? Like her, we
are interested in things that promise to work and have little patience
with details. But someone who doesn't understand the germ theory of
disease could end up with Band-aids in some pretty strange places
and miss out on their real benefits. Similarly, without understanding
something of the cultural setting in which Buddhism arose, we can
have unreasonable expectations as to what Buddhist practice can do
for us, and miss out on some of its truly unique contributions.

With time I came to realize that in my rush to learn techniques, I
was not paying thoughtful attention to information about the milieu
in which meditation was traditionally taught. This information can be
useful in considering how to integrate practice effectively and sensibly
into our lives as Westerners. For example, practitioners on retreat who
come from a highly relational culture that also holds retreatants in
high regard may still feel held by the social fabric even though they are
alone in a cave on a mountain. For alienated, isolated urban Westerners, who live in a culture that values independence, going on retreat
may be a very lonely experience even when they're sitting with three

hundred people in a packed meditation hall. We need to address such an issue, and at least begin to create some social net of relatedness; otherwise, students' natural need for connection will draw their attention away from their spiritual life.

Not only is the social container for meditation decidedly different in traditional and modern settings, but it is also the means by which students are able to make use of guidance from teachers. For example, one Tibetan teacher with whom I have studied, Lama Tenzin Wangyal Rinpoche, tells the story of watching a video on Mustang, Nepal, with some of his Western students in Los Angeles. In one scene, Khamtrul Rinpoche, a visiting high lama, tells a local alcoholic something like, "Don't worry, be happy." One of the Westerners watching the video, familiar with the complex psychological interventions necessary to effect change in an alcoholic, said that the lama's kind words were totally ineffective. Tenzin Rinpoche explained that in Asia, because of the respect for the lama and the people's relationship to spiritual authority, these words would offer solace that might diminish the individual's reliance on drink. The video didn't reveal the fate of the individual in question, but the conversation opened a window on the very different places authority may have in our respective cultures.

As this story suggests, in Asia teachers may be able to use their influence to effect change in ways that will not typically succeed in the West. For North Americans, with our democratic, antihierarchical values, sensibility to a teacher's charisma may initially be less effective in altering our lives. This openness to the advice of a teacher then is a cultural resource available in Nepal or Tibet, but not immediately accessible to many here.

On the other hand, we North Americans may have cultural needs for which the tradition has no established resources. Householders may benefit from guidance in expressing our emotions effectively, enhancing intimacy, and finding meaningful work. This is not part of the Buddhist teacher's traditional repertoire.

We may initially prefer to ignore such cultural differences and go after the spiritual rewards of meditation by following our teacher's instructions. We can make progress with this approach at least for a short while. Over time, with more prolonged contact with the tradition, we cannot help recognizing the differences in what is emphasized traditionally and what we consider valuable. Culture is the container within which our most basic daily decisions about life are made. For example, in traditional Asian Buddhist cultures, monasticism and restraint of sexual desire were held in high regard. In contrast, in our culture, pleasure—particularly sexual pleasure—is considered one of the highest goals.

The realization that traditional Buddhist cultures have resources we can't easily access, and that we have cultural needs that traditional Asian teachers can't fully address, is disquieting because it disappoints a deeply felt yearning that we have for an ideal teacher who will address all of our needs. Our frustration can lead to a more active process of spiritual engagement if we can remain involved. We cannot merely passively expect to have perfect attunement between our desire and its fulfillment. We learn that we cannot simply apply a technique for sitting meditation and expect it to improve every aspect of our lives automatically. The process of realizing this provides an opportunity to step back and freshly reflect on who we are, who the teacher is, and what our pursuit of spiritual experience entails.

Some of the questions that arise in Western Buddhist practice are: What is my sense of individuality, and how does my culture value individuality? What is the Asian/Buddhist culture's understanding of individuality? How do I reconcile my culture's emphasis on self-assertion with Buddhist teachings to abandon pride and ego? Can I engage in Buddhist spiritual development in a way that is respectful of the tradition *and* sensitive to who I am culturally and psychologically?

My own understanding of traditional Buddhism has been molded by my contact with Indian, Sri Lankan, Tibetan, and Mongolian teachers as well as study of the Pali, Sanskrit, and Tibetan canonical literature. Much of what I say about the traditional cultures with which I am familiar applies as well to traditional forms of Buddhism in China, Korea, Japan, Vietnam, and other parts of southern and southeast

Asia. Sometimes I will use information about these latter cultures gleaned from secondary sources, if it seems relevant to the themes I am exploring. Of course there are many significant differences among these cultures, but there are some notable ways in which they collectively differ from those of the modern West. And while I recognize that overgeneralizing is dangerous, if we hold in mind that exceptions and variants abound, there is much to be gained from cross-cultural reflection.

With this in mind, what are some of the key understandings and values of traditional Buddhists that will most set them apart from us and cause us the greatest inspiration, bring the deepest understandings, raise the most questions, and/or create the most difficulties?

CULTURAL VALUES OF BUDDHIST ASIA

Traditional Asian cultures influenced by Buddhist thought understand human life as a cyclical process of birth, aging, sickness, death, and rebirth. Birth occurs in one of six realms, among hell beings, hungry ghosts, animals, humans, demigods, or gods. Throughout these rebirths, we are subject to suffering over and over—aging, disease, and the misery of losing what we love and meeting with uncomfortable circumstances. Even lasting pleasure eventually becomes tiresome. And since everything we know is subject to change and disintegration, it is ultimately unreliable and unsatisfactory.

Until we engage in meditation practice and begin to understand things differently, the cycle of rebirth, which is known as samsara, continues beyond our control. We powerlessly cycle over and over, although the quality of our rebirths is affected by the ethical quality of our behavior. The cause of this cycling is understood to be attachment, fueled by our failure to understand in a deep way the ultimately insubstantial nature of all phenomena. However, this powerless cycling can come to an end if we come to realize the impermanent and insubstantial nature of reality and thereby sever attachment at its root. It is one of the tasks of insight-oriented meditation to bring the practitioner to the point where he or she directly experiences—not merely with thought or words—the changing, ephemeral nature of the world and subjective experience. When we directly and profoundly understand the ultimately insubstantial nature of conditioned phenomena, they naturally lose their appeal.

According to the traditions, insight deepens within a context of ethical behavior and a settled, stable mind. Through such an approach, practitioners reduce and eventually abandon clinging, ill will, agitation, doubt, and mental dullness.[1] According to the Theravadin Buddhist tradition of South Asia, with the mind freed in this way, and possessed of such understanding, the practitioner will finally achieve a state of peace called nirvana, ultimately free from cycling in samsara. In the Mahayana Buddhism of northern and southeast Asia, one aims to understand reality and thereby become a bodhisattva or buddha, beings who are free from the powerless cycling and have the ability and commitment to continue to manifest out of compassion in the world as needed, for the benefit of all sentient beings.

While the ethical and meditative practices of the Buddhist traditions can contribute to a better life, their ultimate goal has been to allow practitioners to understand things in a new and liberating fashion. The purpose of practice is not to improve one's ordinary functioning but rather to achieve liberation from samsara altogether.

Buddhism developed and grew in South Asia, China, Tibet, and northeast and southeast Asia, where traditional cultures have been patriarchal and hierarchical: Men held more power than women, and society was stratified, with either male priests or warrior-rulers in control. The primary tasks of men and women were assigned by the culture, and individuals had limited choices in life. Typically, children of farmers went into farming; children of merchants, commerce. The monastic life was one real choice that was open to both men and women, though in general fewer women participated. Religious practice in the home was also possible.

Those engaged in religious practices would seek to embody the truths of the tradition as much as possible. For laypersons, this might include showing reverence for the monastic vocation by offering food and robes to the monks, visiting the monasteries, going on pilgrimage, reciting mantras or sacred scriptures, and observing ethical behavior. Most monks and nuns more strictly followed ethical guidelines of avoiding killing, stealing, sexual activity, lying, and intoxicants. They preserved the teachings via study, recitation, and instruction of both the lay and monastic community, often at the expense of meditation.[2] Practitioners—monastic or lay—dedicated solely to meditation were few compared to the larger number of monastics and laypersons.

In traditional Asian societies, connections of family, village, clan, and territory are extremely important and serve as significant sources of social support and identity.

Marriages are made between members of similar social strata, with property, clan, and class being taken into consideration and with parents typically playing a prominent role in matchmaking. In the Himalayan region, with its highly isolated areas, clan identification may have a mirror image in the religious sphere, where concern for maintaining a religious lineage in some way parallels secular regard for family and clan.[3]

THE SOCIAL SELF: INTERDEPENDENCE

From my own observations of Indian, Nepali, Sri Lankan, Tibetan, Vietnamese, Japanese, and Chinese individuals, I have observed that there is a strong emphasis on social warmth and connection, particularly among friends and family. In their work *Emotion and Culture*, cultural psychologists Hazel Rose Markus and Shinobu Kitayama look at a variety of studies considering the major cultures of Asia and identify a strong emphasis on connection, relatedness, and interdependence. For example, one study that looked at the sense of "we" among Koreans found over half placed a strong emphasis on feelings of affection, intimacy, comfort, and acceptance, whereas Canadians only mentioned affective connection in 15 percent of their responses.[4] Emphasis on emotional bonding seems common to wide areas of Asia. On the other hand, the researchers found that in North America and many parts of Europe there is an emphasis on individuation as a basis for connection. Once two people recognize each other as separate, they then establish areas of common interest through conversation. Here the emphasis is on bridging the gap between two autonomous individuals.

In contrast to this modern North American and European emphasis on the independent individual, we can see in the classic ethical literature of India and China—whose influence spread widely in the region—a delineation of the way in which individuals participate in a system of interlocking duties and expectations. Works such as the Hindu *Bhagavad Gita*,[5] the Buddhist *Sigalovada Sutta*,[6] and the *Analects of Confucius*[7] show a long-standing tradition of valuing social reciprocity where there are explicit rules that articulate the responsibilities that exist between various segments of society.

For example, Buddhist teachers were expected to provide spiritual guidance, and lay people were expected in turn to offer them alms and robes. Writing of India today, cultural psychologist Richard Shweder presents observations that could apply with some modifications to any of the traditional cultures of Asia: "Like most peoples, Indians do have a concept of a person-in-society, but a person-in-society is not an autonomous individual. He or she is regulated by strict rules on interdependence that are context specific and particularistic, rules governing exchanges of services, rules governing behavior to kinsmen, rules governing marriage, and so on."[8] This is a holistic perspective, in which every individual in society is seen in relation to the whole.

Buddhist doctrine reflects and promotes this traditional cultural value of social interdependence. The particular religious contribution of Buddhism to this cultural view is to provide meditations that move beyond traditional secular boundaries such as clan affiliation and universalize a sense of connection and gratitude toward others.[9]

Buddhist monks and nuns were outside the rules and roles of ordinary traditional society. They did not observe caste distinctions and, as they were celibate, did not have arranged marriages. However, their community created its own internal rules, and they had relationships with the larger community—offering spiritual guidance and receiving material sustenance in return. Even if one dropped out of lay society, one was still within a social fabric.

The Buddha went against the social hierarchy of his day, whereby Brahmins by birth ruled the ritual life of Hinduism. He accepted all equally into his religious community, including women, whom he saw as equally capable of achieving the full fruits of a spiritual life.[10] On the other hand, administratively and organizationally, he maintained the gender hierarchy of his day, giving male monks the authority to guide the community of nuns.[11]

DUTY VERSUS RIGHTS/ROLE VERSUS PERSON

When my wife and I were at Gomang Monastery in south India, we met a monk who was blind in one eye. He told us that he had been involved in building a temple that was being readied for a visit by His Holiness the Dalai Lama, and he got so busy he didn't take time to use his glaucoma drops. Certainly there may have been many reasons for this monk's behavior, but his expression of how he valued his duty and the way he seemed unconcerned by the loss of his sight in one eye seemed very different from what one would hear from a Westerner.

This story points out two further distinctions that are helpful in understanding how traditional Buddhist cultures differ from our own: They were oriented toward duties instead of rights, and they were focused more on roles than on individuals.[12] In duty-based cultures, individuals are concerned with the moral quality of their actions: There is an emphasis on behaving properly.[13] In the Buddhist as well as the Hindu world, an individual's duty is understood to be tied to the quality of his or her life experience through the workings of the law of karma. This law provides an explanatory scheme that connects behavior and life events, linking what is considered positive behavior with pleasurable experiences in the present and the future and negative behavior with painful experiences.

A duty-based society emphasizes the roles individuals have—

whether these are family roles, such as "oldest uncle," or professional roles, such as "monk" or "herbal physician"—as well as the duties and social connections of individuals.[14] By contrast, we in the United States today tend to focus on individuals and their rights in pursuing their personal interests. The next chapter considers this contrast further by examining our society's emphasis on the individual.

The Joys and Perils of Individuality 3

A T A THERAPY WORKSHOP in Houston in the early 1990s, Kim Insoo Berg, a noted innovator in family therapy, observed that in Korea, with its strong value on social connectedness, the punishment of choice for youngsters is to put them out of the house—to separate them. She observed how different it is here in the United States where, with our strong emphasis on independence, the most severe discipline is to be grounded—to be kept inside the home, connected.

A CULTURE OF SEPARATENESS

Our values differ significantly from those of older Buddhist cultures, and this affects our relationship to the Buddhist tradition. Over the past several hundred years, we have oriented ourselves more and more to developing our particular notion of the independent self.[1] Until recently, this self has been modeled on the autonomous, individualistic male "self," although the rise of feminism has challenged this.[2] This Western social self is understood to have individual property rights and inalienable political rights. This self objected to traditional religious authority in the Protestant revolution and all religion in the scientific revolution; it revolted against political hierarchy in the democratic revolution of the French and in the colonial rebellion that led to the Declaration of Independence in the United States. And now feminists are revolting against gender hierarchy and the tendency to define ourselves through separation and individuation.[3] Rather than seeing the self as unique and single in opposition to others and nature, feminist authors see value for the self in developing connection and relationship to others. Up until these more recent feminist trends, the revolutionary quality associated with the self in the modern West could be summed up in the popular bumper sticker QUESTION AUTHORITY.

Markus and Kitayama note that the culture of North America as well as much of northern and central Europe is marked by the wish "to separate one's self from others and not to allow undue influence by others or connection to them."[4] This is in contrast to the attuned type of connection prevalent in Asia. We strive for emotional separateness, articulated in the psychological literature as *differentiation*. The couple therapist David Schnarch, in his *Passionate Marriage*, defines differentiation as our ability to hold our sense of identity while in close relationships with others. Psychologically, this depends on our capacity to soothe our own frustration and not absorb others' anxiety.[5] To be distinct is also to be outstanding. For example, William Safire in an editorial in the *New York Times* states, "he stands the tallest who stands alone."[6]

In the context of world culture, however, this is a minority view of how individuals relate. The anthropologist Clifford Geertz characterizes this still dominant model of self-as-separate-from-other as follows:

> [T]he Western conceptions of the person as a bounded, unique, more or less integrated motivational and cognitive universe, a dynamic center of awareness, emotion, judgment, and action organized into a distinctive whole and set contrastively both against other such wholes and against a social and natural background is, however incorrigible it may seem to us, a rather peculiar idea within the context of the world's cultures.[7]

My colleague, poet Mushim Ikeda-Nash, informs me that this model of the individual set against others and nature with its emphasis on personal prominence is contrasted with what she heard from her parents, echoing traditional Japanese mores: "The nail that sticks up the most gets pounded down the hardest."

Cultural psychologists Richard Shweder and Joan G. Miller contrast the culture of the United States with that of more holistic cultures by pointing out that for us, individuals and their unique preferences matter more than rules of correct behavior or a vision of how the parts of our society relate one with another. Our society is based on the idea that we seek, within the rule of law, our own personal, as opposed to collective, wants and desires.[8]

These values have been absorbed into our psychotherapeutic literature. The development psychologist I studied most in training to be a clinical social worker was Margaret Mahler. Her articulation of the goal of normal child development is "separation and individuation": children should grow up to have their own identity and make choices independent of others' influence.[9]

INDIVIDUALITY BASED ON FEELINGS AND CHOICE

Unfortunately, every day in my psychotherapy practice I am struck by the cost of individualism run amok. I particularly see it in the isolation of single mothers, who struggle to find support in raising their children. I also see it in the physical and emotional isolation of individuals and even couples who, often because of moves related to education or work, feel unconnected and lost, a feeling exacerbated by a social environment that encourages independence rather than support and connection.

Influenced by the vision of European and American romantics, many of us today feel that we have a unique, independent journey. With this belief we feel that each person is uniquely gifted and has an individual contribution to make. This differs dramatically from the way people envision themselves in, for example, traditional India, Nepal, and Tibet. Joseph Campbell states this eloquently: "This, I believe, is the great Western truth: that each of us is a completely unique creature and that, if we are ever to give any gift to the world, it will have to come out of our own experience and fulfillment of our own potentialities, not someone else's."[10]

As a consequence of this particular romantic view, the freedom to choose has great cultural significance for us. We feel better when we feel we have a choice in our lives. Therapists frequently talk about how people can make effective and satisfying choices as opposed to feeling powerless and victimized.

In terms of our identity, the way we choose to express ourselves through our work lives is central to who we are and consequently a critical aspect of our mental health. I had my own wake-up call in this regard in the winter of 1980, while studying with Ga Rinpoche in Clement Town, India. When I learned that I had been denied tenure at the university where I'd been teaching, I realized I had lost my career. I wanted to inform the teacher of my situation, but I realized there was no way for me to say in Tibetan, "I have lost my career." I could only say that I had lost my *work*. Over the years I have thought about this. What did it mean that in Tibetan I could say only that I had lost my work? Why did I feel that saying this didn't really communicate my situation?

Slowly, as I deepened my own personal therapy, studied Western views on developmental psychology as well as cultural psychology, traveled abroad, and had lengthy discussions with others, some clarity emerged. I now see how much of what we hold dear is loaded into the word *career* and how hard it is to convey this to someone who doesn't share our culture's romantic sense of individual uniqueness. It is ultimately this vision of an individually chosen career that matches our talents, interests, capacities, and preferences—so central to our culture and so alien to the cultures of Asia—that makes in-depth discussion of vocational choice with native Asian Buddhist teachers a cross-cultural challenge.

Our sense of individuality and our emphasis on personal choice is often striking to foreigners, who are astounded by the array of options presented for eating lunch at a restaurant or shopping for shampoo.

We take this for granted if we haven't visited places where choices are far more limited. The Tibetan lama Tenzin Wangyal Rinpoche reported his utter amazement at seeing grandparents in a restaurant asking their five-year-old grandchild, "What do you want, tomato soup or split pea soup?" In his traditional Tibetan community, children eat what their parents offer them. On the other hand, Joseph Campbell famously counseled, "Follow your bliss"—epitomizing the values of entitlement, uniqueness, and choice that characterize our culture.[11]

As a translator and practitioner, I've had years of exposure to indigenous Tibetan Buddhists, and as a therapist I have noticed that "making individual choices" is not a prominent value for Tibetans. With that cross-cultural experience as a backdrop, and knowing many Buddhists in the United States who use that sort of cultural model as a support for debilitating psychological passivity (even though Tibetans themselves are not, for the most part, passive), I am particularly sensitive to how in our culture the experience and articulation of preference is significant.

In clinical work, this articulation is often a key area in which individuals have difficulty. For those for whom life's goals and choices come easily it may be hard to appreciate how problematic this becomes when exacerbated by emotional problems. I work with people on this issue every day. While there are certainly cultural differences that seem of slight concern, such as drinking tea or coffee for breakfast, not all cultural differences are inconsequential. The ability to make choices assertively, which has its own unique value in our culture, is extremely important in day-to-day life and can be of enormous consequence when impaired.

I once worked with a nine-year-old boy in the Boston area who was severely depressed following inappropriate sexual touching by his father. The boy's desires and preferences had been ignored and trampled upon. He had been traumatized. He had no interest in anything, was pale and wan, was not participating in school, and was unable to relate to the other children in the residential treatment center. During our first two sessions he merely sat in his chair curled up into a ball.

When I invited him to play with toy figures in the sand, rather than telling me a story about them—as most children his age would readily do—he just moved his hand back and forth listlessly like a zombie. He seemed emotionally dead. By accident I came upon one of the advertising inserts that came with my G.I. Joe toys. I showed it to him and he seemed just a bit interested. I engaged him by asking him which he would choose as his favorite. He gave it some thought and finally picked the one he liked most. When he saw that he could safely say "I like, I want," and that he could be heard and acknowledged, he saw it was possible to express himself without being overpowered from outside. He gradually began to involve himself at school and with the other boys. It marked the beginning of his emergence into the world of our community. His recovery took off from there.

The capacity to evaluate preferences and make choices is a critical marker of mental health according to modern Western psychology. In order to know our bliss and be able to follow it, we must be aware of our feelings. Over the past one hundred years, the institution of psychotherapy has emerged to support the discussion, acknowledgment, and validation of feelings. Such emotional skills help create and support our sense of individuality.[12] In contrast to societies in which togetherness rests on extended family, stable identifiable roles, rules of behavior, shared myths and rituals, and some degree of nonverbal emotional attunement, we create relationships through establishing ourselves as individuals and verbally sharing our separate feelings and exploring our free choices with each other.[13] Richard Shweder shaded this a bit further with the observation that in India emotions expressed are dangerous and don't go away, whereas in Manhattan, emotions unexamined and unexpressed are considered dangerous.[14]

Why are these cultural differences significant to those who wish to practice meditation? Because most instructions on meditation have occurred within a larger discussion about the meaning of life, the place of emotions, an understanding of corporeal sensations, and the significance of human relationships and rules for how they are to occur. We can end up seriously off track, especially when seeking guidance from those from other cultures, if we merely assume that we are one with their cultural vision. This is particularly true with respect to their understanding of the significance of emotions, the nature of relationships and career, and the relation of meditation to larger life questions.

Exploring the cultural context within which meditation was traditionally taught may expose us to perspectives we might otherwise miss if we focus only on the details of meditative technique. For example, if we have certain feelings of agitation while meditating, our traditional teachers might recommend dietary changes and herbal remedies— unfamiliar interventions in our culture. On the other hand, we need to be aware that our culture has resources unique to our way of understanding things. Asian teachers would not try to understand the experience of anxiety within the context of our relationships, but it might be extremely useful and culturally acceptable for us to do so.

I had been clarifying some of these considerations in my own mind when I encountered a vivid illustration of how significant and poignant these issues can be for practitioners dealing with cultural disparities. In Hawaii in the summer of 1995, I had just concluded a lecture on Buddhist meditation on death from a cross-cultural perspective. Afterward, an Asian American woman approached me in the hall. She told me she was a second-generation Korean American and said that my observations about the importance of feelings in Western culture were correct. She mentioned with some frustration that she understood that sharing feelings was important, but in the Western Buddhist group that she attended, they just spent too much time talking about their feelings. I suggested that culturally she might be more at ease in one of the more traditional ethnic Buddhist centers. Her response revealed that she had left her Korean family's tradition behind. "Oh, no," she said with great consternation, "they're impossible." Their concern for decorum and roles was not what she wanted to deal with either. This woman, who was struggling to find a nurturing spiritual milieu, highlighted to me that how a community understands the significance of emotions and what they collectively do with them can significantly factor into whether an individual feels comfortable in a particular Buddhist setting. With her diverse cultural identifications, she was finding aspects of Asian and American cultures both attractive and foreign.

While cultural differences might not emerge during a Dharma lecture or a one-week silent retreat, they do with extended exposure to Buddhism. How we feel, what we feel, and how we prioritize what is significant all reflect and serve to create our culture.[15] When we engage in a spiritual pursuit, it is because we have feelings about what is important. Across cultures, the elements of such choices vary significantly. In Asia, one might engage in spiritual life to honor one's parents' spiritual understanding, to show one's willingness to submit to a discipline, or to deepen one's understanding of liberation and become more loving and caring. For us it may be a way to distinguish ourselves from our parents and friends, to settle our anxieties, to become more individually creative, or to feel greater openheartedness and freedom. We seek personal self-realization in a context of deeper belonging. While elements of these two animating visions overlap, their contexts differ markedly. If a young woman from a devout Boston Catholic community decides to become a Buddhist nun, clearly her relationship to her family, her larger community, and the accepted values of her culture will differ from those of a young Tibetan woman who makes the same decision. At the least, we can say that the Tibetan is working with a narrative of cultural continuity and all that this entails; the Bostonian, a narrative of individual choice, autonomy, and perhaps even rebellion.

The way we value family, compliance, individuality, mutuality, tradition, and emotions all shape the way our spirituality will be embodied. Consideration of culture helps us clarify nuances that affect the particular ways in which our spirituality is understood and expressed.

EXPECTING TOO MUCH

One way in which culture affects our relationship with the Buddhist tradition is our expectation that our teachers will comprehend and appreciate the importance we place on romantic love. For several hundred years in the West, our views of individuality, the significance of choice, and the value of feeling have permeated our romantic lives. We have the sense that there is another separate and distinct individual out there with whom we can fall in love, whom we can choose as a mate, and with whom we can share our inner life. We expect and hope that this combination of choice and sharing will enrich, clarify, and further both of our selves.

Our traditional Asian Buddhist teachers are more accustomed to spousal relationships being based on cultural rules and roles; issues of individuality and communication of feelings are secondary or not considered at all. Thus they do not share our views or expectations of relationships, and this brings us difficulty in communicating with traditional masters about friendship and love relationships. Unless they are acquainted with the art of cross-cultural reflection or have listened to a great deal of country and western music, how can they fathom our expectations of romantic love and the meaning we attribute to it? Furthermore, many Asian teachers—though not all—are monastics who have never had adult relationships of sexual intimacy and see celibacy as the most effective means for cultivating spirituality. It is clearly a challenge for a teacher from such a background to hear about our hopes for love or to be asked specific questions about relationship problems that are rooted in our culture's appreciation of feelings. We expect too much of our teachers when we do this.

SEEING TOO LITTLE

The power of our culture affects what aspects of the Buddhist tradition are of the greatest interest to us. Influenced by our highly psychologized culture, we approach the teachings with an interest in optimizing our ability to function in the world. We are attracted to the psychological aspects of Buddhist teachings on calming the mind, simplifying life, and loving one another. Such instructions promise balance to what we feel is underdeveloped in our lives.

A number of practical, useful recent books introduce meditation to a general audience without burdening them with information about foreign cultural and religious beliefs. Some of the most popular are for improving our emotional reactions to illness and stress.[16] The Theravadin commentator Buddhaghosa points out that when the mind is focused, one naturally experiences pleasure and interest.[17] Initially, it is this natural pleasure and interest that allows long, continuous practice of observing something as seemingly uninteresting as the breath coming and going through the nostrils. It is also this pleasure and interest that contributes to a sense of personal well-being in those practicing meditation for stress reduction and healing. This experience of well-being has tremendous cultural value for us.[18]

Furthermore, psychotherapists have extolled the usefulness of Buddhist mindfulness meditation in conjunction with therapy because it allows us to become more aware of our feelings, which contributes to the resolution of our psychological issues.[19] Psychotherapist Mark Epstein describes a special role for Buddhist insight meditation in resolving the "injured innocence" that he identifies as a remnant of certain successful therapeutic experiences.[20] Some form of focusing meditation is recommended for calming and relaxing in the treatment of depression and anxiety.[21] Meditation is recommended in psychoeducational programs for obsessive-compulsive disorder, borderline personality disorder, anger problems, low self-esteem, and marital discord.[22]

More generally, the effects of Buddhist meditation seem to facilitate our experience of a richness in life and enhance our success. Psychotherapist Jeffrey Rubin notes that Buddhist meditation leads to "unselfconsciousness," which he sees as "necessary in such experiences as appreciating art, listening to others, participating in athletics, and experiencing love."[23] As a psychotherapist, I see significant value in these various presentations for enhancing psychological well-being and growth, and I use some of these insights myself.

However, in those books or seminars where meditation as a technique is abstracted from a larger discussion of its original meaning, or when its cultural context is dismissed or ignored, subtle but significant colorations occur. Meditation is being appropriated for the worthwhile purposes of increasing awareness, reducing stress, and enhancing the quality and functioning of our personal lives. At the same time, it gets woven into the individualistic narrative of our lives.[24] Hence meditation, as it contributes to positive internal experiences, can easily become significant in the service of our individualistic agendas for success. Marcus and Kitayama point out that there is much cultural value for us in being outstanding, unique, different, and better. In light of our appreciation of success and emotional well-being, any intervention that even hints at offering personal improvement will be considered highly attractive.

Such considerations affect what is focused on and presented from the Buddhist tradition. Unfortunately, when we are exposed only to what is palatable, approachable, and easy to assimilate and filter it through our cultural presuppositions, we merely become better at what we already do: orienting ourselves toward individual material success. We miss that which is different and unique—a discussion of a profound freedom beyond the ebb and flow of ordinary temporal existence. We see too little.

INDIVIDUAL OR RELATED?

Our culture also affects the way we attend to Buddhist teachings on social interdependence. Buddhism was traditionally taught in cultures where practitioners were linked with the larger society through an understanding of mutual relatedness. Many North American practitioners are embedded in their sense that it is good and right to realize and express individual selfhood. They often use Buddhism to pro-mote their *individual* health and welfare, to heighten awareness of their own feelings, and to allow for more successful individual engagement. When seen from the holistic worldview of traditional Buddhism, such an approach ignores the tradition's rich interpersonal vision of spirituality.

Training in the capacity to experience our lives more fully through mindfulness, to modulate our inner experience through concentration, or to become more successful due to enhanced well-being through meditation will serve to enhance our culturally constructed sense of individuality. We have taken a traditional Asian discipline that was oriented to spiritual liberation in the context of a community and used it to serve our quest for individuality. This is epitomized by a magazine advertisement for Mercury Sable automobiles that shows the seamless and unacknowledged absorption of these practices into our cultural milieu: "There are many paths to reach independent thought. Meditation. Yoga. Calling 888-748-8812."[25]

The value we place on here-and-now pleasure, wellness, and personal success has created certain filters on what gets transmitted from the tradition. The most culturally assimilated works about Buddhist practice do not emphasize acknowledging the spiritual teachers who have maintained the traditions, the significance of the social duties of a moral life, gratitude and love for others as a basis for engaging in meditative practice, or considering our interdependence with others when engaging in practice. Such teachings may be mentioned, but their significance is downplayed. For example, in Tibetan practice, before teachers give any instruction, they typically say a prayer acknowledging the lineage of masters who have maintained the teachings down to the present, and they will often elaborate the history of the teachers who transmitted the teachings about to be given. This is part of a holistic vision that accounts for spiritual family history and ancestry. In addition, every teaching is preceded by a brief homily reminding students that all sentient beings have been related to us and been kind to us in the past, and we therefore owe them a debt of gratitude. Out of this gratitude, we practice with the aspiration to be able to assist others in their wish to be free from suffering and established in happiness.[26] The teacher will explain that the way to do this most effectively is to attain buddhahood ourselves so that we can instruct others in how to be liberated from the cycle of rebirth. In this way, our experience of receiving teachings occurs in a historical context, and our motivation for practice arises from a vast sea of universal care.

When we assimilate Buddhism, sometimes unconsciously, into our concern for our own individuality and happiness, we lose an opportunity to freshly consider how our norms influence our experience of life and whether we wish to alter our perspective. On a social level, traditional teachings that link our motivation for practice with a heartfelt concern for others mirror the holistic vision common to Asian cultures. Markus and Kitayama poignantly contrast the social sources of happiness in Japan with the individualistic ones of modern North Americans: "Happiness and elation are apparently of a different nature in Japan and seem to require an awareness and assurance of connection and interdependence."[27] Spiritually, the Buddhist teachings on interrelatedness take the cultural vision of interconnection and extend it to all beings. Traditionally, practice is to be grounded in a deep gratitude for what all beings are doing now and have done over the course of many births.

My sense is that as Westerners, we yearn for the sense of embeddedness and connectedness described in the social vision of Buddhism. Yet we have some ambivalence as to whether recognizing our relatedness might impair our sense of individual freedom. How do we consider and integrate Buddhist teachings concerning our profound relatedness? How do we build from within who we are, melding new values and insights into what already exists, rather than merely attempting to emulate teachers and teachings from a different time, place, and culture? We cannot go back to earlier models and earlier times, nor can we move in a simple-minded way from an independence-oriented model to a culture of reciprocal relationship. We can, however, begin to seriously consider how values of interdependence can be woven into our hyperindividualized social structure.

Mirrors and Reflections 4

A s we consider integrating Buddhist psychological and spiritual information into our lives, three questions arise: How did we collectively come to this endeavor? What are the broad issues that confront us in such a process? And how do we understand information from another culture in a sensitive way so as to make use of it effectively?

First, how have we collectively come to this? Our major religious traditions in the West have been heavily influenced over the centuries by Enlightenment rationality. Leaders in churches and synagogues influenced by the rise of science and the age of reason looked with disfavor at the mystical practices of the Judeo-Christian traditions—a complex synthesis of ancient myths, sophisticated contemplations, theories sober and exuberant, alchemy both practical and fanciful, and various magical practices. Clearly some of the material did not stand up to the scrutiny of reason, and for the most part the mystical tradition was frowned upon.

With the rise of science, efficiency and industry became ruling values in much of the West. In the United States, this manifests in extremely high regard for pragmatism and extraverted activity in the world. As reason, science, and pragmatic activity ascend, interiority, silence, and meditation find a mixed fate in the religious landscape of the West. In the sphere of organized religion, the monastic and contemplative orders are losing strength. Among the lay population, however, there is a renewal of interest in matters mystical, mythic, and meditative. This is seen in growing numbers of small meditative groups—traditionally affiliated as well as independent—and large charismatic congregations.

The naïve optimism in science that fueled major intellectual and material development for the last two to three centuries is eroding. The horrific destructiveness wrought by science in World War II showed us that "science and reason" are not necessarily either coterminous or progressive, that science must be tempered with values, imagination, and spirit. Thus, the past few decades have seen a search for something more than material comfort supported through scientific progress.

Into this post-Holocaust, post-Hiroshima world has come an ever-increasing flow of spiritual information from Asia, in part fueled by contact stemming from the three major military conflicts with Japan, Korea and Vietnam. There was a further surge of interest in the 1960s due to the widely held though questionable belief that the altered states produced by various chemical substances resembled the meditative experiences of traditional Buddhist practice.

Easier travel to and from Asia, greater access to original source material in the West, and the thirst for more information on Buddhist meditation have all led to an increase in scholarship, translated literature, and popular books on Buddhism. Growing numbers of Asian teachers have been invited here to teach. There are now rich resources available to us to sustain and nourish our interest. As the Buddhist teachings open new horizons to us, we naturally wish to learn more about, understand, and perhaps even emulate our masters' values, behavior, and attitudes in order to optimize the possibility of experiencing their realization as well.

This brings us to the second question. What are the broad issues that come up in such a process? Consider for a moment what we have highlighted so far. In our culture we question authority, value familiarity with emotions, highly prize the experience of romance, appreciate the robust expression of our unique individuality developed through free choice, and develop our relationships through verbally exchanging our thoughts, dreams, personal histories, and feelings. We then approach teachers who embody the traditional cultures of Asia, where continuity of custom and reverence for those who are old and/or wise is valued; relationships are governed by explicit and implicit rules related to the roles individuals play; and closeness is often achieved through intuitive accommodation to others' moods. Within these cultures, feelings and their verbal expression are not necessarily valued, and certain feelings such as anger may even be seen as obstacles. In these settings, spousal relationships revolve around the social connections of the parents and societal obligations to produce children. Within Buddhist culture it is frequently taught that it is important to subordinate oneself and to practice for the sake of others.

How do we negotiate our cultural values with respect to duty, freedom, assertion, individuality, love, and relationships in the face of very different explicit or implicit expectations from the traditions whose spiritual guidance we are seeking, and whose values we seek to embody? If we are honest, we will inevitably find ourselves bumping up against such cultural issues and their psychological offshoots. Even a vague general awareness of our cultural differences can be very helpful in pursuing traditional practice. Ignoring them can contribute to miscommunication, misunderstanding, or a general sense of not fitting. Bringing these cultural conflicts to light and exploring them fosters deeper understanding and new possibilities.

BRINGING BUDDHISM WEST: USING CULTURAL INTELLIGENCE

We begin with the larger cultural issues, which brings us to the third question. How do we adopt spiritual insights from another time and place in a way that is sensitive, respectful, and effective?

When I was a graduate student in Buddhist studies, my major professor, Richard Robinson, said that it was important to understand the cultural context within which any Buddhist teaching arose. He liked to point out that, for example, at the time of Gautama, the term *nirvana* was used with respect to a fire going out, and it was believed that an extinguished fire went into some dormant, unmanifest state, not a state of nonexistence. For Indians of that time, this understanding of nirvana would have been implicit and unavoidable. When they heard that Buddha attained nirvana, they would understand it to be the attainment of a dormant, unmanifest condition rather than some absolute nullity. Knowing this gives us a more nuanced understanding of this important Buddhist concept.

With the resources now available, we are able to explore the contexts within which various teachings arose, consider their meaning there and then, and appreciate how the teachings changed as they moved from country to country. This is not something we need to do systematically; rather, as our interest and knowledge grow, it occurs naturally. In my own deepening consideration of Buddhist instruction, I have found much helpful in the work of Richard Shweder and Jeffrey Kripal.[1]

Shweder identifies four movements that can occur when we consider another culture—a process that facilitates understanding the other more fully and leaves us richer as human beings.[2] He calls this process "thinking through culture."

1. *"Thinking by means of the other."* This refers to our valuing the expertise of other cultures. We see others as having information that can "reveal hidden dimensions of our selves."[3] We do this when we decide that Asian Buddhist teachers and texts have valuable knowledge for us about areas of spiritual experience—for example, how to cultivate meditative states of mind—that we would like to understand and that have been underdeveloped in our lives up to now.

2. *"Getting the other straight."* This involves seeing the internal logic of the beliefs and practices of another culture.[4] We do this when we turn to the tradition to illuminate the techniques of meditation as well as the moral, psychological, and philosophical worldviews in which these teachings are embedded.

This is where I see the greatest misunderstanding when Buddhist teachings are brought to this country. There is often the naïve assumption that an English translation of a term or concept used in Asian Buddhist texts has the same range of meaning as the original. As a translator, I see my task as providing as much background as circumstances permit so that those interested can get the most accurate sense of the original meaning of teachings.

3. *Seeing areas where others may have limitations.* After seeing how the other "powerfully reveals and illuminates," there come times when we begin to realize what the other culture doesn't address for us, its incompleteness.[5] I had this type of reflection when I realized I could not easily articulate the notion of *career* in Tibetan.

Or, for example, one translator states that she searched hard for a Tibetan translation of *sensitive*, meaning to be aware of nuances, but could only come up with "easily ignited," the negative side of sensitivity. She concludes that being open to feelings, which *sensitive* implies, has no easy positive equivalent in Tibetan.[6] This doesn't mean Tibetans are insensitive. Rather, it gives us information about the limits that Tibetans may have in *articulating* the value of sensitivity. In my own encounters, I have found Tibetans to be rather emotionally attuned, at least when hearing about others' suffering, but not necessarily verbal about their own feelings.

Depending on a student's expectations of the Buddhist tradition, observing certain behavior, hearing particular instructions, or discovering some conceptual incompleteness may be seen as a limitation and in some cases it can precipitate a major crisis with respect to her or his involvement. In optimal circumstances, such moments provide an opportunity for extended reflection on the tradition and ourselves. This then is the next movement.

4. *Being aware of oneself in the context of engagement with the other.* This occurs when we consider ourselves in the act of becoming involved with another—observing, reflecting on, and being in dialogue with them.[7] This may occur in numerous ways. For example, realizing that I could not say, "I lost my career" in Tibetan led me to reflect on the importance of this notion to me personally and in our culture as a whole. As I looked into the mirror of Tibetan language and culture, I

noticed not only what was absent from their culture but also what was prevalent in mine. As I saw their culture more clearly, my own became clarified. As I became more lucid about who I am in this culture, I could then elucidate the differences with theirs more clearly.[8] My experience with not finding a word for *career* in Tibetan has helped me to understand the meaning of individuality in two cultures.

I approach Schweder's movements not as a rigid method to be adhered to but as a reminder that we have a variety of ways to approach and consider the various issues of Buddhism. There is some progressive movement here. We tend to be motivated first by interest and curiosity about a particular aspect of Buddhism and then inevitably encounter its limits. If in our exploration we can maintain a sensitive awareness to our own ongoing reactions, we have the opportunity to find out much about ourselves.

This type of reflection about cultural issues is important because unacknowledged cultural differences can lead to alienation and separation. Openly acknowledged, they can fuel curiosity and creative synthesis. As we hold differences in mind, we consider: What is attractive about Buddhism within our cultural frame? How does it complement our values? What in Buddhist teachings differs from our values? How will our culture want to absorb Buddhism? How might aspects of Buddhism challenge our culture?

I had a glimpse of how this can work when my father died. At that time, my friends offered their support by listening to me talk about my feelings. During the same period, when I talked with Buddhist teachers about my loss, I would feel their hearts open, and they would speak about the inevitability of death. Their response was supportive and included a reminder of my existential situation and the significant chance I now have to practice. There was no specific verbal reflection of my feelings, and in some sense I felt that my personal pain was not being acknowledged. I did not experience my feelings being mirrored or validated as I had with my Western friends. I felt something was missing in the tradition. The discomfort I experienced was a challenge.

Through cross-cultural reflection, I came to appreciate that with Tibetan Buddhist teachers, emotional support is often present nonverbally, yet it is difficult for us to discern because we are not attuned to this style of support. Furthermore, these teachers' nonverbal sympathy focused not on validating my individual suffering but on the pain that is my fate as a human being. On the other hand, while my friends held me in the moment, the existential observations of my teachers gave me something to reflect on later. Being told about the pervasiveness of death and impermanence was nothing new, but in that situation it had rekindled significance.

I came away from these experiences around my father's death with renewed interest in the ways we in North America feel nurtured and consoled through articulating our feelings and having them acknowledged, and how the expression of social support differs in other cultures. One of my interests is how to integrate the best of various approaches in a way that is real, authentic, and vibrantly alive. It has been easy to pick up meditative techniques from other cultures and harder to internalize alternative ways of being subtly attuned to others. It is comparatively easy to set aside time to meditate, more of a mystery and miracle to have ongoing tender, quiet openheartedness in the company of others.

Another area of cross-cultural reflection of particular interest to me has to do with "Dharma loneliness," which can be positively illuminated by cross-cultural reflection.[9] For example, someone was telling me recently about his sense of alienation in not knowing people in his meditation group after years of sitting together. They have been silent! This is a powerful example of the dissonance that can occur when a practice from abroad is adopted here without any consideration of the world in which it arose. When we acknowledge both the strong sense of social interrelatedness in the countries where sitting practice arose and our own sense of social isolation, questions begin to form: What do we do with the loneliness that can arise in the midst of our communal practice? How do we address the issue creatively? These questions will be explored further in later chapters.

Numerous other issues present themselves for reflection. What do we need to address in terms of our own values and expectations? For example:

- What is the place of innovation in practice lineages that emphasize the sacred wisdom of scriptures from another era?

- What is the role of individuality in a system that teaches the emptiness of self?

- What is the place of meditation in an extraverted, "can-do" culture?

- Is compassion developed through inner cultivation or pragmatic action?

- How do issues related to gender or sexual orientation play out in spiritual practice?

Some of the most active and creative cross-cultural reflection undertaken to date has addressed issues related to women in Buddhism.[10] When modern Western women come in contact with Asian Buddhist culture, they cannot help being struck by the vast differences in gender expectations between that culture and ours. There have certainly been issues related to sexual orientation as well for those who are gays and lesbians.[11] More recently attention has been paid to issues of race and ethnicity pertaining to the way Buddhism is practiced in the United States.[12] Comfortable in positions of privilege, Caucasian heterosexual men have been able to close their eyes to intracultural issues related to gender, race, and ethnicity a bit longer than women, homosexuals, and people of color. These differences in the way diverse groups of individuals in the West have encountered Buddhism point up gender, sexual orientation, and ethnic/cultural issues that are ultimately significant to us all. All of us can learn much about ourselves through engaging in a dialogue that articulates the details of Buddhist culture and our own culture. This process allows us to see the larger scheme of values and meanings operative in both contexts. If we can sit with the sometimes disturbing tension of seeing the differences in these diverse value systems, we become engaged in a process of personal and spiritual expansion and growth.

Part of the fourth movement articulated by Shweder is to recognize that as we immerse ourselves in another culture, we continue to be changed. We become ever more aware of our own cultural lenses, our presuppositions and expectations. As part of this process of increasing awareness, we inevitably face questions as to whether we wish to alter how we fundamentally view the world. This is not to say that altering our worldview is anything like going into a department store and trying on a new suit of clothes. It entails considered reflection and can involve anxiety and challenge—but also astonishment and wonder.[13] To the extent that spirituality involves enhancing the meaning of our lives and transcending restricted visions of ourselves and others, the process of cross-cultural reflection becomes a spiritual enterprise. As Jeffrey Kripal so eloquently states, "Thinking through others thus leads to a kind of postmodern religious experience in which transformation and transcendence are discovered not within a particular tradition or culture but *between* at least two."[14]

The material presented in this book is a road map of such an approach. I have been concerned not only with developing my particular themes but with presenting a set of principles and processes that can be meaningfully applied to the variety of concerns that arise in the course of involvement with Buddhist spiritual instruction.

Spirituality: Local and Express 5

BUDDHISTS IN NORTH AMERICA find ourselves practicing in a different way from traditional Buddhists. The latter cultivate meditation within a context of correct moral behavior, with a focused mind and an orientation toward liberation from cyclic existence. Along with these aims, we often harbor a dim expectation that we will do personal psychological work during the course of our meditation sitting. As psychologist and meditation teacher Jack Engler states, "With the 'triumph of the therapeutic' (Rieff, 1966) in Western culture, there is . . . a tendency to confuse meditation and psychotherapy. . . ."[1] In the early stages of meditation, as our minds become clearer, our thoughts and feelings become more evident, and there is a temptation to ruminate and reflect upon these now more vivid internal states during the course of our meditation. Furthermore, if we add the stimulus of psychotherapy to our now more evident internal experience, there can be a proliferation of thoughts and feelings. Attending to the content of these internal experiences, however, temporarily moves us away from the focus of traditional practice.

Traditionally, in developing concentration and mindfulness meditation, the practitioner is interested in clarifying the mind and understanding its *processes*. The goal is understanding how the conditioned phenomena that make us up are ephemeral, insubstantial, empty of inherent existence, and unreliable. This ultimately leads to the transcendent states of nirvana, or buddhahood. Even for those who do not reach these lofty ends, deepening practice brings ever more profound contact with internal spaciousness, freedom, and lightness of heart.

Therapists who advocate using focusing and mindfulness skills to assist in the process of free association are orienting their clients toward the *content* of the mind, not its processes.[2] If we harness mindfulness in this way, we are making use of its attentional capacity. However, to the extent that we get absorbed in the content of our minds and our mental associations, we lose the focus on the fundamental changing nature of thoughts, feelings, and bodily phenomena and their lack of inherent existence.[3]

The ability to use the attentiveness developed through mindfulness training to examine emotional processes is very useful in psychotherapy. But as Daniel Brown and Jack Engler point out in "The Stages of Mindfulness Meditation," this alteration of focus, if carried into meditation practice, diverts practitioners from making progress in the established stages of practice.[4] When diverted in this way, meditators are unwittingly converting their meditation cushion into a psychotherapeutic couch, and in the process they may lose sight of their ultimate spiritual goal. Brown and Engler suspect that paying this type of attention to personal content is fairly common for Western practitioners and may mark a major difference between meditators here and in Asia.[5] For us, the individual feelings, experiences, and observations that arise during our practice constitute the very stuff of who we are and our medium for communicating with others.[6] In light of the importance of the emotional details of our lives in making up our unique sense of individuality, the attraction of becoming more intimate with ourselves is easy to understand.

It is likely that we as Westerners, whether in therapy or not, often engage in psychological self-reflection while sitting, using our heightened awareness to deepen contact with our thoughts, feelings, and fantasies. Mark Epstein aptly cites Donald Winnicott's observation that for those of a mystical bent, moving inward away from contact with external shared reality is "counterbalanced by a gain in terms of feeling real."[7] We certainly can feel our experience more clearly as we sit, and psychological insights may arise because we have become more receptive to them. This is very useful for working through specific life issues and clarifying our sense of ourselves. If, however, our meditation focuses only on content, we'll become sidetracked from traditional training and the rich and meaningful insights it can offer.[8] For those working with visualization and mantra, which are designed to affect subtle energy, following one's thoughts will divert awareness from delicate states of mind and energy. In general, getting absorbed in or identified with the emotional and cognitive content of our experience, without continuing to develop balanced observational skills, can leave us at some distance from the freeing experiences that are possible through Buddhist meditation.

As we meditate, we constantly face the choice between following personally meaningful thoughts and emotions and pursuing the unique insights of Buddhist practice developed through mindfulness—*content* versus *process*. The particular value that psychological self-reflection has in our milieu is hard for many Asian teachers to appreciate, and it is therefore difficult for them to acknowledge and clarify the difficulties in making this choice. Similarly, the freedom of liberation is hard for students to appreciate fully, and therefore it is difficult for them to value the wisdom of the traditional approach and give up what is familiar. Let's consider this in more detail.

TAKING THE EXPRESS

When I was growing up in Brooklyn, it was a great thrill to ride in the first car of the subway, standing against the window, hands cupped around my eyes to block out the ambient light as I peered into the mysterious world of the tunnel. I felt the power of the train as we traversed the darkened underground of rails and shadows, occasionally punctuated by green, yellow, or red lights—turning here, now slowing, and then speeding along in the straightaways. I learned early on to hope for the express trains that would take me quickly to my station. It was thrilling to clippity by the local stops between 36th Street and

Pacific Avenue at full throttle on the way to fascinating Manhattan. As I got a bit older, however, I became curious about some of those local stops and would on occasion ride the local, get off the train, and go upstairs to look at the world around the station. There was much to see and learn.

I think of these experiences as an analogy for contrasting native Asian spirituality and what we as Westerners seem to be drawn to in spiritual practice. A traditional Buddhist meditation master will usually begin instruction in meditation with some sort of concentration practice in order to focus the mind and quiet it down.

⇥ Meditation

Set aside twenty minutes with your phone off. Sit in a chair or comfortably on the floor with your legs crossed. However you sit, it is very helpful to keep the back comfortably straight. Keep your eyes closed or just barely open, looking down about a yard away. Notice the breath coming in and out of your nostrils. If it helps, count gently and silently one with the in-breath, one with the out-breath. Count up to ten, and then begin again at one. Whenever the mind wanders, note it with a mental observation, "distraction, distraction," and with some focus bring the mind back to the breath.

After twenty minutes, observe how your mind and body are feeling. Did you have any emotional or creative experiences that seemed to pull for your attention? How easy was it to push these aside? How do you feel internally—calm, rested, speeded up, tired, spacious?

Meditation has the goal of concentrating our attention and is effective over time in quieting body and mind. However, many of us have found that, on some occasions, engaging in such a practice brings many thoughts to mind. We usually want to pursue the intellectual or emotional experiences that overtake us. If we are practicing in order to develop concentration and we go to a Buddhist teacher who is not psychologically sensitive with a report of our reflections and emotional breakthroughs about our relationships or work, he or she will inform us that it is all distraction and suggest that we return to the focus of our meditation. If we are practicing mindfulness meditation, the teacher will tell us to notice the process of sensation, thought, or emotion and not get lost in the content.[9] We may be asked to examine if thoughts are permanent or impermanent. There is a method and a goal, and we are supposed to go straight toward it. It is an *express* orientation, avoiding all local stops, and it poses a dilemma: Do we pursue the aims of developing concentration and understanding the processes of our mind? Or do we pursue the details of the content of our experience? The former is in accord with traditional Buddhist instructions, the latter with our own cultural value of knowing ourselves.

It is clear that in many ways it is extremely valuable to follow traditional meditation instructions: We gain experience in developing concentration and focusing the mind, and ultimately we understand the transitory nature of our experiences. In these approaches, meditation is focused first on tying the mind to its object, then on seeing the nature of conditioned phenomena, with an ultimate goal of experiencing profound states beyond the ephemeral. This is the path of practice, and we are not supposed to get distracted by content. When successful, this approach leads to deep inner peace and freedom. From the traditional perspective, given the brevity of our lives, the sufferings of rebirth, and the rare opportunity to achieve freedom now, the goal of directly achieving deep liberating meditative insight is paramount.

THE DRAW OF THE LOCAL

Over the years, despite the clear directions of my meditation teachers, my mind has from time to time insisted on making local stops.

Whether they are emotional, intellectual, or creative issues, there have been times when whatever wanted to come through during my meditation and appeal to my attention has done so. I've had some ambivalence about such incidents, since they have been personally rewarding but also a move away from the guidelines I was given.

There now are teachers in the West who do not have a traditional perspective on working with the content of thoughts that appear in meditation. They see working with such psychological content as part of the process of moving toward deeper spiritual understanding.[10] A. H. Almaas has developed a highly elaborated system for using emotional material as an avenue to deeper states of consciousness. His psychospiritual process, which includes close work between teacher and student, while not easily summarized, is described in detail in his extensive writings and taped lectures.[11]

Ira Progoff has created a system that can be easily adopted by people interested in using the content of meditative experience as part of an overall program for enhancing spirituality. Progoff, a psychologist conversant with the work of Sigmund Freud, Alfred Adler, and Carl Jung as well as the major spiritual traditions of the East and the West, has developed a synthetic system that creates opportunities for psychological, intellectual, creative, and spiritual insights, albeit in no predictable order.

❧ Ira Progoff's System of Mantra Crystals [12]

We create a seven-syllable phrase that reflects a mood we wish to explore, an event we wish to consider more deeply, or some value we wish to enhance. The phrase could be as simple as "O silence in, silence out." We then coordinate the phrases with our breath, for example, four syllables in and three syllables out. Progoff states that the primary purpose of coordinating the mantra with the breath is to still the mind. If that is what happens as a consequence of using a mantra crystal, its purpose is fulfilled. In his system, however, we are prepared for all eventualities. Once our mind has quieted beyond its ordinary chitchat, we sit with pad and pen in hand and observe our experience. When images, feelings, impressions, phrases, or thoughts come, we open our eyes just enough to jot down our experiences in sufficient detail to refresh our memory later. We sit breathing with our phrase, aware of feelings and images that arise, making brief notations over the course of twenty to thirty minutes. How does this experience compare with just observing the breath?

The material that emerges during this meditation provides us with information about ourselves. If we maintain a journal of such experiences and read them over, we see that our imagery reveals certain recurring themes that may surprise us. Seeing the emergence of such themes over time allows us a larger perspective on our concerns.

During mantra crystal meditation, personal, interpersonal, psychological, creative, or transpersonal issues may come up. Progoff suggests that through working with his system, which includes several types of journaling exercises along with this meditation, we become more aware of the larger transpersonal issues affecting our lives.[13] This is a *local-stop* approach. In a context of personal and spiritual exploration, we attend to every item of content that comes up. Instead of pushing aside the diverse material that emerges during meditation, Progoff encourages recording, contemplating, and processing it.

Depending on our experience, there may be times when it is most expedient to stop and attend to specific material in order to facilitate our progress toward our final destination. Some may wish to linger indefinitely at certain points. The beauty of Progoff's approach is that it is highly resonant with our culture. The value we place on our own unique experience, our individuality, our feelings, and our creativity are all honored in this approach. The contribution of a practice such as Progoff's for someone involved in therapy and meditation is that it takes the numerous associations that can be stirred up by therapy—

which are regarded as distractions by the traditional teachings—and embraces them in a larger psychospiritual endeavor. The internal settling that arises from the gradual resolution of emotional issues, through following psychospiritual approaches such as Progoff's or any ancillary means such as psychotherapy itself, can in the long run contribute substantially to deeper, clearer meditation. Thus, while in the short run a local-stop approach might court distraction, in the long run a nontraditional approach that brings the attention of mindfulness to the internal content of our experience as needed can benefit our overall spiritual development.

One potential drawback to Progoff's psychospiritual approach, however, is that insofar as he does not link himself to an individual lineage, it is not clear whether his method will reach the particular expressed goals of any specific tradition. Progoff uses mindfulness to develop mental stillness and to deepen perception, allowing the mind to focus on whatever arises in a process that acknowledges the transpersonal. Some psychotherapists, however, abstract practices of Buddhist mindfulness from their original context and suggest their use to clients to help them develop focus only on psychological content. Such "techniques" are taught in workshops and books to help settle, focus, and enhance attention. This practice, however, is outside the context of any spiritual endeavor; it is done for the explicit purpose of clarifying and improving psychological functioning. This is no longer a local stop on the way to a transcendent end.

Although such a restricted application of some aspects of mindfulness practice can be helpful, it lacks a spiritual purpose. Individuals learning how to focus their minds in order to access the content and flavor of their internal experience are not necessarily developing a capacity for clear, nonreactive, even-minded awareness. This skill, which is emphasized in traditional mindfulness practice, ultimately facilitates an understanding of the nature of mental processes. For some individuals, especially those with a tendency to ruminate, following such a secular approach and becoming absorbed in the content of experience, particularly without a mentor, could lead to ever-increasing associations.

By way of contrast, developing facility at evenly observing our internal processes provides a way to ultimately disentangle ourselves from spirals of reactive thoughts, feelings, and actions. A consequent upside to traditional mindfulness practice is that it allows us to see how distractions operate in general and to develop our ability to focus the mind no matter what the content may be.

What to do—observe content or process? While some people may be attracted almost exclusively to either traditional meditation or psychological exploration, many of us may find it useful to develop skill in both. I recommend experimenting with traditional Buddhist approaches *and* those such as Progoff's to see how they both work. It is important, however, to decide beforehand what the framework and purpose of a particular sitting will be and to pursue that as much as possible. It is not realistic to expect to understand the processes of the mind, for example, its subtle impermanence, while in the thick of an emotionally absorbing reverie on our father's behavior, or to expect to resolve the conflict with our partner when carefully observing the mental and physical constituents of the sensations associated with our breath. It is important to learn the types of insight that different approaches provide and of course to be curious about the contribution of surprises whenever they occur. It is extremely helpful to discern how the mind responds to different types of focus, and unless we are clear about the approach we have chosen for a particular sitting, we will never receive the benefit of that information. There are things to be learned about intentionality, motivation, continuity of practice, and mystery that can come clearly only if we are definite about how we are going to meditate.

INTEGRATING APPROACHES

From a traditional Buddhist perspective, the potential danger of attending to material that presents itself in meditation is that we might

get trapped in such an approach and forget that there is a larger existential problem that ultimately merits our attention. There are traditional ways to avoid this danger that can be applied to distractions in
meditation as well as to our ordinary experience, to further our spiritual development.

For example, in Tibetan Buddhism, all spiritual undertakings are
framed by our concern for others. At the start of practice, we establish
that our motivation is to further the welfare and ultimate liberation of
all sentient beings. During practice we maintain focus and insight to
the level of our capacity. At the end, we dedicate the merit of what we
have done to the ultimate buddhahood of all. This attitude can be
brought to awareness before obvious spiritual endeavors such as meditating, or before a deliberate act of generosity such as making a charita-
ble donation, but it can also accompany even mundane activities such
as washing dishes. Such an approach can be utilized to maintain our
spiritual orientation during the diverse activities of everyday life, including any emotional, creative, or cognitive endeavors stimulated by
meditation.

For those who practice Theravadin mindfulness, to the extent that
some mindfulness can be maintained even amid distraction in meditation or during subsequent contemplation of personal issues, to that
extent is their practice integrated with their experiences. When the
practitioner is no longer distractedly absorbed in the rush of thoughts
and feelings and can maintain some degree of self-awareness, this indicates the integration of practice into one's life. Beginners often take
their awareness of their distraction as a sign that they are overwhelmed
by thoughts, but it is actually a sign that they are less absorbed in their
thoughts and more capable of observing them.

The Tibetan tradition teaches specific mind-training exercises to
conjoin the postmeditation experience—virtuous and even unvirtu-
ous—to the larger spiritual endeavor.[14] When it comes to intense emotional reactions, difficult experiences, or even pleasurable feelings that
might distract us from our larger spiritual vision, we can use the fol-

lowing versions of mind-training instructions by the nineteenth-century Kagyu master Jamgon Kongtrul to maintain our orientation.

TAKING AND SENDING CONTEMPLATIONS

When we experience intense emotions—conflict, confusion, excessive desire, hatred, or delusion—we become mindful of this emotional state. We create the aspiration to know, acknowledge, and absorb the disturbances of others through our own. For example, in the case of attachment, we make the following aspiration: "May every bit of every sentient being's attachment be contained in this attachment of mine. May all sentient beings have the seed of virtue of being free of attachment. May this attachment of mine contain all their disturbing emotions and, until they attain buddhahood, may they be free of such disturbing emotions."[15]

With positive experiences that might distract us from our larger purposes, we can offer our happiness, pleasure, and virtue to the full enlightenment of all. We imagine white light spreading to all beings, freeing them of suffering, and transforming them into buddhas.[16]

Through this contemplation, what may start off negatively as an internal drive, need, reaction, or constriction of the heart becomes transformed, imbued with qualities of mindfulness, choice, generosity, and openheartedness. This is one of the most immediate and practical ways that I know of for bringing spiritual transmutation to the shadow experiences of our lives. The alchemist's dream of transforming base iron into pure gold is here effected through the quicksilver of the meditative instructions and the heat of the meditator's sincere intentions. This practice cannot be mere lip service; it should be saturated with awareness of what is occurring in our body and mind.

In sum, if we can be present enough to orient our motivation or mobilize our mindfulness, the breadth of our awareness can give us opportunities to convert what might be ordinary involvement with content into deep and meaningful spiritual movement. What might at first seem ancillary or even contrary to our spiritual development can become central. What is initially in the realm of the ordinary can be transformed through contact with the ultimate goal of practice. The particularities of our experience can become part of the journey to the heart of our practice.

Psychotherapy in the Context of Ongoing Buddhist Practice 6

W E HAVE CLARIFIED how the approach to attention in meditation differs from that in psychotherapy, and this naturally leads us to ask, Are there situations in which practitioners can benefit from pursuing therapy? The answer is yes, particularly if relationship issues, vocational choices, feelings of depression or anxiety, physical complaints of mysterious origin, or psychotic delusions seriously hamper us during meditation. While meditation can help to reduce stress, lower blood pressure, and enhance a sense of well-being, it was not designed to address the numerous difficult psychological dilemmas of our era. There are occasions when we need to pursue emotional and psychological assistance from resources outside of Buddhist practice.

For those interested in developing their spiritual practice, it is advisable to focus on emotional and physical issues as they arise. When such issues do come up, consultation with a therapist or other medical professional or participation in a psychoeducational group can be seen as beneficial to the larger spiritual endeavor. While this may be obvious, often when we find a spiritual practice, we feel it should fulfill all of our spiritual and psychological needs. Our teachers may encourage us to think so.

However, many things can happen to us—accidents, acute illnesses, hurricanes, floods, fires, earthquakes, terrorist attacks, as well as major life transitions—and our lives can become so disrupted that finding a regular period to set aside for quiet practice becomes difficult. Or we may experience emotional difficulties for reasons that aren't clear to us, for example, depression or anxiety, that is hard to fathom. In any case, emotional or physical issues that are not addressed can pervade our meditation period with anxiety, agitation, discomfort, or dullness. In such situations, slower is faster—attending to the matters at hand through psychotherapeutic, medical, or other interventions will move us forward, albeit haltingly. Even if it is difficult initially to integrate such interventions into our larger spiritual pursuit, it is important to make use of them when necessary. If we attempt to ignore the issues that seriously affect us, they will usually just knock louder. Under these circumstances, attempts at barreling through, toughing it out, or just practicing more can lead to derailment. Let's look more closely at how psychological issues manifest in our spiritual life, since so many of us start off thinking that spirituality will dissolve all of our emotional problems.

ASSIMILATING MEDITATIVE PRACTICE

In 1978, when beset by panic attacks while maintaining my meditation, I knew I was wrong to regard Buddhist thought and practice as a cure-all for life's difficulties, but I could not immediately articulate why. I have come to understand this through the French psychologist Jean Piaget's concept of assimilation. I was in some significant ways assimilating my approach to Buddhist practice into my preexistent emotional patterns, some of which were not working very well.[1]

Assimilation occurs in young children when they absorb new information into old patterns. Children who believe that all small, four-legged animals are dogs will experience their first cat as a dog. This is in contrast to accommodation, whereby internal structures are altered in relation to external reality, when the child begins to differentiate cats from dogs.[2] Assimilation applies not only to cognitive processes but also to emotional processes, whereby we respond to a present situation as if it were a past one.

During my first years of involvement with Buddhist practice, I was striving to change internally; I experienced some success, but my prior emotional patterns were powerfully at work. Much like a silent malignancy, these patterns were affecting not only my work and relationships but also the way I understood, practiced, and experienced Buddhist theory and meditation. Assimilation was at work.

Early in life I had learned how to hold myself back emotionally. This now led to a restrained, reclusive lifestyle that I could support with the belief that I was taming my mental afflictions of desire and anger and focusing on my work, my research, and my small spiritual community. My early frustrated need for attention was now being played out in an attempt to be a learned disciple, or a "successful" meditator, and thereby gain the approval of my various teachers.

Unfortunately, in the late 1970s there were few resources to help me sort out why my Buddhist practice was not alleviating my psychological discomfort. Some of the earliest psychological studies of meditation were denigrating and simply reduced it to one pathological state or another.[3] The authors exploring the psychological impact of meditation in the 1950s and 1960s, such as Erich Fromm, D. T. Suzuki, and Alan Watts, saw Buddhist meditation as a form of therapy and were extremely enthusiastic about its therapeutic possibilities.[4] Given the issues associated with integrating a spiritual practice from a foreign culture, there was no way that these authors could foresee all the concerns that developed over the years.

In the 1970s and 1980s, when I recalled the literature that equated meditation with therapy and considered my own psychological turmoil amid the practice of meditation, I had to ask, Was I missing something? But I knew I was not alone. During retreats or afterward, friends and acquaintances would be beset by emotional suffering that was not effectively addressed by the way they were meditating nor by their teachers. As a translator, I was sometimes party to miscommunications between students and teachers on matters ranging from relationship difficulties to altered states of consciousness. In the most troubling instances, people were finding no resolution of deeply disturbing states through either their practice or contact with their teachers. In a variety of ways, this was due to the assimilation of new concepts into old patterns: Individuals with difficulty making commitments found it hard to set aside time for practice; those with an inclination to self-recrimination blamed themselves for not practicing; and some who experienced psychotic episodes had painful visions related to their exposure to Buddhism.

My observations have been echoed more recently by psychiatrist Mark Epstein and psychologist Jeffrey Rubin.[5] Both authors in their reflections on psychotherapy and Buddhist mindfulness mention cases of long-term meditators who were suffering emotionally while maintaining a meditation practice. I agree with their opinions that mindfulness practice done in conjunction with therapy can contribute much to the psychotherapeutic endeavor. However, neither author had occasion to address in depth a significant question: Although scientific evidence shows that, broadly speaking, meditation can reduce physiological stress, why is it that meditation in the absence of psychotherapy does not prevent or reduce mental anguish for some people? I would say that this question applies to meditators in all traditions. Practitioners following a variety of traditional meditative disciplines report still having a variety of psychological discomforts, and problems related to work and relationships. They need help beyond their meditation practice.

Part of my intention here is to consider the cultural and psychological context in which Buddhist practice originated and to contrast that with our contemporary cultural milieu in order to understand how this ancient tradition could not possibly address our modern psychological concerns.[6] By looking at these issues in detail here, we may begin to understand more clearly what Buddhist practice uniquely has to offer us spiritually and what we need to take care of through other avenues because of our own cultural and psychological circumstances. The fact that Buddhism cannot address all of our emotional issues may be disappointing. Using cross-cultural reflection to understand why engenders an enriching self-understanding.

Another important consideration is how individuals with emotional patterns that hinder full self-expression often unconsciously seek support from the Buddhist tradition to maintain what are ultimately unsatisfying or even painful modes of existence. Here the process of assimilation is at work in the spiritual context. This type of assimilation, which casts resistance to change in a language of spiritual growth, is a concern for all of us pursuing psychological and spiritual development.

Often in psychotherapy I will see clients who at one level want everything to change but exert enormous effort at another level to keep everything the same. For example, Tom and Elizabeth came into therapy to work on difficulties in their relationship. When Elizabeth confronted Tom about his flirtation with other women and his moodiness, he informed her that he was codependent and therefore she should understand and accept his behavior. In other words, Tom was saying, "I am coming to therapy because I hope everything will change, but let's not try to do anything different." This is the force of assimilation at work: needing a particular scenario, often painful or disappointing to ourselves or others, to play out over and over. Freud aptly termed this the repetition compulsion.

The critical psychospiritual question is how to stop transplanting new content into old patterns and actually start experiencing things in a fresh way. If we cannot do this, we may be pressured or anxious about getting to work, and pressured or anxious about talking to our loved ones, and then pressured or anxious about getting to our meditation cushion. There is a change in that we now know how to sit, yet we stay the same in terms of how we approach our sitting and our spiritual endeavor altogether. In many ways it is easy to assimilate Buddhist teachings into prior psychological habits, but we can also move into fresher, more self-aware engagement with life and in-depth personal development. The first step in this process is to become experientially aware of what until now have been unconscious processes of assimilation. This step can be followed by more grounded, autonomous choices.

How's the Fit?

When I began suffering from panic attacks, it became clear over time that I needed assistance in understanding how my involvement with Buddhism was being assimilated into my prior emotional patterns. I wanted to begin to live life in a new and different manner, yet I did not want to change anything too quickly. In truth, I was lacking an internal compass for working with seemingly contradictory guidelines from Buddhism and psychotherapy, for example, with respect to anger.

Over the years, I have seen many people abandon Asian spiritual practices because they could not endure such perceived conflicts. I have learned to hold the tension between such opposition and see what results. It can be done. I recently received confirmation for my process in *Tracks in the Wilderness of Dreaming,* by Robert Bosnak, a Jungian analyst specializing in dream work, who states: "I've learned from C. G. Jung that the nodal points of soul are the wringing knots of emotional contradiction. The tension of opposites, Jung teaches, is the source of psychic energy. Whenever I suspect a paradox, the least I can do is look."[7]

I was wrestling with the paradox that Buddhist meditation is a discipline conducive to mental ease, yet I experienced anxiety while maintaining my sitting practice. How could this be? During extended therapy, I came to see that my inclination to restrain my feelings hadn't begun with my exposure to Buddhism; behaviors I had cultivated through my understanding of Buddhism were also serving long-standing and outdated psychological needs. I was forced to examine the motivation behind my behaviors and the covert agendas at work in the way in which I had taken on Buddhist spirituality. The episode of anxiety and panic attacks initiated a new era in my life. My earlier vision of resolving all the major questions of my life solely by immersing myself in Buddhist practice began to crumble. My struggle with panic and stress was thus a double whammy. Difficult and troubling in its own right, it also punctured my dream of perfect success.

In therapy I slowly began to consider these questions: How does my spirituality relate to my sense of who I am and my relationships to those around me? How do my psychological issues predispose me to understand Buddhism? Am I being tight in my body and energy? Are my feelings available to me? If not, why not? Can I become open? Am I well served by retaining habitual ways of coping that date back to childhood? How can I appropriately and effectively work with the experience and expression of healthy assertion? And over the years I have asked, How do the guidelines of traditional Buddhist teachings fit in with the views of modern psychotherapy?

I worked with these questions in later years, when concerns related to life transitions and the accompanying emotional issues became more central. My therapy helped me see clearly how I was denying my experience, particularly my experience of negative emotions such as anger, and understand the large price I paid for psychological denial. In order to avoid the self-deception that led to my panic attacks, I was committed to whatever psychological honesty I could muster. But, at the same time, within my commitment to Buddhist spirituality, I was considering whether my reactions or feelings were reflective of or in tune with guidance in the teachings. I wanted to continue to experience the rewards of meditation that I had felt in the past, and I wanted to be a "good" Buddhist for the long-term spiritual rewards promised by the tradition.

During the early 1980s, a variety of challenges and opportunities affected my psychological and spiritual concerns. I was denied tenure as a university professor, I participated in a two-month meditation retreat that deepened my experience, my father died, I left the community I'd been part of for nine years, I trained as a psychotherapist, from time to time I served as a translator, and I also engaged in my own therapy. In this period, I became ever more aware of my own psychological needs and those of my fellow Dharma students. I was also witnessing through friends and colleagues that sometimes Buddhist teachers' compassion and concern for Western students, along with the meditations they taught, were not enough to resolve long-standing or acute psychological distress.

It slowly became clear that despite my longing for an ideal being who could address my every need, the expertise of teachers born and trained in Asia is the content and culture of Buddhist philosophy and practice. The emphasis in Buddhism is on attuning one's life to spiritual principles in order to free oneself from the cycle of suffering and to establish others in freedom as well. Calm, flexibility of mind, and self-knowledge are encouraged within an ethical lifestyle of inner discipline and altruistic behavior. Teachers extol the virtues of living simply, offer ethical guidelines for helping us lead a principled life, and teach us meditations for calming the mind. They are uniquely qualified to offer inspiring advice on compassion and the consequences of excess attachment. When offering deeper teachings, they point the way to understanding the nature of reality and attaining liberation from our cyclical patterns. However, when it comes to the details of modern relationship and career concerns, the differences in our cultural experience and expectations are so great that, aside from their values of honesty, simplicity, and care for others, Buddhist teachers have little to draw on in addressing the peculiarities of our situation in the West today.

Through the intervention of psychotherapy, I came to appreciate the emotional conflicts that I was consciously and unconsciously trying to resolve or eliminate by adopting Buddhist values and meditation. Psychotherapy led me to feel my feelings, whatever they might be. It encourages self-knowledge, self-acceptance, and communication. It promotes the values of conscious, expressive, effective individuality. Through my professional training as a psychotherapist, I became more aware of the expectations of our own culture and how these had been problematic for me and for others who were also attracted to Buddhist culture.

While therapists have been eager to incorporate the isolated practice of mindfulness into the therapeutic process, they have typically not highlighted discrepancies between Buddhism and therapy, at least not in terms of cultural differences. Since I am conversant with some of the original-language source texts of Buddhism, with contemporary Buddhist culture, and with the emotional issues predominant in North American culture through being a therapist, I am in a unique position to consider the textual prescriptions of Buddhism, see how they are lived by modern practitioners in Asia, and reflect on the cultural concerns that can occur for North American practitioners in adopting Buddhist teachings.

At the same time, practitioners in North America face personal emotional issues in taking up practice and these can benefit from extended psychological reflection. The following questions can stimulate and facilitate this process.

ᐁ Psychological Reflections

As I hear teachings, how are they affecting me psychologically? What are my spiritual goals? Are they being met? How does my psychological history affect my aspiration and engagement?

Is there a way in which these teachings seem to fit my personal psychological style? Can I discern any subtle differences between what I am already doing and the challenges of practice? Are there some teachings I ignore? Why?

How does my psychological and spiritual mode of being in the world affect me in my relationships and work? Am I experiencing depression, anxiety, or repetitive disappointments? Am I seeking help for these? If not, why not?

Do the ways in which I internalize the teachings seem to bring me further difficulty? Can I distinguish difficulties that stem from habitual psychological tendencies from those that arise from spiritual choice? Are all difficulties to be avoided? Are any difficulties to be sought?

Can I allow pleasure and success into my life? How and where do I experience these? How does this mesh with my spiritual values?

Am I adopting Buddhist cultural values out of psychological need and in a way that seems to deepen limited assertion, alienation, withdrawal, or dependency? Or is my practice contributing to an air of superiority and alienation from others?

How do indigenous practitioners (whom I know) appear in their lives with respect to issues that concern me? How are my psychological expectations different from theirs? How do such differences influence my day-to-day spiritual choices?

Am I feeling that I have psychological autonomy, freedom, and openness of heart? Are these my psychological and spiritual goals? How does my practice relate to them?

What are my spiritual values and how do I come by them? Am I prepared to question deeply cherished presuppositions?

Do I have psychological concerns that are not addressed by Buddhist teachings? Are my values in conflict with Buddhist teachings or Buddhist culture? Do I have satisfactory ways of considering and holding such tension?

If I have resistance to teachings, can I explore the reasons for my resistance internally or with someone I trust? What happens as I become aware of my resistance?[8]

Do I have resources to consider such questions? Can I discuss these questions with my teachers, fellow students, friends, mentors, partner, or therapist?

While these questions are by no means exhaustive, they can support our curiosity and initiate an exploration that allows us to remain at home in our culture as we begin to import practices from another. With cross-cultural awareness and ongoing psychological examination, our practice feels more grounded. As our knowledge of traditional Buddhist practice and culture continues to deepen and our social environment continues to change, cultural and psychological reflection becomes constant. Within this, we can integrate practice so that it becomes more and more part of our everyday experience. In the light of such reflections, let us now consider the traditional teachings on ego, anger, love, and attachment.

Ego, Ego on the Wall: 7
What Is Ego After All?

ONE OF THE MOST SIGNIFICANT and startling Buddhist insights is that *no self* is to be found in the elements of our experience. When this is realized directly, not as a mere concept but with the full force of a focused mind, it begins the process of liberation. Understanding that our sense of "I" is not as solid, permanent, or substantial as we habitually hold it to be ultimately uproots clinging, attachment, and hostility. Understanding this burns up the fuel that runs our repetitive habits and the cycle of powerless rebirth. Those who have understood this report a sense of spacious lightness and freedom. They exhibit deep concern and tenderness for others.

Yet there is perhaps no other Buddhist teaching that creates more confusion. Experientially, it is often at the deeper levels of practice that the full meaning of this teaching is realized, which leaves beginners struggling for at least an intellectual understanding. In order for us to develop such an understanding, it is necessary to clarify and distinguish several philosophical and linguistic issues. The unique cultural and psychological misunderstandings that can arise in relation to this topic can obstruct any further engagement in practice.

Part of the difficulty in comprehending the concept of absence of self is that its meaning in the languages of Sanskrit, Pali, and Tibetan is very different from that understood from its translation into American English.

THE NATURE OF SELF

Much as the word *habit* means something different to a nun and a smoker, so too the Sanskrit word *atman* (*atta* in Pali; *bdag* in Tibetan) and the English words *self*, *ego*, and *I* mean vastly different things in different contexts. Confusion can occur when we are not mindful that we are taking concepts out of a Buddhist historical and linguistic context, translating them, and depositing them into our own cultural-linguistic framework.

Historically, in India, the discussion of *atman* can be found developing as a central position in the Hindu Upanishads, philosophical expositions roughly contemporaneous with Gautama. In that context, *atman* is best translated by "soul" or "inner self." Leaving aside a detailed analysis of the various meanings of *atman* in the Upanishads, we can minimally say that it is used there primarily as a philosophical term, not a psychological one, in our sense of the word. It occurs in an ontological context, that is to say, in the deep exploration of the substantial or metaphysical substratum of the individual.

Peter Harvey, in his meticulously researched *The Selfless Mind*, states that the picture emerging from the early Theravadin discourses shows the Buddha encouraging his disciples to explore their own experience and see if they can find a self, defined as: "[A]n unconditioned, permanent, totally happy 'I', which is self-aware, in total control of itself, a truly autonomous agent, with an inherent substantial essence, the true nature of an individual person."[1]

For example, consider the following conversation between the Buddha and his disciples:

> What do you think, O monks? Is form . . . feeling . . . perception . . . the conditioning mental factors . . . consciousness permanent, or transitory?
> It is transitory, Your Reverence.
> And that which is transitory—is it negative, or good?
> It is negative, Your Reverence.

And that which is transitory, negative and liable to change—is it possible to say of it: "This is mine; this am I; this is my Self"?[2]

Historically, the endeavor to explore the nature of the self was done in close relationship with another. Even if we go off and spend months or years meditating alone, the questions we work on in meditation come from our teachers. Our internal experience of cultivating insight is ultimately nestled in a dialogue.

Gautama's disciples never do find a self in any of the elements of their experience, and therefore the Pali term *anatta*—"not self"— applies to all phenomena.[3] My Theravadin meditation teacher, Goenka-ji, would often chant the teaching ascribed to Gautama Buddha in the *Dhammapada, sabbe dhamma anatta ti*—all phenomena are not self.[4]

Gautama's revolutionary message, which went against the received wisdom of his day, was that no matter how deeply he probed with the power of his meditative vision, there was no element of the person that constituted or was related to a persistent, permanent self. It is important to recognize here that twenty-five hundred years ago in India, personhood as it is culturally constructed in the West today had not been conceived. Therefore, the Buddha was not oriented to the concerns that we have in terms of articulating our unique individuality. Rather he was addressing a different question: What is the fuel of human suffering? His response was that attachment to a misguided belief in an enduring self fuels it.[5] This belief can be held consciously as a philosophical position, and it is operative at subtle levels of consciousness.[6]

The practice of Buddhist insight meditation aimed at this belief does not explore the contents of personal history but rather evaluates the very nature or essence of personal experience. The Buddha was not merely putting forth an intellectual position. Rather, he was encouraging his students to explore whether any of the aspects of their phenomenal experience had the characteristics of autonomy, permanence, and so forth that would be associated with a metaphysical self. His guidance was leading to a corrective spiritual experience. When one realizes the absence of self, the craving, clinging, and attachment to phenomena that are in service of a purported self become attenuated, and this leads to spiritual freedom.[7]

Buddhist insight meditation is ultimately a radical reevaluation of subjective experience. Many of us initially have difficulty moving beyond the abstract, objective descriptions of our experience, such as I have a "body," or an "arm," to feel the sensations that give rise to those beliefs. This type of exploration opens up a whole new possibility of seeing experience freshly and ultimately freely.[8]

Peter Harvey brings to our attention how subtly and precisely Gautama is depicted in the Theravadin discourses. While engaging his students in the equivalent of a Socratic search for a metaphysical self in personal experience, Gautama did not explicitly affirm or deny the existence of such a self.[9] To affirm the self would have contradicted his realization that all phenomena are not-self. However, his unwillingness to deny the existence of a metaphysical self may be at first somewhat puzzling. When asked by the monk Vacchagotta, Buddha refused to accept the proposition that the self does not exist. When pressed on why, he responded that disciples hearing this might wonder, "formerly my self existed, (but) now it does not exist?"[10] Unfortunately, it is this latter type of confusion that often occurs in the West. It was to avoid just such misunderstanding that Gautama refused to take a categorical position when asked if the self does or does not exist. It is not unusual for people in the West to misunderstand the teachings as leading to "a loss of self." Author Annie Gottlieb observes that some students hear the word *selflessness*—an abstract term common to Buddhist English but with no equivalent to my knowledge in at least the Theravadin discourses—and fear that teachers will take something away from them.[11] Here, students are having reactions due to attachment to their *self-image*, about which I will say more below.

SELF AS A NAME

But if no self can be found in our experience, how is it that the Buddha as well as his followers could talk about themselves and use names to distinguish themselves as individuals? This question is explored in the famous dialogue between the Greek king Menander and the Buddhist monk Nagasena. I am particularly fond of this dialogue, which is the earliest record of an Indian Buddhist trying to communicate with a Westerner. The monk Nagasena tries to clarify for Menander the importance of using the name *Nagasena* without meaning that there is a "permanent individual" implied in the use of his name; a name is just a label and does not refer to any substantial, abiding entity.[12] Nagasena elaborates his point using a chariot as an example, but we can update this and make the same point using an automobile.

If we had a contraption consisting of an engine, chassis, steering wheel, upholstery, and gasoline and it functioned to move us around, would we feel that an "automobile" is a substantial, permanent entity that is somewhere to be found in that arrangement of things, or would we feel that "automobile" is simply a name given to the combination of parts? For Buddhists, "automobile" is just a name given to a collection of parts—it itself has no essence or substance that can be found. The same would be true of "self," "ego," and so on, in relation to constituents such as form and functions such as memory and intention. The functioning of the constituents is evident without the need to attribute substantial existence to the name that labels the whole.

The Buddha and his disciples made use of conventional terms and could talk of things such as chariots—the automobiles of his day—as well as persons. "Chariots" and "selves" are true on the conventional level. When subject to analysis, "chariot" or "self" is merely a name attributed to the collection of functioning parts—it does not exist in an ultimate way.[13]

NO SELF, YET FUNCTIONING

This Buddhist critique of the self does not discount coherent mental operation. The detailed Buddhist analysis of mental functioning called

Abhidharma shows that mental activity can be accounted for without a self. If we are mindful and begin to look at the various functions operative in our mental states, we may notice that feeling, perception, intention, focus, and attention are present.[14] By paying close attention, we may get some sense of the nature of each of these in turn. At the same time, we begin to observe that these are impermanent, arising and ceasing, and there is no permanent self to be found in any of them. The ontological self we presume ourselves to have is understood as a fiction. This is not ontological loss; it is seeing through a misconception. But what a hold this misconception has! During the course of practice, there can be deep fear, profound grief, or other potentially disturbing emotional responses related to letting go of these deeply held misconceptions.[15]

EGO

In modern American English usage, *self* and *ego* are not necessarily synonymous and each has a broad range of uses. Each, however, has (1) a technical psychological use, (2) a meaning associated with pride, and (3) a usage referring to "I."

Confusion occurs when people mistakenly think that Buddhism is negating self or ego in the technical psychological sense. As to the "ego," Freud in the early twentieth century began to employ "*das Ich*" ("the I") as a description of one part of his tripartite psychological structure of ego, id, and superego. This refers to the structure of consciousness that cognizes, thinks, remembers, chooses, exercises voluntary control over impulses, discriminates, assesses, and operates in the world.[16] It is an artifact of translation history that Freud's translator chose "the ego" rather than "the I" as his equivalent for *das Ich*.[17] It has a rather different effect to read psychoanalytic materials and replace "the ego" with "the I." Lay people with only a passing familiarity with Freud's theories tend to reify this ego into some sort of quasi-material thing. Nonetheless, ego in this technical sense refers to a hypothetical structure of psychological functions and entails no ontological claims as to their essential nature. This ego has no physical location in the brain. Historically, there is no way that the Buddha could have addressed Freud's conceptualization. Furthermore, if we look at a content analysis of this technical use of *ego*, the functions attributed to it were never denied in Buddhist psychology, and the evidence suggests that subsequent to realization, practitioners continued to function with the mental capacities that we today would ascribe to the psychological ego.

PRACTICE TO BECOME NOBODY?

In an essay on Buddhism and psychotherapy, psychologist and meditation teacher Jack Engler, a dear colleague, sums up the relationship between psychological development and meditation by stating, "You have to be somebody before you can be nobody."[18] Even though Engler has since clarified the meaning of this statement, particularly with respect to the temporal relationship between psychological and spiritual development and the nature of the latter, the statement is often cited out of context. Without Engler's carefully nuanced presentation, it is exceedingly misleading.[19]

Let us leave aside for the moment the often-debated issue of the implied temporal relationship between psychological and spiritual growth, which I will discuss shortly. In context, "somebody" in the first part stands for a person having some psychological identity and independence, values enunciated by Margaret Mahler in her discussions of childhood development.[20]

It is the second part of the statement, when taken out of context, that creates a grave misperception of the traditional goals of Buddhist practice. Engler himself understands and in fact emphatically argues that the realization of absence of self does not negate the continued existence of the psychological self.[21]

It is true that in order to practice meditation productively, we minimally need sufficient psychological selfhood to sustain self-reflection, maintain personal continuity, apply ourselves, and tolerate a certain amount of frustration—in brief, to be a somebody of sorts.[22] However, we do not need to have completed our psychological work prior to exploring Buddhist spirituality. With successful practice, we begin to realize there is no ontological self in the elements of our experience, even as we continue to function psychologically.

Unfortunately, Engler's statement "You have to be somebody before you can be nobody," taken out of context, implies that with realization there is some ontological loss of personhood or of the psychological self. This is not so. What is lost is the erroneous conception of self. Emotionally, this may be experienced transitionally as a deep loss; however, through realization there is no loss with respect to the reality of our nature, since we always lack a metaphysical self. Nor do we lose our psychological functioning, the "empirical self," through insight.[23] It is this type of easy confusion between the metaphysical self and the empirical/psychological self that prevented Gautama from making a categorical denial of self to the monk Vacchagotta.

When people misunderstand the teaching that no metaphysical self can be found in the elements of experience and take it to mean that we do not have an empirical or psychological self, they are straying into a type of nihilism that Gautama always insisted he was against.[24] Indeed, the core task of meditation is to enhance the psychological functioning of wisdom. Engler himself says, "Clinically, meditation *strengthens* the ego rather than transcends it."[25] As our insight deepens through realizing that the empirical self or ego is ontologically less, we become psychologically more.

In sum, when taken out of context, Jack Engler's epigram is unfortunately misleading. First, it implies that practitioners undergo some ontological loss through practice, when actually what transpires is realization of an ontological status that has always obtained. Second, it does not highlight the psychological enhancement that occurs with realization.

SELF, ONTOLOGICAL AND PSYCHOLOGICAL

How do Buddhist teachings about the absence of a metaphysical self relate to "self," "oneself," or "I"? When we talk of "self," we are talking primarily about a highly differentiated, historical, and psychologically complex individual. There is even a rich branch of psychoanalytic psychotherapy, known as self psychology, that explores the growth and development of the self. Following in the footsteps of pioneers in this field, Arnold Goldberg states of the self: "[T]he pattern of ambitions, skills, and goals, the tensions between them, the program of action they create, and the activities that strive toward the realization of this program are all experienced as continuous in space and time. . . . [T]hey are the self, an independent center of initiative, an independent recipient of impressions."[26]

Heinz Kohut, who is credited with originating this school of psychoanalysis, states: "The self, however, emerges in the psychoanalytic situation and is conceptualized, in the mode of a comparatively low level, i.e., comparatively experience-near, psychoanalytic abstraction as a content of the mental apparatus."[27] James Masterson and Ralph Klein take off from where Kohut began and clearly delineate several specific capacities of the "real self," by which they mean the functioning psychological self. Under the real self's capacity for separation come functions of sharing, commitment, empathy, and intimacy; and under its capacity for individuation come the functions of self-soothing, self-acknowledgment, spontaneity, self-assertion, aliveness of affect, and creativity.[28] Several of these latter characteristics are reflective of the True Self, a psychological rather than metaphysical concept articulated by the British psychoanalyst Donald Winnicott that probably served as one historical source for Masterson and Klein's formulation.[29]

There are several functions of the psychological "real self" that contrast notably with the classic Theravadin analysis of the person,[30] which does not include the specific categories of sharing (of feelings), commitment (in a social sense), empathy (in the sense of understanding another's thoughts and feelings), intimacy, self-assertion, aliveness of affect, or creativity. While sharing, commitment, and empathy are related in some ways to psychological functions such as generosity, love, intention, and right speech, which are included in the Buddhist analysis of mental functioning, the meaning, context, and significance of these three categories are unique to our culture. While affect is addressed under the Theravadin categories of feelings (which are counted as three: pleasurable, painful, and neutral) and conditioning mental factors (such as anger, love, pride, sloth, torpor, and vitality), the notion of "aliveness of affect" is not singled out for discussion in the Theravadin analysis. The remaining three constituents of psychological selfhood enumerated by Masterson and Klein—intimacy, self-assertion, and creativity—are specifically reflective of our cultural values and are absent from the Buddhist account. (The absence of particular functions from the Theravadin elaboration does not mean that these attributes are completely absent from the traditional cultures, just that they were not singled out for particular attention in their articulated psychology.)

Buddhist psychological analysis of the person enumerates fifty-two diverse functions such as contact, perception, feeling, volition, attention, vitality, application, agitation or tranquillity, delusion or wisdom, and so on.[31] It is interesting to note that both modern self psychologists and classical Buddhist authors enumerate functions in their discussion of how the mind or psychological (empirical) self works. While they may differ as to the types of functions the mind/self performs, neither is making claims about the ultimate reality of these functions. In fact, Kohut, in the above definition of the psychological self and sounding much like a Buddhist, says that the self is an abstract concept.

The various Buddhist schools differed somewhat in how their philosophies assessed the nature of mental functions, but they all agreed that the mind operates through the conjunction of a variety of functions without a superordinate personal self that has ultimate existence.

EGO AS PRIDE OR CONCEIT

One way to further clarify the Buddhist teachings on self is to explore in detail how they relate to teachings on ego in the sense of pride. *Ego*, unfortunately, is used to mean both self and pride, and this leads to confusion. Looking at Buddhist and psychological material on ego, self, and pride can give us a clearer sense of the intricate ways in which these relate one to another. In English, the word *ego* can refer to (1) conceit and self-love, (2) our core functions of consciousness (the psychoanalytic usage), or (3) the conscious subject.[32]

Literally speaking, ego in the sense of conceit or pride is not the direct target of Buddhist discussions of absence of a metaphysical self. It is true that a goal of practice is to give up conceit or pride; it is on the standard list of things to abandon.[33] However, in the Pali/Sanskrit texts, pride is referred to by the word *mana* and not by the term *atta/atman* (self). Interestingly, *mana* at core means "measure."[34] In the early scriptures, Gautama glosses *mana* by saying it is the sense "I am higher, I am lower, I am equal."[35] Sometimes it refers to the concept or conceit "I am"—the deep-rooted sense of "I" with respect to all the constituents of the personality.[36] Etymologically this word is connected to the verbs "to honor" (*maneti*) and "to measure" (*minati*) and comes to be related to the verb "to imagine, conceive" (*mannati*).[37] This then covers a range of meanings related to our conceit and false imaginings about our social and ontological status. According to the technical distinctions of the Theravada, pride is a mental factor (*caitta*) that, when present, affects our subjective experience. In that system, pride, though impermanent, is an actual constituent of our experience, one of many possible conditioning mental factors. On the other hand, "self" is merely a concept (*pannatti*) with no actual correlative, no ultimate existence. It is often identified as having all of the ontological reality of a snake mistaken for a rope seen in the dark.[38]

Pride as haughtiness. Pride is present when we are in the grip of some static image of ourselves and our status, when our mind holds on to an inflated sense of "I." Buddhist teachings about pride are mostly moral, as opposed to psychological, in nature. We are instructed to give up a sense of superiority, because it will have negative future consequences. This emphasis on haughtiness is seen in the Tibetan word for "pride," which literally means "I king" (*nga-rgyal*). Holding ourselves as superior is certainly an issue in our narcissistic culture. Work on this attitude can proceed through moral education, self-restraint, psychotherapy, or ultimately spiritual development.[39]

Pride as inferior status consciousness. While pride, or status consciousness, in the sense of "I am lower, or less than" is certainly part of the technical definition of this term in Buddhist psychological literature, this form of self-denigration does not receive as much attention in the literature as self-inflation does. It is precisely this form of inferior status consciousness, a debilitating sense of inability or unworthiness, that is frequently evident in my psychotherapeutic work with Westerners, Buddhist and otherwise. The British psychoanalyst Harry Guntrip identifies this sense of inferior capacity as central to psychological dysfunction:

> There is a greater or lesser degree of immaturity in the personality structure of all human beings, and this immaturity is experienced as definite weakness and inadequacy of the ego in face of the adult task of life. . . . *The struggle to force a weak ego to face life, or even more fundamentally, the struggle to preserve an ego at all, is the root cause of psychotic, psychosomatic and psychoneurotic tensions and illness.*[40]

Self-hatred, which arises in relation to this sense of inadequacy, is extremely common among those who seek psychotherapy.[41] And even among those for whom it is not of immediate concern, it can emerge under acute stress or become clear during the course of therapy. One of the most poignant realizations for us as Western practitioners is to realize that the low self-esteem and associated self-hatred that afflict so many of us and hold us back are extremely difficult for Asian Buddhist teachers to understand and address.[42] Because of its centrality in our experience, and the way it draws energy away from our productive pursuits—spiritual as well as material—healing this sense of inferiority often becomes crucial to the Western students' psychospiritual development.

Pride as the conceit "I am." The concept "I am" is a deep and subtle attitude that is thoroughly abandoned only with full liberation.[43] According to the Theravadin masters, this conceit may be present in many unwholesome states of mind, but it is not operative in every state of consciousness.[44] For example, it is absent when we are present with mindfulness, openhearted in generosity or love, or clear with wisdom. The early Buddhist masters saw pride as always associated with attachment, deludedness, and some element of restlessness.[45] Such states of mind are unwholesome. On the other hand, any virtuous state of mind is free of this conceit.[46]

As we cultivate insight, it becomes evident that the subjective experience of clinging, or fixating on getting something, has a very close relationship to creating and sustaining the concept "I am." Bhikkhu Bodhi, a contemporary Theravadin monk, points out that the conceit "I am" arises from craving.[47] The dualistic tension of want is intrinsically related to creating the sense of "I."

The modern spiritual teacher A. H. Almaas illuminates the intertwined relationship between want and the sense of "I" when he says that desire is driven by a rejection of our present real state that doesn't match our image of ourselves, and an attraction to an ideal image of ourselves that we are trying to make real.[48] Thus, with a self-image of what we would prefer to be, we move out of the real present, as we compare present reality with an image of who we think we should be or what we think we should possess. In a sense, there are two self-images born in this movement—one with a sense of deficiency and one with a sense of imagined fullness. We reject the deficient, desire the ideal, and move out of presence and into a sense of "I."[49] Rejection and hoping are inextricably linked with creating a sense of self. From the perspective of mindfulness, this is the equivalent of the Fall.[50]

We can thus understand in meditative terms that the teaching on the sense of "I am" refers to the *subjective* way we filter and constrict our experience through moving out of presence into a world of concepts or self-images. These teachings complement the Buddhist critique of the notion of a substantial self wherein, objectively, those who critically search cannot find a substantial, permanent self in any of the constituents of experience.[51] Emotionally, when we are clear that there is nothing that is self, we realize that there is nothing to aggrandize by holding on to things and nothing to defend by pushing things away. Our minds become free from grasping or rejecting in a fixated way, and the subjective, static, constricted images of "I" and "mine" can be given up.[52] When thoroughly liberated from the conceit "I am," the fully liberated one "does not 'lean' on anything for support. . . . [H]e has a boundaryless *citta* (mind), not limited by attachment or I-identification, and immeasurable with such qualities as lovingkindness."[53]

GIVING UP YOUR EGO

Unfortunately, some teachers in talking about "selflessness" will conflate pride (*mana*) and self (in the sense of *atman*) and say, "Give up your ego." A complex set of messages are promulgated by this instruction, and interestingly enough they are not limited to Buddhist spirituality, but I will limit my comments to this context. There are two glosses that are often associated with the prescription to abandon the ego.

1. Give up pride, conceit, and arrogance. This is a message that is seen in the traditional teachings. Pride is one of the afflictive emotions, and it is morally desirable to give up a sense of superiority. A more subtle psychological/meditative aspect to the teachings on pride is that as we give up static self-images associated with pride, we get to observe present reality more clearly as it is.[54]

2. Give up self-love, or self-cherishing. Traditionally, favoring or preferring oneself, or clinging to a sense of self or to things as "mine,"

can be related to pride or attachment and ultimately is to be rooted out.

This requires a nuanced reading. For, on the one hand, self-love is valued in Theravada as the touchstone for understanding how every individual wishes to be happy.[55] In this tradition, the meditation on love begins with ourselves.[56] In Mahayana Buddhism as well, there is an appreciation for the way self-love alerts us to how all beings seek happiness for themselves.[57] In the Mahayana meditations on removing the suffering from beings, we begin with ourselves.[58] In these ways, care for oneself is acknowledged and validated in the traditions, and self-love is a ground for practice.

On the other hand, psychologically, individuals with an inclination to self-hate can misunderstand calls to "give up ego," in the sense of self-cherishing, as license for their psychological tendencies to self-recrimination. For these individuals, there is no ground for supporting these teachings in a sensible way.

In addition, there are four common misinterpretations of the call to abandon ego.

1. Give up self-assertion. Psychologists in the West would distinguish between false pride and healthy self-assertion. Traditional Asian teachers, culturally, may not be able to make such a distinction easily with respect to their Western students. Students with issues related to assertiveness may confuse it with "ego" and, seeking to "give up ego," sustain an unassertive posture in life.

2. Give up ego functioning in the technical sense. Without ego functioning, we could not negotiate our lives at all. Sometimes this misunderstanding is related with the previous one to rationalize giving up decision making in favor of passivity.

3. Give up the metaphysical self (atman). As we have seen, it is not that we have a metaphysical self that we give up; rather, we see that such a self cannot be found. We give up clinging to or conceiving of something that is imaginary.

4. Give up being a conscious subject. This is not even really possible, aside from drug-induced stupor. Advanced practitioners clearly are aware and conscious. However, this notion, coupled with the first two misunderstandings, can be assimilated to support withdrawal.

The idea of abandoning ego can be significantly misinterpreted psychologically and metaphysically.[59] Is it any wonder that we sometimes feel confused listening to teachings? Even when people hear the traditional meaning of this phrase, that is, to give up pride and arrogance, cultural and psychological issues can arise when they internalize the teachings.

> The teacher says, "You are too concerned with yourself. Maybe you need to disidentify with your sense of self." The student, although he might outwardly agree, will feel deep inside, "This guy is not talking to me. I am suffering because I feel worthless. I feel my self has no value. I need to deal with this before I can even think of having or not having a sense of self."[60]

As a therapist, I have sat with individuals bedeviled by compromised self-esteem who resist even the slightest encouragement to assert themselves appropriately, saying it would be unjustifiable pride or selfishness. People with severe inner critics or those struggling to develop a sense of autonomy need to deal with their self-blame in the process of cultivating self-assertion. One tool in this larger project can be the practice of mindfulness, in that clarity and acknowledgment of what is present support psychological healing. If mindfulness is relatively strong and self-criticism relatively weak, we can move from being a critic to observing that this attitude is just made up of moments of experience that arise and cease; it is ultimately impermanent and insubstantial.[61] In this disidentification there is a newfound freedom.

ABANDONING PRIDE, DO I LOSE MY VOICE?

In the spring of 2000, I gave a Dharma talk on the East Coast, in which I spoke about the Buddhist understanding of pride and that ultimately it is given up. Afterward, a longtime practitioner asked me, "I spent twelve years finding my voice in therapy. How does that fit with this talk you just gave about pride and giving up a sense of 'I am higher,' 'I am lower,' or 'I am'?" This is an excellent question. It encapsulates the way we in the West will inevitably place Buddhist philosophical teachings within our own psychological frame. Initially, the tradition looks to be on a collision course with our psychological work toward achieving a fluid expression of our selfhood. We need to distinguish our modern Western discussion of healthy self-assertion from the traditional moral/philosophical/meditative narrative related to abandoning pride that is ultimately based on understanding the absence of a metaphysical self. The Buddhist critique of pride is specifically based on the error of holding to a permanent, substantially existent, conceptually static "I."

As frequently as Buddhist teachers deny that an ultimate self can be found and say that the very constituents of our experience are empty of solidity, permanence, and substantiality, so too do they eventually confirm conventional experience within an understanding that it has no ultimacy. In the famous *Heart Sutra* of Mahayana Buddhism, the solidity of form is questioned with the teaching "Form is emptiness," yet nihilism is refuted through an assertion of the functioning of conventional reality, as "Emptiness also is form."[62] When Khetsun Rinpoche says to me, "There is no self," I experience this in the context of his aliveness, his coherence, his history, and his capacity for asserting, "Emptiness is form." We may not exist with as much permanence and solidity as we would like, but we do not fail to function at all.

Psychological work is aimed at improving our functioning. I have explored with clients their psychological need to feel higher or lower than others, and they get less stuck in the reactive need to adopt either of these positions. They grow more familiar with appropriate self-assertion. As a therapist, I see clients needing to develop a clearer sense of internal value and personal agency. This is particularly true of women and men who have been abused, neglected, or raised by alcoholic parents. Such people begin therapy with a persistent need to take care of others and feel unentitled to make legitimate requests for themselves. Such a capacity falls under Klein and Masterson's functions of the real psychological self in terms of aliveness of affect, self-acknowledgment, self-activation, and self-assertion.[63] These functions include the psychological sense of "I am."

Certainly at the end of any successful therapy, we would hope that a client could say, "I am." And from what I can see, this psychological capacity is not absent among the enlightened. They have understood that there is no self to be found in the constituents of their experience, which is an ontological realization. They therefore do not hold the "I" to be permanent or substantial, yet they are quite capable of full psychological functioning and using conventional language to refer to their empirical functioning self. A look at any discourse shows Gautama, who is identified as one who has understood things in the way they are (*Tathagata*), clearly asserting himself. However, healthy self-assertion is not singled out for discussion in Buddhist psychology. We can identify its presence by reading between the lines. The following excerpt is particularly noteworthy because it shows Gautama being assertive about having given up pride, indicating that assertion can occur without pride: "I say the Tathagata [Gautama] is liberated through the destruction, fading away . . . of all imaginings, all mental churnings, all predispositions to pride or conceit (*mana*) such as constructing an 'I' or 'mine.'"[64] As this passage shows, Gautama has agency ("I say"), identity ("the Tathagata"), self-assertion ("is liberated"), and self-expression. While he psychologically identifies his uniqueness and functioning (an empirical, functioning "I"), he is not holding or being bound by any concepts of substantiality or permanence (a metaphysical "I"); he is free of pride. One way to understand the Buddhist usage of pride in the sense of "I am higher, lower, or

equal," or "I am," is that these constitute what are called self-representations in psychoanalytic literature.[65]

Self-representations are subtle, fixed lenses through which we experience ourselves, for example, such tightly held beliefs as "I am entitled
to be cared for by others" or "I am incapable of initiating activities
that may put me in a positive light." Such lenses prevent us from
having direct, unmediated contact with reality.[66] The message in the
Buddhist teachings on pride is that identifying with self-images is an
obstacle to being immediately and directly present.[67] The enlightened,
by way of contrast, are not obstructed by any coarse or subtle sense of
themselves, yet at the same time they are able to retain a functioning
sense of identity.

In the Buddhist context, we can understand the process of spiritual
development as a process of (1) disidentifying from unchanging, con-
stricting self-images and thus (2) seeing things ever more clearly as
they are, while (3) still being able to sustain, though not in a limiting
way, a sense of psychological identity. This is a more psychological—as
opposed to the traditional moral/philosophical—way of describing the
Buddhist path of concentration, mindfulness, and insight leading to
an understanding that the constituents of our experience cannot be
identified as self, nor are they related to self.

When we consider personal development from the perspective of
self-representation, we can see that psychotherapy is oriented toward
preventing us from staying stuck in rigid roles of superior or inferior.
For example, in order to weaken a sense of inferiority, therapeutic
interventions help clients gain flexibility about who they are through
disidentifying from a sense of deficiency. These interventions include
but are not limited to affirming the client's inherent value through
positive attachment in the therapeutic relationship; making conscious
in an emotively significant way the historical antecedents to his or
her current sense of self, which leads to more personal freedom; and
attending to overlooked strengths. Buddhist practice takes disidentification a step further, in that it leads to states of being that are free
from being bound by such identifications altogether.

To the longtime practitioner who asked about the relationship between therapy, finding her voice, and Buddhist teachings on pride, I would now say that developing flexibility in feeling competent is extremely important if we have been stuck in a rigid self-image of unworthiness. As a complement to this, the process of meditation and spiritual development allows us ultimately to disidentify from any self-representation and move into clearly and directly seeing things as they are.[68]

· The relationship between Buddhist meditation and flexibility of self-representation is complex, however, because practitioners clearly can make some progress in giving up certain kinds of self-representation while still being limited through others. A number of authors have pointed out that it is quite possible for students (and teachers) of meditation to have the initial realization that self-representations have no substantial basis—an ontological realization—while retaining areas of less than optimum psychological flexibility.[69] In the initial stages of practice, individuals can understand in some ways that no self is to be found in the constituents of our experience, yet retain behavior patterns that are governed by identification with a static self-image. In theory, at the conclusion of the spiritual path, practitioners will have become free from filtering experience through dualistic, limiting concepts such as "I'm a superior practitioner," or "I can't make any progress," or the most subtle, static "I am."

This then is the Buddhist context within which it makes sense to talk of abandoning the sense of "I am." One is giving up the automatic, reactive, inflexible identification with and attachment to self-representations. Because of this, the sage is said to see things "as they are" (*yathabhutam*); and the Buddha is called "One who has understood things just as they are" (*Tathagata*). Those who have realized things as they are can still use names and labels such as "I" or "Tathagata" to refer to themselves, but they are not bound by them internally. Their sense of identity and their psychological functioning do not imply any investment in a sense of ontological substantiality.

Because the Western psychotherapeutic venture of creating flexibility in self-image differs in context, language, and modes of intervention from the traditional Buddhist goal of ultimately giving up limitations associated with self-representations, I think it is well to assume that individuals engaged in both endeavors may from time to time hear prescriptions that seem to conflict. However, to regard therapy as oriented toward *loosening*, and Buddhist insight practice as oriented toward *freeing ourselves from*, fixed self-images provides a productive way for understanding the relationship between them.[70]

NEWTONIAN AND QUANTUM PERSPECTIVES

We in the West who are engaged in personal growth face a variety of psychological and spiritual tasks. Those with a disorganized sense of self can benefit from creating some sense of coherence. For those with inhibited or inflated self-representations, therapy can provide an opportunity for opening into a more flexible experience of themselves. In addition to these psychological tasks, spiritual work and insight can affect how tightly we hold our view of ourselves and the quality of spaciousness in our experience, and it can ultimately lead to states that are free from these distorting lenses.

How do we integrate the discourse of psychotherapy, which deals with flexibility of self-representation, and that of the traditional meditation literature, which speaks of giving up self-representation altogether? As therapy deals with relationships between individuals, it is often a macro, or we could say a Newtonian, type of intervention. On the other hand, those meditations oriented to careful epistemological inquiry are often micro investigations, or, to borrow a term from modern physics, quantumlike. Physicists recognize the efficacy of Newtonian and quantum modes of describing the world, even though two very different sets of principles predict the operation of macro and micro reality. In some ways, such differences apply as well when we move between the psychotherapeutic and Buddhist views of reality.

When I was practicing Theravadin meditation under Goenka-ji's guidance, enormous pain would arise during vow sittings. After years of practice, I was on occasion able to see with deep and sustained focus that the "pain" was not a Newtonian solid mass but rather a frothy, changing, evanescent, bubbling energy with hardly any quality of discomfort. This was a quantum vision, to see what had been substantial and impermeable as waves of changing experience.[71]

Therapy does not question the ontological status or substantiality of our psychological functions. Interpersonally and socially, we may need to understand why we hold ourselves back, put ourselves down, or puff ourselves up. A therapist can provide the context to help us find out who we are when freed from a variety of defensive postures that we adopted early in life. In practical terms, to the extent that our work and relationships are adversely affected by our feelings of inferiority or superiority, we can benefit tremendously from psychological interventions. Furthermore, as A. H. Almaas so insightfully shows, the insights and approaches of psychodynamic psychotherapy can be of particular use in working with inner weakness and our need for accurate acknowledgment as these emerge during spiritual practice.[72] Meditatively, at the same time that psychological work is going on, we can be exploring the nature of our feelings, the very nature of that sense of "I"—ultimately realizing that we are less substantial and solid than we thought. Mark Epstein suggests that for those who have completed therapy, Buddhist insight meditation can alleviate the residual narcissistic wounds that remain even after a successful therapy, to the extent that the practitioner realizes that the subject of such injury, a solid graspable self, is ultimately illusory.[73]

It is clear that Newtonian therapy and quantum meditation have much to offer, individually and jointly; as they see different aspects of reality, both have validity. I am reminded of the old woman who greeted Atisha, the eleventh-century Indian Buddhist master who taught in Tibet. She saw the reality of suffering and cried, and saw its insubstantiality and laughed.[74] Both positions have their merits. What can feel deeply out of tune is when a teacher or fellow student tries to help a practitioner in distress by imposing a quantum vision on what is a decidedly Newtonian experience—responding to loss, grief, or hurt by denying its ultimate reality.[75] However, if we slowly deepen our insight, we may find that we can oscillate between both perspectives or ultimately hold them simultaneously.

Newtonian work in therapy helps people to find their voice and the capacity to articulate this in love and work. Developing compassion alongside insight (the quantum view) within Buddhist practice gives us a broader sense of how we are all worthy of care, and a deeper understanding of what is ultimately real, within which vision we may then use our own voice.

DEFERENCE, PRIDE, AND SELF-ASSERTION

It is a psychological expectation in our culture that we have some sense of who we are and express this in the world.[76] Psychologists do not hold that we need to feel better than others in order to do this, yet our culture does support such feelings of superiority. Cultural psychologists have found it is normative for Americans to feel smarter, more considerate, and more in control than three quarters of their peers.[77] This feeling of superiority is documented in children as young as four.[78] Cultural psychologists Markus and Kitayama believe that this sense of being better serves the core psychological tendency toward independence and difference prevalent in our culture.

With an immersion in Buddhist teachings on pride, we become a lot more sensitive to such information. It seems clear that Buddhist teachings to abandon pride will challenge typical Americans, who consider themselves better than most of their peers. Through awareness of this pressure on us to feel that we are better than others, we become much more sensitive to our own conditioning. The nature of our entanglement becomes clearer, and this itself opens the possibility for release.[79]

With this clarification, it becomes easier to consider how presentations by traditional teachers may create cross-cultural confusion for their Western students. It is natural for Asian teachers to present their cultures' behavioral prescriptions under the Buddhist rubric of abandoning pride. The traditional deference to authority and family values translates in a religious context into deference toward teachers and traditions, knowing one's role, and following the rules. Despite what our initial reactions to such customs may be, this behavior may be very rewarding in a culture based on interdependence.[80] On the other hand, our appreciation of self-assertion is not found in cultures where group cohesion is an accepted value. In such cultures, "good feelings may be a function of good social relationships (i.e., fitting in, belonging, maintaining harmony in one's relations, occupying one's proper place, engaging in appropriate action) while at the same time regulating one's inner personal thoughts and feelings so as to ensure interdependence."[81]

There is some tension in the Buddhist traditions around deference to tradition and authority versus valuing individual vision and religious innovation. In the *Kalama Sutta* of the Theravadin tradition, Gautama exhorts students not to alter their conduct through relying on "the authority of religious texts," nor by thinking "this is our teacher," but rather through knowing for themselves that certain things are unwholesome and to be abandoned, and others wholesome and to be taken up.[82] Gautama was an innovator in creating a religious order for women, and in the various lineages of Buddhism throughout Asia, from time to time there have been teachers who have initiated major changes in practice. At the same time, a great deal of effort has been concerned with honoring, conserving, and maintaining the teachings through activities of recitation, printing, and teaching, and honoring those who have held the teachings the longest, or with the utmost care. The predominance of deference to hierarchy and authority in the religious world mirrored similar feelings toward parents and ancestors to be found in the society at large.

In the West today too there is tension between valuing tradition and challenging it. For the most part we lean toward the latter. We value change, independence, questioning, and originality. Imagine our Asian teachers, with their appreciation of deference and social harmony, encountering a culture in which most of us feel we are above average and revel in challenging authority. Of course they are struck by our pride. For traditional teachers who do not reflect on these cultural issues, it can be easy to include in their teachings on pride implicit messages to defer to authority and restrain self-expression. Yet this cultural bias may actually be counterproductive for Westerners.

In relating to Asian teachers, we naturally wish to cultivate an appreciation of their cultural expectations with respect to deference and restraint in the spiritual sphere. But we need to integrate our spiritual understanding into our lives. We may, for example, be working psychologically to move from self-loathing to self-love, from self-thwarting to self-awareness and self-expression. In this aspect of our work, we become more aware of what we are feeling and how it connects to our past and present. We may be doing this at the same time that we are cultivating spirituality. Here we are looking at our deeper nature. The more clearly we understand what we are experiencing physically, psychologically, and emotionally, the more we are able to investigate its ultimate nature. The more clearly discriminated our experience, our feelings, and the various ways we hold or represent ourselves, the more easily we can be mindful, observe, and disidentify from our experience and reach deeper levels of mindfulness, wisdom, and presence.[83] We seek the psychological capacity to experience life fully, while we seek spiritually not to be bound by it.[84] It is important to recognize that each of these tasks is distinct and different, may initially be cultivated in different spheres, and receives a different emphasis at various times.

Our psychological needs may at times be at odds with the implicit cultural imperatives of our Asian teachers, even though we agree on our spiritual goals. When we authentically develop our practice, we may reduce our pride yet remain distinctly oriented toward knowing and expressing our feelings, asserting our individuality, and displaying our creativity. This may look very different from traditional Asian models of spirituality. It remains to be seen whether the behavior of spiritually mature Westerners will be perceived as proud from an Asian cultural perspective.

Women in our culture may face double jeopardy from the implicit cultural messages from male Asian teachers. While Western women historically have been discouraged from expressing their selfhood, women's status in traditional Asian cultures was generally even lower. Though there are exceptions, male monastics often favor male students and may refrain from teaching individual women students. Scholarly Western women sometimes find it difficult to establish working relationships with learned monks and to sustain social relationships in which much informal learning can occur. Unfortunately, there are few learned female Asian teachers. Due to the absence of a continuous lineage of ordination in most Buddhist countries, full ordination of women as nuns has not been possible for hundreds of years.[85] Given the modern Western movement for women to redefine and assert themselves, implicit cultural messages toward self-restraint in general and restraint of women in particular, all tucked under the umbrella of giving up pride, can give rise to significant personal dissonance for Western women practitioners.[86]

In addition to women, those who have historically been oppressed due to their race, ethnicity, religious belief, sexual orientation, or medical disability or for any other reason may find implicit or overt messages encouraging self-restraint similarly onerous. Such individuals are seeking social equity and need to give voice to their just demands. Work for social justice, done from a spiritual perspective with a wholesome mind, can be undertaken without any harmfulness, and it need not involve the thrall of pride or any consideration of status whatsoever.[87] Such engaged activity can be motivated by love and compassion. We have a wonderful historical role model for this in Gautama and his students, who did not go along with the inequities of the caste system of the day. Those who are socially or psychologically oppressed may substantially progress spiritually through achieving flexibility of status consciousness by doing what it takes to reach equality. Such flexibility is a key ingredient in the project of ultimately letting go of being bound to any self-representation whatsoever.

THE SELF IN SUM

In considering issues of selfhood, we need to be aware of the following points. Buddhism denies that an ontological essence or self (*atman*) can be found in what we experience. It does not, however, deny human functioning. In fact, its doctrine of change was an attempt to understand ethical responsibility within the process of change.

We need to be aware of how traditional societies adopted Buddhism and how cultural dictates are melded into traditional presentations of basic philosophical and psychological teachings. As we assimilate teachings from our Asian teachers, certain attitudes such as those toward self-expression and gender hierarchy may need to be reconsidered carefully in the light of our own cultural understandings and expectations.

Anger: Abandon It or Express It? 8

RICHARD HAD LONG BEEN CURIOUS about Buddhism. During his first visit to a Buddhist center on the West Coast, the teacher told him, "You should never get angry." Finding this instruction unworkable, Richard lost all interest in pursuing Buddhist practice and to this day feels a sense of moral indignation about Buddhism. He does not see it as a viable resource for spiritual growth. Richard's experience epitomizes a problem that occurs as Buddhist teachings on anger are presented in the West. Asian teachers operate within their own cultural assumptions and use words whose English translations have different meanings in our culture. Western students, for their part, lack both familiarity with how the teachings made sense in their original setting and insight into how to apply them effectively here.

In the West, we all struggle with anger. This goes back at least to the time of Aristotle. In *Emotional Intelligence*, Daniel Goleman cites Aristotle's *Nichomachean Ethics*: "To be angry with the right person, to the right degree, at the right time, for the right purpose and in the right way—that is not easy."[1] As we attempt to integrate Buddhist teachings—including those on anger—into Western culture, it is useful to first consider this emotion from cultural and psychological perspectives. We can then explore the practical implications.

I continue our cross-cultural and psychological reflections on Buddhist teachings with a discussion of anger because the acknowledgment and validation of this emotion in my own therapy marked a confusing but crucial turning point for me. Over the years, my appreciation of the context for understanding anger, both in traditional Buddhist cultures and the modern West, has deepened, and I draw from both sources to develop effective ways of attending to this emotion.

This section begins with an exploration of how anger means different things in different cultures as well as different contexts within a given culture—including our own. This is followed by a discussion of how healthy anger, or assertion, differs from the intent to harm, which is the traditional Buddhist meaning of *anger*. Chapter 8 presents ways of working with anger to minimize its harmful effects and discusses how, grounded in Buddhist and therapeutic values, effective means of communication conducive to harmonious relationships can be developed.

THE CONFLICT

The following material drawn from Theravadin texts illustrates the Buddhist scriptural position on anger.

> To repay angry men in kind
> Is worse than to be angry first.
> Repay not angry men in kind
> And win a battle hard to win.[2]

> Now you who get angry, has not the Blessed One said this, "Bhikkhus [monks], even if bandits brutally severed limb from limb with a two-handed saw, he who entertained hate in his heart on that account would not be one who carried out my teaching."[3]

Representing the Western view, psychotherapist Leigh McCullough Vaillant states: "Angry feelings have evolved as responses to our need to prevent intrusions, to right wrongs, or to obtain something that is lacked. If patients are not able to set limits when attacked, give voice to what is wanted or not wanted, feel deserving of things desired, or walk into a room with their head high and feel a right to be there, they have missed a huge component of healthy adaptive functioning."[4]

At first glance it appears that modern psychotherapy and Buddhist teachings take widely disparate approaches to anger. Let us look into this further.

WHAT DOES ANGER MEAN?

The first consideration is that the word *anger* and words associated with it, such as *hate*, have different meanings in Buddhist teachings and in modern Western thought. Buddhism identifies hate (*dosa, dvesha*) along with desire and delusion as one of the three roots of cyclic existence. Hate and anger constitute the wish to harm someone else.[5]

In the Buddhist view, the intention to hurt is a root cause for remaining enmeshed in repetitive experiences of pain over many lives. All Buddhist traditions agree that with the understanding that all things are insubstantial, the support for hate is eroded and eventually destroyed. For when the light, evanescent quality of our mind and body is experientially understood—when we realize in a deep way that there is ultimately nothing permanent to hold on to—it substantially alters our defensive reactions. Harmfulness naturally withers away. This freedom from hatred is experienced as profoundly liberating.

Buddhist teachings on anger, hate, and hurtfulness are part of a larger discussion of how pain and pleasure come to be in the world through the operation of the law of karma.[6] The basic principle is that harmfulness in the present brings about pain in the future.[7]

In Buddhist discourse in the West, the word *anger* is typically used to cover emotions involving the wish to cause harm. In ordinary American English, however, *anger* has a broad range of meanings:

- Outright intent to harm: "I'm so angry I could kill somebody."

- Strong reactive dislike: "When the caterers burned the food, I was so angry, I screamed at them in front of the guests."

- Assertiveness, proclaiming difference, creating independence, and setting boundaries: "My roommate assumed I wanted the same pizza she did. I got angry and made it clear that she should have called to check instead of trying to read my mind."

- Protesting injustice: "We were angered by the bigoted behavior of that organization and decided to create an informational picket."

This range of meanings can cause difficulties when *anger* is used in translations of Buddhist teachings to mean the specific intent to harm. Both the Theravadin and Mahayana traditions emphasize that harmfulness needs to be abandoned.[8] Yet when Western students hear Buddhist teachers proscribing anger, they believe that this refers to all the meanings of the word. This is a major misunderstanding, one that probably contributed to Richard's indignant rejection of Buddhism. The focus of Buddhist teachings on anger is the injunction to abstain from *harmful intent and action.* This definition clearly relates to the first meaning listed above—but not necessarily to the others. The second and third scenarios could just be expressions of strong assertiveness, not necessarily the wish to harm. In considering these situations, we need to understand that traditionally there is no proscription against assertiveness, proclaiming difference, establishing autonomy, or setting boundaries. For example, we can see Gautama exhibiting all of these qualities in talking to a new student when he says, "Profound, O Vaccha, is this doctrine . . . and it is a hard doctrine for you to learn, who belong to another sect. . . . Therefore, Vaccha, I will now question you."[9] If we imagine some hypothetical teacher emphasizing receptivity, unity, and togetherness, it becomes clear that, by way of contrast, Gautama was able to delineate differences, take a position of leadership in guiding the student through questioning, and clearly identify the uniqueness of his vision.

Although behavior that is direct and independent clearly is not proscribed, and is in fact exhibited by the spiritually mature, it is useful for us as practitioners to monitor ourselves to see how reactive or agitated we become around others, as this may reflect a form of unawareness. For example, a shouted "Why did you buy me peaches when you know I hate them" is more than a simple expression of difference, and might be experienced as harmful.

It is also helpful to examine ourselves when setting boundaries to see if we are influenced by a wish to harm. Those who grew up amid frequent invasions of privacy often find that their initial attempts at separating from others include some hostility—a legacy from past intrusions. For example, when your partner walks in on you when you are working on an important document, it may be hard not to bark dismissively, "What is it?" This may be unavoidable if we have not paid much attention to working with our emotions, but eventually, with awareness, we can define our need for space more graciously.

The fourth sense of anger, protesting injustice, can also be viewed in a variety of ways. In 1995, when His Holiness the Dalai Lama was asked in Houston, Texas, about the appropriateness of voicing objection to unjust behavior, he said that this is not anger and it is appropriate. This type of assertiveness received further validation from Thich Nhat Hanh, who told a *New York Times* reporter, "You have to have the courage to speak out against social injustice, the violation of human rights."[10]

Tibetan teachers speak of "ferocious compassion," such as a mother shouting and grabbing her child out of harm's way. When this type of energy is used toward a compassionate end, they don't see anything wrong with it. In fact, in tantric Buddhism, there are enlightened compassionate deities who manifest in ferocious form to benefit beings. Buddhist teachers see no element of anger in the sense of hurtfulness in acting for justice or energetically protecting the helpless.

WHAT IS EMOTION?

Understanding the meaning of a term like *anger* in its traditional Buddhist context helps us reflect on the related concept in our own culture and language and on the relationship between these two meanings. This is especially helpful if we are trying to integrate traditional teachings about anger into our lives. To that end, it is also useful to examine the broad definition of emotion. Are there ways that emotions are valued differently in traditional Buddhist cultures and our own?

Emotion words such as *guilt* or *anger* refer to an interpretation of feelings and physical sensations that arise in response to events that we experience and the actions we envision as a response.[11] There are thus two aspects to an emotion. First, events in the world lead us to have certain perceptions, sensations, and feelings. For example, when you insult me, I feel heat in my face and perceive that you are threatening me. Second, in response to this perception and sensation, I react with an impulse to insult you back, which completes the emotion. Much of this split-second reaction may occur subliminally or almost outside my awareness, yet all of it constitutes my experience of anger.

Every culture has its own way of evaluating the relevance of particular behavior. In some cultures, it might be considered an affront to say certain things about a person's relative; in others, to say something about a person's honesty. In one culture, people might deal with an insult by confronting the offender; in another, by ruining the person's reputation through gossip. The sense of urgency associated with a given offense will vary, with some cultures having a high tolerance for insult and others requiring an immediate forceful response.

Given the variability of what provokes anger, how it is subjectively experienced in different cultures, and how people express it, the question arises: How valid is it to compare the experience of two cultures? For example, in North America, the open expression of disagreement is common and accepted, whereas in Japan it is quite unusual and frowned upon. While the Japanese word for this type of muted disagreement (*ikari*) is usually translated as "anger," our image of what anger looks like and its acceptability are quite different from what the Japanese understand by *ikari*.[12]

It is only through appreciating the different place of anger in our culture and related ideas and behaviors in Asian Buddhist settings that we can sensitively consider how to assimilate spiritual guidance from that tradition into our lives.

Proclaiming Our Individuality

The expression of anger in the sense of expressing difference, autonomy, and personal rights is common in the West. When our rights, goals, or needs are obstructed, this can lead to anger, and we feel entitled to express our upset. This is in line with our appreciation of independence and the articulation of our needs and what is due us.[13]

Because of our deep love of independence, we value differences between individuals. For example, Rabbi Jacob Neusner, a noted scholar of Judaica, illustrates this appreciation for respectful disagreement by imagining how he would respond if he were to meet Jesus: "I can see myself meeting this man, and, with courtesy, arguing with him. It is my form of respect, the only compliment I crave from others, the only serious tribute I pay to the people I take seriously."[14] As problematic as harmfulness may be for us in the West, we approve of anger in the sense of vigorous expression of difference because this is a vehicle for us to embody our value of maintaining separateness and individuality while retaining contact with one another. Indeed it is this peculiar blend of difference and contact that is singled out in the following observation on the place sports talk has in the psychological development of young boys: "Our first strongly held opinions were about players or teams, and the way in which they differed from those of our friends were among our earliest intimations of a self."[15] Anger, in the sense of forceful disagreement within a relationship, is part of what helps us in the West develop as discrete individual selves.

Our cultural construct of anger is seen in bold relief when we contrast it with aspects of Asian culture. For example, Japanese culture places great significance on building relationships and attending to others' needs and goals.[16] The emphasis in that culture is on attunement and alignment between individuals.[17] Anger, in the sense of strong disharmonious expression of individuality, is understood to disturb the sought-after sense of interdependence and is viewed very negatively.[18] Thus, one sense of anger—the emphatic assertion of difference—has a potentially positive connotation here but a distinctly negative connotation in Japan. Some similar appreciation of social harmony was part of most traditional Buddhist cultures.

This was illustrated to me clearly when I was in graduate school at the University of Wisconsin. My major advisor, the late Richard Robinson, was often frustrated by the unwillingness of his Japanese students to confront and question him. He was looking to be disagreed with in a rigorous manner. This was a clash of cultural expectations at a fundamental level.

The particular model of harmony exhibited in the island culture of Japan is not necessarily found throughout Asia. For example, Tibetans have a deep appreciation of a good argument and there is a fair bit of polemic dispute between religious lineages. However, the picture is complicated. While there is debate in their educational system, if we look a bit more closely, most of the monastic debates are reenactments of traditional arguments, some of which go back over a thousand years. Within the monasteries, there is tolerance and encouragement of a certain amount of playful differentiation, but it typically does not go beyond a certain range.

Let us now look at the larger context for understanding anger in traditional Buddhist and Western settings, for an appreciation of differences here will ultimately facilitate a more thoughtful approach to working with this emotion.

DIFFERENCES OF NARRATIVE

When considering anger in a cross-cultural context, it is important for us to appreciate that there are different ways of portraying our human experience. For example, we all have experienced having feelings that don't make any sense. For example, if for no apparent reason I were feeling blue, I would tend to look back on what happened emotionally in my relationships over the past few days. If I were queasy, I might wonder if I had eaten something bad. If I felt really sick, I might wonder whether something was physiologically wrong with me. As a modern

Westerner, I tend to understand my experience in terms of my psychological or medical condition.[19]

However, this is not the case the world over. In other cultures, my unexplained sensations might be attributed to a curse that someone had put on me.[20] In Buddhist cultures, certain physical conditions, such as symptoms associated with anxiety, might be understood in terms of an imbalance in the humors. Other experiences might be understood as due to the moral quality of one's past actions. For example, the inexplicable shaking that I experienced during a meditation retreat was explained by my teacher Goenka-ji as the ripening of some negative action I had performed in a prior life.

Traditional Buddhist discussions of anger predominantly understand harmfulness in terms of how it affects our current spiritual state in relation to our future experience (karma). Harmfulness is identified as an unwholesome state of mind that leads to painful experiences in the future. It is critical to appreciate the karmic context in which this emotion is discussed. As we consider practical issues related to anger, we will see that in contrast to the Buddhist schema above, the way we in the West understand anger has to do with its place in our present emotional and social life. This in turn affects the way we address this feeling.

Do We Respond Emotionally or Physically?

Another issue in the cross-cultural consideration of an emotion such as anger is the relative significance a culture places on emotional versus physical experience. In a groundbreaking work, Arthur Kleinman identified the Chinese as responding to life stressors in a markedly different way from Westerners.[21] The participants in one study developed a set of complaints that were primarily physical: headache, fatigue, dizziness, insomnia, weakness, and muscle tension. Chinese physicians call this set of symptoms neurasthenia, based on earlier models of Western psychiatry.[22] Neurasthenia is understood in terms of frayed nerves or tired blood—physical causes.[23] It is understood to be distinctly different from depression, where the picture is primarily of sadness, hopelessness, and self-deprecation. For example, in over 50 percent of the cases in a Taiwanese sample, individuals suffering from the primarily physical complaints of neurasthenia did not meet the emotional criteria for depression set forth in the *Diagnostic and Statistical Manual of the American Psychiatric Association,* the accepted standard for diagnosis in the North American mental health profession.[24] Interestingly, researchers in an Indian psychiatric clinic had similar findings.[25] In both China and India, a careful look at those suffering from somatic complaints showed they were not necessarily "depressed" according to our current criteria.

This research shows that people from certain cultures are inclined to express their experience primarily in physical (or somatic) terms; others, in emotional terms.[26] Yet Westerners who haven't studied cross-cultural psychology may naïvely assume that people everywhere create similar links between their perception and the meanings of their sensations and discuss their experience in terms of emotions, such as sadness, hopelessness, or depression.[27] However, this is only one way to have life experience. If I am Chinese or Indian and lose my job, I may not get sad or depressed, but instead I might feel that my nerves are frayed, get tired, and feel dizzy. These differences are highlighted in the following account:

> A fellow psychiatrist . . . was at a conference about depression in developing countries. The essence of the lectures was that people in those areas commonly expressed depression as physical symptoms. They "somaticize" their depression, to use medical parlance, complaining of malaise, stomachaches, dizziness, and other symptoms that are hard to pin down.
>
> Techniques were discussed for dealing with the patient who insists her only problem is a heavy head or a squeezing sensation in the belly, but who is clearly depressed.
>
> Toward the end of the meeting, a doctor from India stood

to speak. "Distinguished colleagues," he said, "have you ever considered the possibility that it is not that we in the third world somaticize depression, but rather that you in the developed world psychologize it?"

His comment, my colleague reported, was met with stunned silence.[28]

Even as we recognize that individuals in Asia may respond to life experience in a different way, it is also important to remember that the way they understand the *origin* of their physical experiences is not universal. In China, the condition of neurasthenia is seen to arise from the experience of oppression. In the clinic in India, those suffering from similar symptoms mostly understand their condition in relation to something they did in the past, their karma.[29]

Knowing what we do now of modern India and China creates some suspicion that physical experiences, as opposed to emotional responses, may historically have had greater significance in these countries and other regions where traditional Buddhism developed. This marks a contrast with our current situation in the West, where emotional experience and its discussion is critical to the way we construct ourselves and our relationships. This difference is further evidenced in the fact that while specific emotions are certainly discussed in Buddhist texts, these texts have no single morally neutral term for our abstract concept "emotions."[30]

Our way of understanding our experience is then very different from that of traditional Asian cultures. For example, faced with a variety of life stressors, I might talk about a lack of meaning in my life, a sense of emptiness or confusion, whereas an Asian might speak of her fatigue, dizziness, and lack of energy. I might attribute my condition to the emotional experiences of current and past relationships or perhaps my need for an antidepressant. If the person is Chinese, she might attribute her symptoms to overwork; if Indian, to the karmic result of having committed harmful actions in the past. If we each talk only about our symptoms, which already differ, we may not even realize

the dramatically different ways in which we understand the very workings of our lives.

DIFFERENT INTERVENTIONS

When we wish to follow Buddhist teachings and develop a sensitive
model of practice, it is helpful to understand the place of emotions in
traditional cultures.

My guess, based on the research I cited, is that in many circumstances there may be a preference for physical rather than emotional
expression with respect to circumstances that would provoke anger in
the West, such as being treated poorly by a superior at work. However,
I am cautious about overgeneralizing. There may be broad variants in
what stimulates hostility, the frequency of its experience, and how it is
expressed—both here and there. For example, I have noticed in my
own encounters with Tibetans that many from the eastern Kham area
are quick to voice intense hostile feelings, especially in the face of a
threat to family, clan, or religious lineage. Many from central Tibet
are more prone to indicate displeasure through indirection, silence, or
avoidance.

Despite these open questions, there are some clear differences in
how anger is expressed in, for example, Tibet and here. Typically in
Tibet, hostility is expressed with the intent to actually harm the other
party. One lets others know that one wishes to harm and ruin them,
or does so indirectly through gossip or withholding support. The Tibetans whom I have seen angry will express their anger by venting
their emotion with shame or blame—"Losang is unreliable; he says
one thing and does another"—or with a physical threat or actual violence. This type of hostility is also very common in the West, of course.
However, Tibetans will not "own" their feelings as we in the West
currently seek to do: Those of us who have made an effort to optimize
our communication will self-reflectively report what we are feeling in
relation to another's behavior, for example, "I am deeply frustrated
that you didn't call and tell me you were going to miss our committee

meeting." Instead of blaming or shaming, we turn the focus on the subject, ourselves. This way of disclosing our current experience is rooted in our appreciation of individuality, the value we place on emotion, and the way we create closeness through sharing our personal feelings.[31]

In sum, individuals in many traditional Buddhist cultures may have been more likely to experience physical symptoms rather than emotions in response to the ups and downs of life. Furthermore, these cultures did not encourage individual expression of feelings as we do or to an extent that produces disharmony. The Buddhist narrative about anger is primarily concerned with explaining suffering in terms of moral cause and effect.[32] The meaning of anger in this context is harmfulness, and it was historically the subject of moral instruction by teachers to students who took such instruction quite seriously.

We in the modern West are much less familiar with and open to moral guidance than those in traditional cultures.[33] We are also much less likely to respond unquestioningly to a teacher's moral authority. Recall the Western student's strong doubt about the effectiveness of Khamtrul Rinpoche's advice to a Nepali man with a drinking problem. We must recognize that the internalized voice of moral authority, which is effective in Asia for working with harmfulness, will not be as influential for Western students. Richard's experience in the vignette at the beginning of this chapter illustrates how an authoritarian stance is often met in our culture with a certain kind of rebellion. To work constructively with feelings of harmfulness, Westerners require something other than the time-honored prescriptions of a venerable spiritual tradition.

The clear differences between traditional Buddhist and modern Western views of anger make it evident that we must consider a variety of interventions for dealing effectively with this emotion. Given our preference for understanding things in emotional terms, interventions that acknowledge our psychological reality will be most effective for us today. Our Western contribution to working with difficult feelings is the understanding that they may be opened up through carefully structured discussion into a means of connection. I have not seen anger used in this way in traditional Buddhist culture.

ANGER IN THE WEST

In terms of both spiritual development and interpersonal relationships, anger is a high-stakes emotion. If handled ineffectively, it can have severe psychological, legal, moral, and physical effects on our lives—and, from the Buddhist perspective, consequences for our future lives as well.

Even in the West, where we value emotional expression, many people do not allow themselves to feel anger. This may be especially true of women, who historically have not had the legal, financial, and political capacity to wield power equal to men. Until recently, women were not given access to positions where they could exercise assertiveness, leaving many in the older generations inexperienced in effective expression and unable to model it for their daughters. Individuals, both female and male, who are uncomfortable with self-assertion may not voice anger if they feel it. If they voice it, they may do so ineffectually, resorting to blaming, guilt-tripping, or nagging.[34]

On the other hand, many people in modern Western society—especially men, who are the creators of contemporary cultural norms—are quick to express aggressive anger, through shaming, violent behavior, and more subtle forms of aggression such as stonewalling or undermining others' self-confidence—often women's.[35] Men may gain temporary control through such means, but ultimately they undermine the quality of their relationship to themselves and others. With both under- and overexpression of anger, there may be dire consequences for relationships, health, and safety. Aristotle's concern for balance in the expression of this emotion is one I share, and this informs my consideration of anger.

The modern West's psychological epoch begins with Sigmund Freud, whose views on aggression and anger were never finally settled.[36] For a time, he considered aggression to be instinctual. But it is important to realize that Freud was looking at bare data and then applying metaphors to try to capture the essence of that data. The metaphors Freud chose were those current to his day, particularly to then-emerging sciences. In our day-to-day lives, we often confuse metaphors with actual experience.

In identifying sex and "aggression" as instincts, Freud took a complex mix of social, emotional, and behavioral components and presented them in terms of the supposedly immutable biological mechanisms that control the behavior of animals. Furthermore, his writings on instinct were replete with metaphors of energy, storage, and flow that were related to the studies of electromagnetism and hydraulics emerging at that time. Some common phrases we use today to describe anger, such as "bottled up" or "stored up," reflect the language of those fields of study.[37]

It was part of Freud's philosophical anthropology to present humans as engaged in an ongoing struggle between the force of instinct and the restraining forces of civilization. One of his major contributions, whether we ultimately agree with him or not, was to see human action as deriving from the biological basics of the body. At times, Freud considered aggression one of these irreducibles, part of our human genetic endowment.[38] From this perspective, we humans are seen as biologically driven and destined to constantly struggle to tame our base nature.

After Freud, there was a gradual shift among some psychoanalysts toward seeing human connection, rather than sexuality, as the primary source of human motivation. These analysts saw sex and aggression as related to issues in our relationships rather than as our primary drives.[39] For example, Harry Guntrip, a British analyst, identified anger as a response to social threat.[40] For him anger was not an irreducible feature of human nature, as Freud had originally proposed, but rather an understandable reaction to danger. If we follow this view, then interventions that lessen intimidation in our relationships are possible, and anger can be dealt with through altering the way we communicate.

In this view, we are not condemned to the aggressive biological destiny theorized by Freud.

Of more practical consequence, however, have been the cultural influences of therapeutic practice. In Europe, Freud developed a system of free association in which clients were encouraged to let their attention move where it wished and then describe whatever associations arose. This was a calm, reflective, and genteel practice in early twentieth-century Vienna. When it crossed the Atlantic and eventually arrived in California, however, many variants of therapeutic practice developed. The theory and practice of psychotherapy included forms such as Gestalt, which encourages an intense, cathartic expression of feelings. Here the prescription is for the full verbal expression of anger in the controlled environment of the therapy office or workshop space, using either empty chairs or surrogates as recipients. There can be much therapeutic benefit to such exercises in the therapy office, particularly for individuals who are overly restrained or have blocked energy.

Whether or not Fritz Perls, the originator of Gestalt therapy, intended it, this approach has devolved in popular culture to the attitude epitomized by the expression "Let it all hang out." Perhaps we have become entranced by the metaphor of "bottled-up anger" and hope that by uncorking the bottle and emptying out the anger, we may then be rid of it. Unfortunately, this is not the case. Outside the controlled environment of a therapist's office, the unchecked, unconsidered expression of anger leaves a deep wake of shame and emotional wounding that is difficult to heal. Such discharges seem only to hasten further destructive interchanges.[41]

Recent work by Leigh McCullough Vaillant on short-term psychotherapy concisely articulates the critical distinctions that I have been discovering through a comparison of psychotherapeutic and Buddhist concepts of anger.[42] She cites recent research that convincingly establishes anger as a feeling that arises in response to conditions, not as an instinct or a predestined biological necessity. Furthermore, Vaillant makes an important distinction between aggressive behavior, which must be monitored by morality, and the feeling of anger, which occurs inside our own bodies.[43] Aggression is a defensive, unreflective venting, often loud or violent, that occurs with little forethought, is not mixed with any positive feeling, and often leaves a trail of damage in our relationships.[44] Aggression is the manifestation of the harmful intent of which the Buddhist teachings speak.

Vaillant contrasts aggressive, harmful anger with the constructive expression of anger, or assertion. She highlights the importance of anger for maintaining personal boundaries, energizing our emotional strength, and allowing us to set limits, pointing out that the constructive expression of anger entails some restraint while still allowing us to express our wishes. It involves both positive and angry feelings, is oriented toward solving a problem, and often improves relationships rather than destroying them.[45]

Much in Vaillant's work on anger is in accord with Buddhist values, and other writers have also synthesized the salutary and effective from modern psychotherapy and the traditional spirituality. For example, Buddhist author and social activist China Galland is widely known for her impassioned stance against child prostitution. Her unique vision, developed through her personal journey and informed by a Buddhist worldview, includes a sense of compassion for perpetrators, mindfulness, and patience, as well as energetic commitment to right and just action.[46] Galland is an excellent example of an individual who has mastered the Western art of constructive anger and connected it to the larger frame of Buddhist mindfulness and compassion.

Two Extremes of Anger

My experience participating in spiritual communities beginning in the 1960s and my work as a psychotherapist since 1984 have shown me that anger takes two extreme forms in the modern United States. One extreme is underexpression. Rules that we internalized in childhood can lead some of us to minimize not only our expression of anger but even our conscious experience of it. Underexpressers often use a religious, spiritual, or "New Age" framework to reinforce their inclination to suppress anger. This is the case with underexpressers drawn to Buddhist practice. They may cloak themselves in an air of invulnerability that they justify with traditional Buddhist teachings on anger.[47]

If sustained underexpression of anger in our culture could be reliably or effectively achieved without harmful consequences, this discussion would not be necessary. But underexpression often takes a heavy long-term toll. Those in the grip of underexpression often have a deep wish to be free from the sway of any disturbing emotion, a hoping for a pure, cool mental life that is unperturbed by messy feelings—much like the character Spock on *Star Trek*. Driving this fantasy of emotional inviolability, however, is often the powerful fear that feelings—any feelings—will inevitably lead to impulsive action or loss of control.

Underexpression of anger becomes apparent in relationships that lack liveliness. Underexpressers may be unable to set boundaries or to define who they are and what they want. They may suffer from obsessive worry, compulsive behavior, or somatic complaints with difficult-to-trace physical causes. They may lack direction or vision in their work lives. Underexpressers often stay isolated and rarely complain—except that they sometimes have unexplainable eruptions of disagreement that seem far out of proportion to the issue at hand. Typically, serious anxiety, depression, or a major breakdown in relationships is the catalyst for an underexpresser to seek help.

For underexpressers, the danger of not learning how to hold, understand, and deal constructively with angry or harmful feelings is self-blame and/or agitation, lack of energy, an absence of zest and fullness of life, and, in the most extreme cases, passive or active suicide. These are common issues among clients seeking psychotherapy, and they are not uncommon among Western Buddhists.[48]

At the other extreme are overexpressers, whose emotional responses are expressed in explicitly harmful behavior. This pattern develops notably among those who have grown up amid domestic violence, abuse, chemical dependency, or emotional uproar. After an outburst, many overexpressers say they are surprised by what they did; they weren't aware of a buildup of feelings. I know of people who "practice" Buddhism while continuing to hit their partners or control them by push-ing, shoving, and screaming. Clearly they have not properly assimilated the teachings.

It is typical of the overexpressers with whom I've worked in therapy to disbelieve that their tone of voice is loud or threatening, even when others tell them that it is. Sometimes overexpressers find nothing sub-jectively wrong with their behavior until they face extremely adverse social or legal consequences.

BUDDHIST AND THERAPEUTIC APPROACHES

In his discourses, the Buddha often counsels his followers not to "en-tertain" hate, or to abandon it, which I understand to mean not to encourage or become absorbed in it, which could lead to harmful ac-tion. Contemporary teachers will similarly call for an almost instanta-neous abandonment of this emotion. This is what alienated Richard in the incident described at the beginning of this chapter. Without any discussion of rationale or means, such advice can feel quite off-putting. On the other hand, within the context of ongoing consultation with individual practitioners, I have seen teachers being sympathetic to the reality that effectively managing harmful emotions requires effort and time.

The most fundamental skill in working with anger is mindfulness, which allows us to know our present emotional state. The first devel-opmental milestone in mindfulness meditation is the ability to discern the difference between getting lost in a feeling, or identifying with it, and merely observing it. Successful observation offers us the opportu-nity to choose how to proceed.

When cultivated well, mindfulness allows us to observe the feeling of anger so clearly that we can recognize it as just a changing experi-ence that doesn't have to overcome us. We can clearly note the entire process of the rising, presence, and eventual dissolution of the emo-tion. Cultivating mindfulness to the point of being able to observe the process of the rising and falling of anger—without acting it out and without getting lost in its content—is one effective way of working with and lessening emotion. In this practice, the feeling is not consciously suppressed but simply observed for the duration of its natural manifestation and dissolution.

The goal of Buddhist interventions with anger is to diminish it. In this approach, it does not matter why we're angry, only that we are. This is in contrast to many Western therapeutic approaches that emphasize the exploration of both recent and past history in order to understand the origin of the anger, which in some instances can help bring the feeling to resolution. From the Buddhist perspective, we should abandon anger in order to prevent harming others, to diminish our own immediate mental discomfort, and to avoid future negative karmic consequences.[49] Harmfulness is a hindrance to meditation and is to be abandoned by those wishing to further their meditative practice.[50] Furthermore, mindfulness and insight will themselves in the long run cut the root of harmfulness, ultimately leading to liberation from cyclic existence.[51]

The therapeutic world makes no such claims. Leigh McCullough Vaillant's work provides a clear contrast to the Buddhist approach. It exemplifies the best that the field of psychotherapy has to offer with respect to working with anger.

Vaillant emphasizes awareness of physical and emotional aspects of anger as it develops as a way to activate its constructive expression.[52] Our physical sensation and internal feeling provide us clues that we may need to take appropriate action. This approach provides an opportunity for clients to begin to feel the physical or emotional components of anger and to voice the concerns associated with these feelings.

Here, as in Buddhist practice, the most critical first step is mindful awareness of our experience, which creates space for choosing how to proceed. What distinguishes therapy from traditional Buddhist mindfulness, however, is the positive value therapy places on being able to understand the origins of our anger, its encouragement to stay with the emotion long enough for some understanding of the feeling to emerge, and the constructive use of anger to motivate appropriate action.[53]

It's important to note that totally giving up anger is not a therapeutic goal. On the contrary, for Vaillant the constructive uses of anger—as opposed to the harmful behavior that may be associated with it—are necessary for maintaining a healthy emotional life. Therapeutically, Vaillant further differs from Buddhist psychologists in encouraging her underexpressive clients to train, within the confines of therapy, in becoming angry—even if this includes voicing harmful thoughts and feelings. She does this in order to free her clients from the inhibition that hurts them and renders them numb to the entire realm of human feeling. Vaillant acts as a substitute for the parents and friends of underexpressers who ideally would have helped in such a process earlier in life. She provides a safe environment for her clients to become familiar with their negative feelings.[54]

I see the importance of this type of work in particular with survivors of physical, sexual, and emotional abuse, who often unfortunately hold themselves, rather than the perpetrators, responsible for their abuse.[55] Adult survivors often mislabel this "forgiveness" and even try to support their stance with spiritual teachings. However, if this is forgiveness, it is premature, as it rests on a childhood distortion of reality. What's more, burying the outrage at the harm done leads those affected to believe that they don't deserve any better as adults. Underexpressers who do not develop skills in the constructive expression of anger may and often do become victims again. As Vaillant states, "If our patients are ridden with guilt or shame at the arousal of anger, they will be crippled in the tasks of setting limits, asserting themselves, or defending themselves."[56] Only when such clients are allowed a safe space to begin to feel and understand that it is all right for them to feel angry can they stop being victims. As psychoanalyst Jane Goldberg writes, speaking of encouraging the awareness of negative feelings in relationships, "Making hate conscious is the only way to reduce its power over us."[57]

Therapists, parents, and friends offer us a precious gift when they listen to, acknowledge, and contain our angry feelings—which may, on occasion, be tinged with harmfulness. They create an opportunity for us to voice, explore, and ultimately productively resolve these feelings rather than act them out. Sensitive listeners can actively contribute to the diminution of harmfulness and in this way support the values articulated in Buddhism. One of the gifts I receive from being a therapist is that on a daily basis I get to see what British psychoanalyst Adam Phillips calls the "transformative effect of listening."[58]

Once her clients have gained some facility in recognizing and acknowledging their angry feelings, Leigh McCullough Vaillant teaches them constructive methods of expressing such feelings so that they don't hurt others. This is critical for understanding therapeutic work with harmful emotions. The goal is to teach positive, nonharmful behavior. Anything else negates the therapeutic process.

After years of fine-tuning, I have arrived at an approach to anger that concerns itself with the process of reducing and minimizing the harm clients can do to others and to themselves while optimizing their capacity for rewarding relationships. Nonclinicians may not fully appreciate how difficult it is to change harmful patterns and how profound the effect on their quality of life when people do so. It can mean breaking cycles of abuse and hurtfulness and coming back from depths of hopelessness. Working with anger in an interpersonal way, which includes encouraging its expression in a contained environment in order to move toward assertive expression of difference, clearly distinguishes the therapeutic approach from traditional Buddhist methods.

We turn now to a discussion of how the therapeutic and Buddhist approaches can work together, informing and complementing one another.

A Middle Path on Anger 9

I SUPPORT THE BUDDHIST VALUE of minimizing harmful actions of body, speech, and mind, and I include within my concern ways in which we harm ourselves as well as others. I am interested in both traditional and modern ways of minimizing harmfulness. How do we proceed with respect to anger when we wish to engage in psychologically grounded Buddhist practice?

As I consider how to work with anger constructively, it has become clear to me that those with extreme under- and overexpression can be blind to their issues. Furthermore, those of us engaged in Buddhist practice may be unaware of how we absorb or ignore the teachings to suit our psychological needs. One of my aims here is to alert those interested in personal development to a variety of emotional issues that can arise in spiritual practice and detract from it if not skillfully attended to.

It is clear that both the therapeutic and Buddhist traditions have wisdom with respect to anger, with the former encouraging constructive self assertion from the psychological side and the latter emphasizing restraint of harmfulness from the spiritual side. Because of my concern for emotional well-being in developing an approach to working with anger, I have considered elements that reduce reactivity, strengthen autonomy, promote emotional sensitivity, enhance understanding of historical sources of our hurt, and provide guidelines for safe, effective communication. From the spiritual perspective, I have been interested in how to optimize mindfulness, reduce harmfulness, promote care for ourselves and others, and create an approach that both expresses and supports ongoing meditative practice.

Working with Anger

Avoiding Acting Out

In working with anger, it is extremely helpful to avoid (1) violent, harmful behavior, (2) threatening postures motivated by harmful intent, and (3) verbal shaming and blaming forms of criticism or contempt.[1]

Here Western psychotherapy and Buddhist teachings are fully in accord. Both agree that violence, shame, blame, and contempt are inimical to positive, harmonious relations. Shame involves criticism of another's character: "You are lazy." "You're a slob." "You're a bitch." Blame places fault on others' shoulders: "If it wasn't for you, I would have gotten that job." "You're wrong. It's all because of you." Contempt consists of verbal and nonverbal behavior that conveys that another is inferior.[2] Shame, blame, and contempt are exceedingly powerful ways to move from a smoldering smoker of a disagreement to a full-blown firestorm. They are extremely corrosive to relationships. Avoiding them is an uncomplicated but powerful way to minimize the negative cycles of attack, defensiveness, and acrimony.

Becoming Aware of Feelings

Although their inner dynamics are different, both underexpressers and overexpressers need to develop awareness of the physical and emotional experience of their feelings. Underexpressers will say they are not angry in the face of an emotional assault but will talk of feeling empty or depressed or enumerate a range of unexplained physical symptoms such as anxiety or dizziness. Overexpressers, on the other hand, will frequently say that they are not aware of feeling angry before they explode. They typically mistakenly see their own feelings in their partner, a mental activity known as projection. In this case, there may be an absence of awareness of internal sequences of perception, sensation, and behavior followed by a disavowal of personal responsibility. We can see this type of sequence in the following typical scenario.

Phyllis comes home late from work. Frank sees the clock is one hour past the time Phyllis normally comes home (perception). His dinner has been delayed. Frank feels slighted and hurt but is actually unaware of this (emotion). He begins to feel hot and pressured (physical sensation). Phyllis walks in the door and Frank screams at her, "Where have you been? I've been waiting for over an hour for you to get home!" (behavior). When Phyllis tries to explain that she was talking to her friends after work and then got caught in traffic and asks why Frank is so upset with her he says, "Bitch, you're punishing me, it's your fault I'm angry, you were hanging out with your goddamn friends who you take better care of than you do me" (shame, blame, projection, disavowal of responsibility). He then picks up the phone book and slams it on the table and walks out of the room (threatening behavior). Neighbors hearing the loud noise call the police. When they arrive Frank insists, "It's her fault, she made me angry because she came home late."

Mindfulness and awareness can be very helpful in slowing down this process. The practice of mindfulness of breathing begins with paying attention to the physical sensations of breathing. Doing this develops skill in becoming more aware of our physical experience. An unheralded piece of Buddhist spiritual wisdom is that awareness of our mental and emotional states becomes clarified through ever subtler attention to our physical experience.[3] Thus, through ongoing work with sensations related to the breath, we can slowly become increasingly sensitive to our angry thoughts and emotions, and this gives us an opportunity to decide how we will behave.[4]

If we have some tolerance for experiencing anger, mindfulness practice can heighten our awareness of this feeling. This then creates an effective context for further work with this feeling. But what if we have trouble tolerating it?

Underexpression

Those who lack internal permission to know their feelings or assertively express themselves and who undertake traditional Buddhist meditation will find few tools to help them develop these specific skills. There is little focus in the sutras on seeing the downside of inhibited emotion or stifled self-expression, nor do they offer any explicit guidance on these issues. This is not to say Gautama or other teachers lacked assertiveness. Rather, they saw no spiritual or cultural need to single out this issue for attention.

On the other hand, there are many explicit Buddhist doctrinal messages against harmfulness, which is often translated as "anger." As we have seen, contemporary English-speaking teachers who encourage students to abandon anger inadvertently condemn assertiveness. (I admit that as a translator I am often unable to point out these subtleties of meaning during the press of a teaching.) At some level, students understand that they are getting a message that goes counter to our cultural expectations with respect to self-assertion. However, underexpressers, not yet fully aware of how problematic this stance may be, find such teachings attractive because they are presented along with a spiritual message about liberation and freedom. When imprecise translations create the erroneous impression that teachers are suggesting we stop asserting ourselves, those trapped in patterns of emotional and personal inhibition exult in receiving a spiritual stamp of approval for their tendencies. They remain emotionally stuck.

A question with respect to anger is, Can we have right attitude—goodwill and abstention from harm, one of the branches of the Buddhist eightfold path[5]—for the wrong reasons? For example, what about someone who refrains from harmfulness because he was taught not to express himself in his family, or because she wants to receive the appreciation of her teacher? This is clearly reactive. Of course it is good to refrain from harmfulness, but if this is done because of internal restraints and inhibitions that are not consciously chosen and are part of a pattern that limits one's capacity to function effectively in relationships, the situation may need to be considered carefully. While the behavior may be positive, the dynamics underlying it may be counter productive in the long run. People can appear to be "good" or "spiritual" while slowly undermining their own psychological well-being.

Underexpressers who do not have internal permission to know their feelings or be assertive may need specific psychological work to develop tolerance of anger, which will not typically develop through meditation practice. Our emotional issues related to assertiveness are firmly rooted in our culture's emphasis on individuality. In another culture, difficulty knowing one's feelings or articulating one's individuality might not be considered a problem; it might not even be noticed. In our culture, significant help for resolving such issues can be found in Western psychotherapy or psychoenergetic work. Individual, family, or group psychotherapy is useful because, in an optimal situation, it creates a safe social environment in which we can begin to explore our feelings and our sense of who we are with others, understand the roots of our current reaction patterns, and explore alternative behaviors. Body or energy work can be helpful in increasing physical awareness of feelings and exploring habitual patterns of emotional numbing. In general, underexpressers do not feel entitled to full-bodied experience.[6] Whatever approaches allows us to be in our bodies, increases balanced awareness of our sensations and feelings, and gives us inner permission to develop choices that will make significant contributions to our feeling meaningfully alive.

Therapists address issues of anger and harmfulness in ways different from that articulated in the Buddhist discourses. In the Buddhist context, the concern is that practitioners not get lost in these feelings and act them out. In this regard we are taught (1) to be mindful of feelings of anger and recognize when they are present and (2) to reduce them as effectively as possible using a variety of methods.

In contrast to the view articulated in the Buddhist discourses, psychotherapists understand that the expression of anger, rage, or hatred in the contained environment of therapy can help lead some clients to greater compassion toward themselves as well as forgiveness and love for others. Perhaps a client will experience the wish to harm others and discuss this with the therapist. Therapeutic discourse makes a significant distinction between what people are feeling internally and what is considered appropriate physical and verbal behavior.[7] In my work with clients, we spend a lot of time facilitating the emergence of feelings into awareness. It is a developmental milestone when a client comes to know the difference between being out of touch and being aware of feelings. Anything that therapists can do to facilitate their clients' knowing and owning their feelings counters destructive tendencies to deaden, internalize, or erratically act out negativity.[8]

If we have grown accustomed to being numb, then recognizing, accepting, and holding our feelings in mind is very different from our usual experience.[9] The contained environment of therapy, the awareness that is cultivated therein, and the overall goal of resolving harmful feelings distinguish the nature of harmfulness experienced and explored in the therapeutic context from habitual reactions of anger, hate, or harmfulness. In therapy, we have the opportunity to use our present anger to explore and understand its roots in the past, which can in turn help us determine our future course of action. This particular self-reflective way of sitting with anger—relating the *content* of our anger to past history or anticipated future behavior—is what distinguishes the therapeutic from the Buddhist approach, which focuses on the *processes* of anger.

My years of working with adults and children in therapy have made it clear to me that providing clients with the tools to work with anger in this way often yields dramatic positive changes and is absolutely essential. The capacity to be aware of our feelings that is developed in therapy, even if not amplified by skills developed through mindfulness practice, provides the basis for all further steps discussed below in working with our feelings in a productive manner.

Some may feel that this approach, encouraging the experience of anger in therapy, goes against the teaching. I would respond that there is no need to give up our long-term orientation to minimizing harmfulness within therapy. Rather, such work allows us to free ourselves so that instead of being obsessively driven to behave in a certain way, we feel that we are more consciously able to choose what we consider is the right course of action.

Interestingly, one of the subtle but significant ways in which Western psychotherapeutic values have subtly been assimilated into the practice of Buddhist mindfulness relates to the question of how to work with anger. The traditional discourse on mindfulness has Gautama instructing practitioners to *know* what is present in the mind, with the ultimate purpose being to understand its unstable and insubstantial nature. Here the practice is to observe the process of becoming angry.[10] Yet many contemporary Western teachers of mindfulness, with a firsthand knowledge of psychotherapy, unknowingly alter the tradition by telling their students to know *and accept* their feelings. I think it is important to acknowledge that this is a departure from the traditional teachings, which encourage *observing* the impermanence of anger as effectively as possible. This subtle but significant shift may also contribute to the way in which many Western meditators engage in psychological reflection on their cushions rather than the more traditional observation.

In order to optimize what we are trying to achieve, it is very important to consciously choose how we are going to proceed in our practice of meditation. Traditional instruction emphasizes balanced observation, noting the way a particular feeling lacks enduring substantiality. I recommend that in working with anger off the cushion, outside of formal mindfulness practice, we develop skills not only in *knowing* or *observing* the feeling but also *accepting* it (but not, of course, acting out harmful intent). According to circumstances, we can emphasize one or the other of these skills. I suggest working with both, because both are critical to the way we construct ourselves emotionally in the West.

In order to know fully who we are, we need the capacity to observe and to accept, to protect our boundaries, and to voice our concerns assertively. When we observe in the context of mindfulness, we are impartial and disidentified from what we observe; when we accept, we are immersed in and can own the emotion, which in turn facilitates our life choices.[11] While razor-sharp observation skills are necessary for making progress in understanding the nature of reality in a profound way, for appropriate day-to-day engagement in the world some dynamic mix of awareness and capacity to accept is useful. In time, we can come to know a "sweet spot" where knowing and acceptance are balanced, which occurs when we are open to our feelings in a direct way and our mindfulness is very clear.

Overexpression

For overexpressers, those who have trouble tolerating their feelings of anger without acting them out, both therapists and Buddhist teachers would counsel restraint and adoption of harmonious speech.[12] For such individuals, breath-mindfulness can enhance awareness of the physical sensations associated with becoming angry, creating more opportunities for de-escalating intervention before an eruption.[13] Furthermore, in some instances, this type of mindfulness can be used by overexpressers to quiet themselves down before attempting to resolve conflict with others.

Once we have awareness of our feelings, there are both Buddhist and psychological approaches we can make use of.

Using Buddhist Approaches

Individuals aware of their anger and, particularly, harmfulness may need to moderate it before they can fruitfully communicate with another person. A most basic approach would be to become mindfully aware of the mental and physical states associated with this feeling, not getting absorbed in the reasons for it but watching its arising and ceasing.[14]

A general approach in the Buddhist discourses for turning away from harmfulness is to cultivate universal love.[15] In both Theravadin and Mahayana teachings, meditations on love and compassion are taught as preventives to the arising of anger, with Mahayana teachings also emphasizing patience as a significant antidote to harmfulness.[16] These meditations will be discussed in the next chapter.

Buddhist teachers recognize that in developing such preventive meditation, students will encounter difficulty when they try to love their enemies or those for whom they feel anger. They may get in touch with their harmful feelings. The thorough Theravadin compendium of meditation, Buddhaghosa's *Path of Purification,* contains several detailed contemplations for defusing these harmful feelings that can be of service in moderating our hostility.[17] These contemplations presume an acceptance of karma and rebirth.

- Consider that the karmic ramification of harmful intent is pain in the future. Is this a consequence you desire?
- Reflect on how you have been related to all beings in the past through relationships you have had in prior rebirths that extend back infinitely. The person with whom you are angry now was your dear loving parent in a prior life. Is this a way to repay his or her kindness?
- Consider all the aspects of a person's behavior; that is, consider the aspects that are inspiring.
- If it is not easy to find anything inspiring about the other person, recognize that due to the operation of karma, he or she may have a very unfortunate future. Use this thought to get in touch with a sense of compassion for the person.
- Reflect on inspiring examples from the tradition wherein teachers avoided getting angry, and use this inspiration to motivate abandonment of your own current hostility.

Working with any of these interventions requires a union of feeling and thinking, with the reflections gaining force over time.

Jamgon Kongtrul's mind training practice can be used here as well. This approach is based on the understanding that practitioners are trying to minimize harmfulness. When one is aware that a harmful emotion is present, one is mindful of its presence and furthermore aspires to absorb the harmful intentions of all beings into one's own afflicted mind. The practitioner's immediate experience is a touchstone for recognizing the pain, anguish, and bewilderment of all beings. Implicit in this practice is the willingness to relinquish attachment to the story that justifies one's harmfulness. Instead, the practitioner is challenged to hold the emotion in awareness without acting it out, and to offer it as a kind of black hole into which the afflictions of all others are absorbed. This practice can bring a searing, direct recognition of the pain that is shared by all sentient beings and the concomitant heartfelt wish that all be free of this pain and established in a state of enlightened clarity and peace.[18] Strength of intention and unwavering mindfulness are necessary in this practice, lest it become mere license to become absorbed in ordinary emotions.

Using Psychological Approaches

In addition to psychotherapy, there are two lesser-known Western approaches that I find very helpful for working with anger once we are clearly aware of it. One is found in the Big Book of Alcoholics Anonymous, which suggests that we look for the fear that underlies our resentment.[19] It takes a while for most of us to let go of the externally oriented narrative of our anger. Most of us habitually think this way: "Jayne lost the book I lent her. She is irresponsible and awful." It is a lot harder to acknowledge this feeling: "I fear I don't matter in her eyes. I fear she doesn't care for me. I fear I'm not very worthwhile." Doing this creates a tremendous opening to the source of the anger. I find it very powerful to couple this form of exploration with Jamgon Kongtrul's practice of relating our experience to others'. The movement from anger to acknowledging our vulnerability to empathetically considering that others feel similarly has a profoundly grounding effect while at the same time opening the heart to a sense of tenderness.

Building on the capacities developed in the Big Book approach,

overexpressers with a chronic sense of resentment (and underexpress
ers suffering depression) can learn to modulate their emotions and
soothe themselves using the HEALS approach developed by psychologist Steven Stosny.[20] In his approach, once trainees are aware that they
are upset, they reflect on what core value is being challenged in a particular situation.[21] They reflect on whether they are feeling unworthy,
unlovable, or unfit for human contact. These feelings about ourselves
are what fuel our anger.

They then ponder, "Am I really unworthy?"[22] Posing this question
is important because it creates a certain openness and curiosity. In my
experience, authentically sitting with this question has more force than
a mere affirmation, which seems to impose a sense of value but lacks
conviction. In gently considering this question, we can arrive at a realization that every human being, including ourselves, is worthy from
birth. Sometimes, remembering the fresh preciousness of being with a
newborn can allow us to recognize our intrinsic value and lovability.
Another avenue to such realization comes through meditation, when
we experience certain states that give us an incontrovertible sense of
value. These qualities of intrinsic worth are not granted through the
emotional whims of others. There is something deep, moving, and
spiritually rich in acknowledging our fundamental nature.

His Holiness the Dalai Lama uses a similar approach in *The Art of
Happiness* when he suggests that as an antidote to depression, discour-
agement, or self-hatred, individuals reflect on their intrinsic buddha
nature or the rich possibilities of their human potential.[23] We need to
explore what taps into a fundamental and real sense of worthiness
for us.

Stosny suggests that we deepen this sense of worthiness by bringing
it into our present lived experience.[24] The easiest way to do this is to
kindle our own compassion. As Stosny insightfully intimates, when we
feel compassion for others, we naturally have a sense of our own value.
A resource for enriching our own deep sense of value can be found in
the Buddhist practices that enhance love and compassion. From Stosny's perspective, when we are working with anger, the easiest and most

relevant way to bring compassion into our experience is to consider how the other person's provocative behavior is based on his or her own fear of being worthless.

For example, I was in a group of people planning to drive to Austin. James made the sarcastic comment, "Yeah, if you go with Harvey, you'll get to see a lot of Texas, but forget about getting to Austin on time." James departed before I had a chance to talk with him, and I was left feeling hurt and angry. I allowed myself to be aware of that for a few moments. Then I realized this brought to mind a sense of being unworthy. I felt a sunken sense of heaviness in my body and dryness in my mouth. I asked myself, Am I at core unworthy? and slowly I got in touch with a sense of intrinsic value. There was a hint of joy, almost a curl of a smile on my mouth. Then I considered James. I thought about what core value of his was being threatened so that he was sarcastic toward me, and I saw that he was not feeling worthy himself. Based on my own experience, it was easy to see how wound up in pain he had been to strike out as he did. At that, I felt an opening toward James and with it a firmer sense of my own value, and my hurt and anger became something else—if not full compassion, then at least an openhearted sense of James's pain. Stosny's approach, based as it is in psychology, is a variant of Jamgon Kongtrul's teaching. Here, by moving through the layers of my own experience of anger, I find my own suffering, and through this I am able to feel compassion for the suffering of others.

If we initially take the opportunity to be with ourselves rather than reactively lashing out or getting depressed, can we tolerate experiencing the pain that is under the anger or heaviness that we feel? Though this isn't easy, it can be extremely rewarding. When we take responsibility to sense and ameliorate the anxiety or deficiency we feel in relation to our core sense of value, it takes a lot of pressure off a relationship.[25] Instead of trying to control the other person's behavior or seeking relief through an eruption of disappointed rage, we can approach that person with respect and ultimately openheartedness.[26]

Ultimately, the underpinning of Stosny's training program is that no matter what another's behavior or intention, our core nature of being valuable, worthwhile, and lovable is intrinsic to us and not dependent on another's opinion. For those who seek confirmation of their worth from others' approval, gaining familiarity with such a grounded sense of intrinsic value will mark a major departure. While Stosny does not directly credit Buddhism, his method parallels ways of developing mindful compassion found in traditional practice.[27]

Expressing Feelings

Having developed the skill of attending to their experience through meditation and/or therapy, practitioners can now use it to help them become aware of their current feeling, and couple this with guidance from the assertiveness model of Western psychotherapy to help them communicate effectively with others.[28] This model involves using a clear, nonjudgmental description of another person's objective behavior and its effect on us. For example, "When you say you will be here at noon but come at one o'clock, I feel uncared for and outraged."

My purpose in making a statement about my experience is to inform the other of my own unique experience and create an opportunity to figure out how to avoid this situation in the future. Following such an approach, individuals are sharing their feelings as an act of self-revelation, instead of initiating a cycle of shaming or blame.

To prevent this cycle, we can have compassion for ourselves by accepting that we have a variety of feelings and then recognizing and mindfully acknowledging whatever feelings we have, first to ourselves and then to our partner or friend.[29]

Ultimately, for underexpressers, the task is to effectively bring emotion into the relationship. For overexpressers, the additional first task is to monitor themselves and when overly agitated make use of some way to calm themselves down, such as meditation, reflections on the fears or hurts underlying their anger, taking a walk, or listening to music, so that when they are in face-to-face contact they can safely communicate without escalating into blaming, shaming, threatening, or actual violence.[30]

AVOIDING TWO EXTREMES

To integrate Buddhist values and insights on anger into daily life, we need to figure out how to work with the teachings in a way that makes them real and effective while honoring our cultural and psychological realities. If utilized carefully, the skills of meditation can contribute to our psychological well-being, while the insights of psychology can create the milieu within which our meditation can continue to develop.

This integrated approach avoids the extremes of overexpression and underexpression. Rather than act out our harmfulness and inflict injury on others, we acknowledge our feelings. This is an extension of Buddhist mindfulness practice, in which we acknowledge feelings internally. The further step beyond traditional mindfulness practice is that instead of just silently observing the emotions and physical sensations arising as anger, we use these observations as a basis for reporting about ourselves to others. By internally and externally acknowledging our anger, we also avoid inflicting pain on ourselves. Through sharing our feelings, our vulnerability, and our awareness of our anger, but not acting out the intent to harm, we deepen our personal connection, thus creating the possibility of loving contact with others.

Does this approach psychologize the Dharma, merging Buddhist teachings with a purely psychological agenda? On the one hand this approach is useful and effective in and of itself and could be used for strictly psychological purposes. For some that will suffice—the resultant improvement in relationships will be reward enough. I, however, see these steps not just as ends in themselves but as opportunities in daily life for developing the qualities of mindfulness and awareness necessary for deeper freedom, richer love, less clinging, and ultimately liberating insight.

Embodied Love 10

IN SEPTEMBER 1972, I attended a thirty-day retreat with
Goenka-ji, the Theravadin meditation master from
Burma, in an old colonial hotel perched high over the
valley in Dalhousie, India. By then I had become comfortable with
the structure of retreats and with the practices of concentration, self-
observation, and cultivating love. Although I experienced a lot of physical difficulty during meditation sessions, for three days after leaving
the retreat, I was suffused with an unusual feeling of love, a full-bodied
presence of care for others, rich in tenderness, vibrant, and kind. In
the language of traditional Western theology, I felt touched by God's
grace. I was deeply moved by practicing the Buddhist meditation on
love and compassion, which is called *metta*, "a divine way of abiding"
(*brahma vihara*) because deep, focused love toward all beings is said
to be the very nature of divinity. This opened me to a new dimension
of emotion: delicate, sweet, and oriented toward others in a profound
manner. These initial glimpses have continued to sustain my interest
in deepening and opening my heart. Because I wanted to understand
as much as I could about the teachings on love in this tradition, upon
returning to the United States I chose Theravadin *metta* meditation as
the subject of my Ph.D. thesis.[1]

While I recognize that all religious traditions value love and offer
avenues to its enhancement, the practice that I have been most exposed to and affected by is that of the Buddhist tradition.[2] My interest
in this led me to explore beyond the Theravadin tradition and attend

teachings on the Mahayana practices of cultivating love and compassion given by the late Geshe Rabten in Dharamsala in the fall of 1972. At that time, Geshe Rabten talked about the interconnection of all beings and how valuable it is to develop a sense of gratitude for all that others have done and continue to do for us. He pointed out that the foremost gratitude is owed to our parents, particularly our mothers, because of all the work that went into carrying us, feeding us, and teaching us rudimentary skills such as eating, talking, and walking. To help us understand our interrelatedness further, he spoke of rebirth and the supportive relationships we have had with others in the past, when in past lives others have been our kind mother as well. He also pointed out the ways in which our every activity in the present is supported by the activities of numerous others.

From the Mahayana perspective, the recognition of our indebtedness to others and the wish to help them serves at the outset as the motivation for undertaking practice. Once we acknowledge with heartfelt gratitude all that others have done for us over the course of many lives in their role as our parents, and generate a compassionate and loving wish to repay this kindness, we slowly come to realize that the deepest help we can offer others is to show them the way to become free from all suffering and endowed with full understanding—the achievement of full enlightenment. In order to do that, first one needs to become awakened, to become a buddha. In this way, love is what actually animates our practice on the path to full realization.

Tibetan teachers often mention that the openheartedness that emerges with ongoing practice is what allows more subtle understanding to emerge. In a significant way, love and compassion are a necessary support for liberating spiritual understanding. Then, with the emergence of new transformative wisdom, our care is deepened yet again, and we are moved to assist others, now guided by gnosis. In this way compassion and wisdom form the two interdependent wings of our spiritual flight.

Care for others is thus significant in Buddhist practice in general and central to the Mahayana tradition, in which all aspire to buddhahood. However, for Western students, the foundational Mahayana meditations on developing love and compassion, while inspiring, are not without their difficulties.

LOVE, INTERRELATEDNESS, AND REBIRTH

Some students find it difficult to believe in rebirth and assume this is an obstacle to further practice. For Tibetan Buddhist teachers, the notion that we have benefited from our relationships with others over the course of innumerable lives is simply a description of the way things are. Empirically oriented Westerners may feel they lack sufficient data to convince them absolutely of the truth of rebirth. At the same time, such firm belief is not necessary to engage in this meditation.

I often find Western students approaching Buddhist ideas with an understanding of faith that is borrowed from more familiar religious traditions. Even those who are not active Christians understand that Christian ministers may make central an avowal of faith that Christ died on the cross for the sins of humanity. They then mistakenly assume that some similar decisive expression of faith is necessary for engaging in Buddhist practice. For example, they feel they must have faith in rebirth or the Buddha or karma in order to practice meditation. This is not what I was told by my teachers, and I do not teach in this way either. I have been given all the room I have needed to play or wrestle with new ideas that are difficult to understand. I am therefore uncomfortable when people ask me for simple yes-or-no responses about something like rebirth, since I find myself still actively engaged with this issue, and it is difficult to reply in a way that does justice to the nuances of my engagement with these ideas.

Also difficult for many of us is the idea of rebirth as beginningless. For Buddhists this is an article of faith. The Buddha, who is understood to be omniscient, looked and stated that he could find no beginning to the process of rebirth. It is quite interesting to consider that the very basis of St. Thomas Aquinas's logical argument for God throws out as illogical the possibility of an infinite regress of causes. He argues there needs to be a first cause, namely God.[3] On the other hand, Buddhism, based on the vision of its founder, finds it quite logical to accept a causal sequence that has no perceivable beginning.

Another issue concerns the way Asian teachers frequently use our relationship with our parents as an example of the helpful, loving relationships that we had with others when they were our parents in previous lives. Some students then ask, "How can we do this meditation if our parents were neglectful or abusive? We don't have the model upon which to base the meditation." It is hard, sometimes impossible, to feel love toward one's parents in the face of such painful history. The short answer is that one can do the meditation using any being who has been kind to us and realizing that all beings have been similarly concerned for us in the past. The longer answer is that in the process of working with and internalizing any of the Buddhist meditation teachings on love and compassion, we may face a variety of issues that relate to our psychological history and cultural context. These deserve extended consideration, and that is what we will turn to now.

DEVELOPING THE MIND OF ENLIGHTENMENT

Jeffrey Hopkins, professor of Buddhist studies at the University of Virginia, describes a Mahayana system of contemplation for engendering compassion as passed from Manjushri to Shantideva. One considers the following:

"I am only one. Like all sentient beings I want happiness and not suffering. In this sense we are all equal. Because I am only one, and others are many, they are to be valued even more than myself."[4] And Shantideva says further: "[B]y oppressing oneself for the sake of another, one meets with success in everything."[5] The eleventh-century Tibetan Buddhist master Gampopa says of generosity: "What is the essence of liberality? It is an unattached and spontaneous mind and the dispensing of gifts and requests in that state of mind."[6]

In a completely different context, Timmen Cermak, who has written about the impact of alcoholism on the family, describes the Dependent

Personality Disorder in a book on codependency: "Assuming responsibility for meeting others' needs to the exclusion of acknowledging one's own is a classic symptom of Dependent Personality Disorder. At its root is the fear of being alone or abandoned, which is so great that violence against one's own needs is tolerated."[7]

These quotes clearly illustrate the cultural divide in considering the guidelines of Buddhist texts beside the definitions formulated by our psychiatric establishment. A very superficial reading of these would pathologize Buddhist teachings on love, compassion, and generosity and equate them with dependency or codependency. This is a cross-cultural travesty.

Once again it is important for us to reflect that the general appreciation of interdependence and social reciprocity in traditional Asian cultures is as prevalent as the quest for individuality and personal independence is here. The understanding of interrelatedness dominant in traditional Asian cultures, with the attendant appreciation that one is responsible for others through rules and roles of mutual engagement, goes more than halfway toward supporting the reflections that engender the mind of enlightenment. Given the acceptance of rebirth and the general sense of love and care for relatives and elders, in a traditional setting, it is very easy to talk about an attitude of care for others. In Asia, the major work teachers have to do is to emphasize the significance of loving *all impartially*, pushing students beyond narrow concerns for family, clan, region, or sect, and to explain the ways in which buddhahood is the most loving way of being. Much of the rest of the meditation on developing the altruistic aspiration to enlightenment is quite natural to that cultural setting.

For us in the West, meditation that develops the mind of enlightenment poses several cultural challenges. Philosophically, it involves belief in rebirth and in beginninglessness. Furthermore, it contravenes our concern for our own individuality, independence, and freedom. We are moving into new territory as we begin to consider how we rely on others and owe them a debt of gratitude. These notions can be considered over time from a variety of perspectives, for example, anecdotal evidence regarding rebirth, the nature of our interdependence, and so forth.

Some of us may have little or no difficulty with these hurdles and find ourselves attracted to this vision because of its spiritual expansiveness and the way it meaningfully relates us to others. Sometimes, however, even as we feel this, we may be moved by this vision because it resonates with deep-seated psychological agendas that pressure us to see others as more important than ourselves. To deny that some Western Buddhists who engage in Shantideva's vision do so under a cloud of deep emotional need would be a psychological travesty. Of course there are individuals who can practice the contemplations of love and compassion and engage in generosity without being fueled by a buried sense of inadequacy. These concerns do not apply to every practitioner, of course, but those who are so motivated need to be able to discern their actual intention and work at understanding and resolving it. Failure to do so can cause them to feel underappreciated or misunderstood and ultimately to become depressed, physically symptomatic, anxious, enraged, or burned out, with little understanding as to why.

Anger, hate, and harmfulness are obvious obstacles to cultivating love, and they are relatively easy to detect; Buddhist teachings do address this. The way in which love and generosity can be undermined by our unconscious need for approval and attention is harder to detect and understand, and the psychological dynamics involved in such instances are not discussed in the tradition. Love and kindness can be somewhat like a Trojan horse: They appear attractive, yet over time, if covert needs are at work and not addressed appropriately, they may eventually bring forth a bewildering array of symptoms such as anxiety, depression, numbing, or overwhelming fatigue that can be as surprising and noxious as the Trojan army.

In my own life, an experience of deep, embodied love for all, with its presence, warmth, and reverent, grounded connection, inspired me to undertake further study and practice to encourage these feelings to reemerge. My efforts included practice of the Theravadin meditation on love and the Mahayana contemplations for developing compassion.

During the course of my daily responsibilities, I reflected on the relatedness of beings. My behavior was further guided by teachings from
the Theravadin and Mahayana traditions emphasizing generosity
(*dana*) and kindness to others.

As much as possible, I tried to be kind in my physical, verbal, and
mental behavior. In retrospect, I may have been trying too hard to "be
spiritual," using willfulness to recapture an experience at once fulfill-
ing and evanescent.[8] Perhaps I was overly mindful of my goal and
inattentive to my body and emotions; I don't know that I appeared
especially supportive, precisely because I was putting so much effort
into my intention. Can we appear warm, open, and supportive if we
are *grimly* determined to be kind?

When I began to experience panic attacks, I slowly realized how I
had been stifling my own voice. I saw how hard I had been working,
for the most part unconsciously, to remain unaware of my likes and
dislikes—my authentic feelings—out of awareness while being "kind,"
seeking the approval of those around me. Over the next several years,
with the help of psychotherapy, I began to understand the emotional
baggage that I was importing into my contemplations and behavior
related to love, compassion, generosity, and kindness. These Buddhist
values and practices were not at fault, and these are meditations and
values that I still hold dear. However, over the years I have undergone
the psychological equivalent of microsurgery, whereby the entangled
malignancy of unresolved psychological issues has slowly been disengaged and removed from the healthy, growth-sustaining tissue of spiritual aspiration. Through my work as a teacher and translator and my
involvement in a variety of Buddhist groups, I have come to see that
others bring similar psychological issues to their development of love
and compassion.

One danger in subjecting our spiritual concerns to therapeutic exploration is that our larger spiritual vision can be interpreted to be
related to mere psychological issues—for example, seeing something
like meditation as relating to frustrated needs for maternal union versus some real transformative state.[9] My sense is that many therapists

can be respectful of our spiritual concerns without lapsing into simple-minded reductionism. Fear of such reductionism, however, leads some to shun therapy altogether and seek alternative interventions, such as particular diets or supplements, for their emotional and physical distress. Some of these interventions may offer relief to a lucky few. Sadly, however, if we fail to explore and work through our earlier psychological issues, we could find ourselves experiencing a limited range of feelings and suffering from inexplicable physical and emotional problems.

In reflecting on Buddhist teachings about love and compassion, I would like to suggest a both/and approach, whereby we appreciate the vision of interrelatedness and compassion that underlies Buddhist practice and at the same time honor and engage those roots of hurt in our childhood that might undermine our attempts to embody these values. If these sources of pain are not adequately addressed, they will motivate a sequence of behaviors that can lead us to crash and burn spiritually. What are the roots of spiritual burnout, or "compassion fatigue"?

True Self and False Self

In considering how family-of-origin issues may play out on the spiritual path, I turn to the writing of British pediatrician/psychoanalyst Donald Winnicott.[10] In his work with families and children, Winnicott observed that some parents support their child's spontaneous self-expression and personal exuberance, which he termed the True Self. He also observed that some parents set up a dynamic with their children whereby the children are informed either overtly or covertly that their behavior must conform to parental expectations or there will be a withdrawal of love and affection. This generates behavior that complies with parental expectations but does not reflect the child's inner impulses, and therefore he called this the False Self.

More recent researchers doing systematic observation have found that as early as the second half of their second year, children are capable of displaying emotions they are not feeling. In cases where the parent is withdrawn, children can learn to inhibit expression of their own feelings and substitute false positive feelings.[11] In doing so, the children are attempting to purchase the attention of their parent with the reassurances that everyone is happy. Having learned early on that affection does not come easily or predictably, such children become restrained and evasive when their parent does sporadically attend to them.[12] They want closeness yet fear it, since it has been withdrawn in the past. With caregivers who are hostile or demanding, children learn how to limit their own desires and do exactly what is demanded of them; they become compulsively compliant.[13] This childhood pattern is often linked with overachievement.

False Self dynamics are not at all uncommon, the reality being that probably few of us have been exposed to completely "good enough" parenting.[14] In adulthood, individuals raised in a way that discourages their own self-expression will be vigilant in observing the social horizon for any lack of approval from others. As psychotherapy clients they will excel at reporting about everyone in their social or family network or addressing their therapist's needs, but they will often be frustrated by not knowing their own desires. When such individuals look within, they are greeted initially by silence, some sense they have preferences but don't enact them, or awareness of pressure to attend to the crises affecting others around them. Often as adults, they try to perform a three-step dance: scanning for what needs to get done, "doing the right thing" to perpetuate approval, and rescanning to see if they have succeeded. At core, they may feel that they are not okay, or even feel shame, but if they were just *doing* enough right things they might elicit consistent approval.[15]

Those who are motivated by such dynamics are perpetually seeking others' approval. Their generosity is initiated by their need to get something in return. The vast literature on codependency that sprang up in the 1980s describes these issues. The fact that this label has become faddish, glib, and overapplied on TV talk shows in no way negates the painfulness of False Self dynamics and behavior. Although we may not talk about codependency as much as we used to, these issues have not gone away for Buddhist practitioners.[16] What is most difficult is that the anxiety behind False Self behavior is rooted in the earlier desperation of the child seeking approval, and it is thus deep, powerful, and often unconscious.

REPETITION COMPULSION

How do False Self dynamics play out for those developing love, compassion, generosity, and the altruistic aspiration to enlightenment?

Our motivations are complex. We may be attracted in a very reasoned, mature way to the traditional vision of developing universal love, and at the same time we may take up such spiritual practice in part to please a surrogate parent, the teacher, and thereby receive his or her admiration and blessings. It is certainly important to be open to the spiritual love of a teacher, which can provide great solace and inspiration in times of difficulty and on occasion may touch us so deeply that it opens an entirely new vision of human experience to us.

It is clearly heartwarming to receive love and support from other adults. If, however, our predominant—but covert—motivation for doing the practices described in this chapter is to secure the love and approval of our teacher, we may be setting ourselves up for intense disappointment. If what moves us is the frustrated need for the validating attention of an adult, we may be creating a situation that is sure to fail.

In communal situations such as spiritual communities, people often replicate issues they first experienced in their family of origin. Whether our community contains twenty or two hundred other students, how much of our teacher's attention and time can we realistically expect when we want to report on our practice of developing love, compassion, and generosity? It is natural to feel yearning toward teachers as if they were parents and to see other members of the community as either supportive or obstructive siblings and relatives. But what do we do with our disappointments, upsets, and sibling jealousies? To the extent that these have not been resolved, what often occur in spiritual

organizations are intense re-creations of childhood dynamics—
conflicts, departures, and incomprehensible emotional pain. I have
witnessed this as a student, a translator, and a teacher.

Although Freud's work has certainly come in for reevaluation, his
identification of the repetition compulsion attests to the acuity of his
observations of human behavior. Over and over, in spiritual settings
and in therapy, we engage in new situations hoping for better endings
to old stories. We compulsively repeat. What is so confounding is that
we look forward to a different outcome but re-create in some measure
the psychological components that prevented a happy ending to begin
with. We are motivated by an unacknowledged wish to repair the past
through the present. If we experienced deep disappointments in childhood, the sad reality is that even if a teacher were moved by compassion to offer us all the time and love we seek, we are no longer
children. Time and love we lost as a child cannot be replaced. When
students face frustration with one teacher, they often move on to another teacher or a different group, motivated by a vague hope of finding that one teacher who will finally fulfill their inner longing and heal
their wounds. Unfortunately, however much attention we get as adults
will never be enough due to the nature of our unresolved pain. Ralph
Klein and James P. Masterson, psychiatrists working with the issue of
early loss, explain that without emotionally working through our pain,
our contact with others may make us temporarily *feel* better, but we
will not *get* better.[17] It is relatively easy to feel better temporarily
through contact with inspiring teachers and a lot harder to become
better psychologically through such contact. Attachment to feeling better can unfortunately lead to unfulfilling dependency.

A related issue arises when we wish to deepen our capacity for love
through following our teacher's exhortation to reflect on our parents'
kindness in order to inspire a sense of gratitude toward others. Emotional wounds experienced at a parent's hands may prevent us from
seeing our parents as the touchstone for deepening our appreciation
of others. While this type of obstacle shocked Tibetan teachers when
they first heard about it, they have indicated that it is possible to use

any individual who has been kind to us as a stimulus in developing gratitude toward all beings. At the same time, the recognition of difficulty in feeling tenderness toward a parent alerts the practitioner to an opportunity to look anew at an issue that may be closing him or her off to a variety of significant emotional experiences.

In working through disappointments with respect to teachers, and blockages felt in the cultivation of love and compassion, some grieving may be inevitable, and some assumption of emotional responsibility for the psychological work entailed may be necessary.[18] In such situations, therapy is a valuable resource. It facilitates a growing acceptance of who we really are emotionally. Working through our past losses and hurts within the therapeutic relationship allows a different type of care to become part of our personal history. To the extent that we become open to ourselves, we authentically feel more empathy for others. In some instances, it may be very difficult to ever feel any gratitude toward a particularly abusive parent. However, emotional work can serve the larger spiritual purpose of deepening our appreciation of the meaning of our experience and open us to empathy for others, sometimes reaching up to even the less than adequate parent.

PRACTICING GENEROSITY

In addition to seeking approval from a teacher, practitioners may seek similar approval from peers by acting generously. The giver may feel that she is acting kindly, but she may in fact be more interested in the other person's emotional response than anything else. The recipient may appreciate her generosity, but the giver may unfortunately feel depleted when the recipient leaves and she no longer has the approval she sought. When the giver realizes how much she depends on others to feel good about herself, she may feel rage at the recipient, herself, or both. These dynamics can be much easier to identify in others than in ourselves.

The Buddhist tradition is of some help here in alerting us to when we are about to go off track. Lacking the elaborated developmental psychology of the modern West or the concerns that we have for emotionally grounded individuality, the tradition still provides some pithy observations about the nature of unqualified self-offering. Shantideva wrote: "In fact, through acting for the good of others, there is neither intoxication nor dismay, nor even desire for the reward, with a thirst solely for the well-being of others."[19] And Gampopa wrote:

> A Bodhisattva does not give . . . in order to gain fame and praise.
>
> To avoid an improper manner of giving means that we should not make a gift if we do not rejoice at doing so . . .
>
> [A] Bodhisattva . . . feels no regret after making the gift.[20]

One story from the tradition involves Shariputra, one of the Buddha's eminent disciples, who was challenged by someone who wanted to spiritually humiliate him. This deceitful individual asked Shariputra to cut off his right arm and offer it, which Shariputra did. But when the recipient then changed his mind and refused the gift, Shariputra became enraged and fell from his bodhisattva vow to help all beings. Though they did not use the language of True Self and False Self, the storytellers in the tradition understood that we can give with a dubious motivation, with all sorts of unarticulated strings attached. If our desire to give is linked to the recipient's response to our gift, we may be seeking emotional gratification for ourselves rather than offering a gift in a pure spirit of generosity. Both the Buddhist and the therapeutic traditions would agree that we are on solid ground if we are clear that our giving does not involve expecting something in return.

AM I OVERDOING IT?

Kindness, generosity, love, and compassion are all significant constituents of evolving spirituality. But is it possible to do too much of a good thing? Much of the world's religious literature provides examples of spiritual behavior that expands our notion of what is humanly possible.

Out of devotion, Abraham was said to have been prepared to offer his son. In India, Asanga, motivated by compassion, was said to have been prepared to lick the maggots off an infested dog. There is something both inspiring and frighteningly awesome in these images. If we are driven to emulate such behavior with the covert psychological agenda of finally winning parental or social approval, we may be sorely disappointed.

To the extent that we unconsciously act out of False Self dynamics, we do not listen to ourselves but anticipate something from others. When we look outward in this way, we do not pay attention to our own motivations or reactions until we feel overwhelmed. Due to unfulfilled earlier needs, we may engage in activity that is really beyond our capacity. If we find that compassionate activity is followed by feelings of rage or despair, it may be a clue to unresolved earlier issues.

How can we know whether our actions are coming from an internally grounded motivation rather than buried need?

❧ Self-Reflection

Examine yourself honestly and ask: When I perform a particular act of kindness or do something considerate, am I seeking a particular response from others? Can I be mindful and aware of such wishes and have some sense of how they are working within me?

After an act of generosity, am I disappointed because I did not get the social acknowledgment I anticipated? Do I find myself feeling depleted? Do I end up thinking things like "People never appreciate me," "Why don't people love me," or "I do so much for them"?

Even if we find that we have complex motivations for our altruistic behavior, this does not mean we should give up being kind or generous or stop meditating on love. Rather, it means that we use our practice both to engage in behavior that is positive and to become aware of our intentions. Practice goes on and at the same time clarifies our psychological issues. If we answer these questions in the affirmative, it may be a clue to an inner need that might be best addressed in therapy rather than acted out with consequent feelings of disappointment, despair, depression, or rage. We can see how these issues played out in the life of one of my clients.

Jerome came from a tight-knit Italian family. His mother suffered from multiple sclerosis and depended on him to take care of some of her medical needs. Jerome found himself dabbling in a variety of meditative traditions and feeling particularly drawn to the meditation on love and compassion. Jerome's girlfriend, though capable, had a terrible job and frequently asked him for large sums of money to buy costume jewelry, which he gave her. She also spent about fifteen dollars a week of Jerome's money on lottery tickets, explaining that she had really strong hunches. Jerome asked his Buddhist teacher if it was helpful to give gifts from his earnings rather than keeping it all for himself, and his teacher enthusiastically affirmed that generosity was a very positive virtue. Jerome volunteered to repair the leak and stain in the reception area of his meditation center. No one seemed to notice the beautiful, careful work he had done. At the end of that task, his teacher asked him to consider working on the roof of the meditation hall. Jerome noticed he was feeling stressed, tired, and anxious. A friend suggested that therapy might help him out.

In therapy we explored his feelings of needing to take care of his girlfriend, his mother, and his teacher and how he felt trapped in his caregiving and generosity. While initially talking of his commitment to love and generosity, we gradually began to see that his "love" felt unfree, programmed, and like bondage. He felt no joy in giving and actually harbored a growing bitterness. Jerome slowly came to understand some of what he did not get in his family of origin and to grieve those losses. He saw how the attention that he did not receive as a child affected his current quest for approval. He got in touch with long-buried feelings of resentment that helped him to set limits with respect to how much he offered of himself. As a consequence, Jerome felt freer to make choices about volunteering to work at his meditation center. He also became clear about what he could reasonably do for his mother and sought ways of sharing this responsibility with others. He decided that he was no longer going to support his girlfriend's lottery purchases, and he cut back significantly on his purchase of presents.

To the extent that we are conscious of our motivations, we are more able to make informed choices. Once we begin the process of attending to and validating our sensations and feelings, we can slowly reverse the False Self process. Meanwhile, it is important to examine whether we are attempting to do something beyond our capacity, in the hope of some anticipated reward, and decide whether to proceed or not. It is helpful to understand that there will be awkward periods as we come to know ourselves emotionally.

In considering the effects of these various psychological issues on our spiritual practice, we might become disheartened and consider abandoning it. This would be the least productive response. Such issues need not be insurmountable obstacles to our development of love and compassion. Rather, they can become a most powerful fuel for making our empathy for others real and alive. The mind-training instructions of Jamgon Kongtrul can help us use our own difficulty to develop compassion for others.

❧ Enhancing Compassion through Empathetic Contemplation

If we feel that our knowledge of ourselves is limited, we can make this heartfelt aspiration: "May my difficulty in this area absorb the similar difficulties of all others." If we overextend ourselves and then find we are depressed, regretful, or angry: "May my emotional turmoil absorb that of all others." If we get in touch with our own poignant need for others' approval: "May I absorb this

similar need from all others." If we do this not merely as an intellectual exercise but grounded in our bodies and feelings, it is a
powerful way to open our hearts to the dilemmas of all other
beings. A natural tenderness ensues.

If during our practice we experience a heartfelt feeling of love,
compassion, or generosity, we can share this quality through
imagining light spreading out from us and establishing all others
in liberated buddhahood.[21]

CONTEMPLATIONS ON LOVE AND COMPASSION

I find the following two Buddhist contemplations particularly helpful
for enhancing our care and appreciation for others. The meditation on
love, drawn from the Theravadin tradition, is simple and can be done
by itself or as the conclusion to another practice. I have developed a
slight variation on the traditional approach, based on trial and error in
working with Western students.[22] The meditation on interrelatedness is
based on teachings I received from Geshe Rabten in Dharamsala,
India, in 1972. This contemplation is an especially accessible approach
to developing openheartedness, as it does not depend on belief in rebirth.

Meditation on Love

We begin the meditation with ourselves, for if we do not love
ourselves, it is difficult to love others. In *The Path of Purification*,
this is explained in the following way:

> [I]f he develops it [love] in this way "I am happy. Just as
> I want to be happy and dread pain, as I want to live and
> not to die, so do other beings, too," making himself the
> example, the desire for other beings' welfare and happi-
> ness arises in him.

Who loves himself will never harm another.[23]

Especially in the West, where so many of us struggle with issues of low self-esteem, it is important to begin the process of developing universal love by starting with wishing ourselves well.

In a very gentle and relaxed way, we wish for ourselves:

> May I be happy.
> May I be free from suffering.
> May I be free from all abuse, internal and external.
> May my life be rich in meaning and centered in purpose.
> May I be blessed to see the challenge of my adversity.
> May I be at peace.[24]

We then take the positive feelings that arise from doing this and see if we can extend them to some spiritual mentor or teacher for whom it is easy to feel love and compassion, calling this person to mind and making these wishes on his or her behalf: "May my spiritual mentor be happy" and so forth.

We then expand further by seeing if we can extend our positive feelings to someone who is near and dear to us and then do the same for a neutral person, for example, a stranger we see in the supermarket.

Finally, we see if we can do the same toward an enemy. If this is difficult, there are many suggestions enumerated in the previous chapters for reducing our anger. With approaches like those, we attempt to ameliorate resentment and extend to our enemy the love that we felt for the near and neutral. If this is successful, we can then expand our love to all people in our neighborhood, town, city, state, country, and then the whole world. We can also expand our focus to include not only humans but all beings that we comfortably believe in—for Buddhists, this typically includes hell beings, hungry ghosts, animals, humans, demigods, and gods.

✑ Deepening Gratitude toward Others through Reflecting on Interrelatedness

Begin by settling comfortably into a meditative state either through relaxation or mindfulness of the breath for a short time. Begin to consider the loaf of bread that you bought at the store today. Consider how it is in dependence on the person who owns the store and the people who work there that you were able to buy it. Isn't it appropriate to feel gratitude to these people?

Now think of the people who constructed the store where you bought the bread; the people who deliver the bread; and the people who built the road as well as the truck in which the bread was delivered. Isn't it suitable to feel appreciative toward all of them?

What about the people involved in creating and shipping the parts that make up the vehicle that delivered the bread? And if some parts come from abroad, consider all the people involved there in manufacturing, assembling, and delivering the parts. Then consider all the people and beings involved in feeding those involved in these manufacturing and delivery positions—the farmers, the cows, the animals that contribute to fertilizer, the insects involved in pollination. Isn't this loaf of bread related to all of them as well?

In light of our understanding of photosynthesis, we can go even further. Think of all of the beings whose exhalation contributes to supporting the plants that go into making the food that ultimately feeds us. Even the exhalation of our enemies supports these plants. Are we not connected to and dependent upon all of them?

Can we feel a sense of gratitude that includes innumerable others through understanding that they all contribute to our welfare? When we experience an emotionally grounded sense of appreciation, we sit with it, settling into the felt sense of positive relatedness.

MIND OF LOVE/MIND OF ENLIGHTENMENT

Since starting graduate school in 1966, I have had occasion to receive oral teachings on love and compassion from a variety of Tibetan, Burmese, Mongolian, and Western teachers.[25] From the Mahayana Buddhist perspective, the deepest love is to take on the responsibility for the care of all beings. This can be fully accomplished only by beings who have the wisdom, compassion, and capacity of a buddha. Deepening our love and compassion then serves as the emotional basis for engaging our motivation (*citta* in Sanskrit) toward awakening, or enlightenment (*bodhi*). Such teachings are typically presented as instructions for developing "the mind of enlightenment," or *bodhicitta*.

Khetsun Sangpo Rinpoche tells the story of a famous Tibetan outlaw who decided to kill a pregnant mare. He slashed open her stomach, and as she lay dying the foal emerged. With whatever life was left in her, the mare immediately started licking the foal clean, using her last dying energy to care for her offspring. The outlaw was so moved by the sight of this motherly love that he turned toward religion and the cultivation of love and compassion and went on to become a famous and inspiring religious teacher.

Teaching at the University of Virginia in the mid-1970s, Lati Rinpoche suggested that if it is difficult for us to get in touch with our sense of connection to our mother, we can go to a desolate place and with great abandon repeatedly shout "Ma! Ma! Ma!"

The contemplations included here are meant to create a deep sense of connection to others and a concern for their welfare. Although they have a cognitive aspect, it is the feeling with which the teachings were imparted that touched me most. The printed word may not be up to the task of conveying this experiential aspect of the instructions. Minimally, I can hope to serve as a conduit to these teachings and the sources of inspiration that have touched me. I would encourage anyone who can to attend lectures by realized teachers such as His Holiness the Dalai Lama on the mind of enlightenment. It is a powerful experience to be in the presence of a teacher who embodies these teachings, and this can serve as a significant experiential touchstone for returning to these contemplations over and over.

◌ Cultivating Love and Compassion Leading to the Mind of Enlightenment

For this meditation, see if you can adopt an attitude of experimentation and open yourself to a variety of views that may not be in full accord with your current beliefs.

We begin by considering someone who is dear to us in this life. If we can entertain the possibility of past lives and accept, even temporarily, that the process of rebirth goes back without beginning, then it makes logical sense that this person who is most dear to us today was in some difficult relationship with us in the past. Because rebirth goes back without limit, there has been enough time for any given being to have been in multiple relationships with us over the course of innumerable lives. There is really no need to single out this friend today from all other beings as specially positive. He is dear today, but he was probably our enemy at one time in the past. Similarly, someone who is an enemy in this life was in the past probably our best friend, so there is no reason to single her out as negative in this life. We stabilize in our meditation when we have some feeling that we can bring an equal level of engagement to all beings. This step enhances the attitude of equality toward all.

We then deepen our sense of connectedness to others by considering that over the course of innumerable births, each being has been our mother or a particularly helpful friend.[26] We reflect that our mother, or a particularly helpful person, has been beneficial to us not only in this life but in previous lives as well. Because rebirth is without beginning in the past, there have been numerous opportunities for this currently helpful person to have been so in the past as well. Not only has this particular individual been kind to us, but other beings have as well: our father, siblings, neighbors, neutral people, enemies, animals, and insects—all beings whom we can think of have been significantly helpful to us in some previous life. We stabilize in our meditation with this realization.

We then consider that they have cared for us deeply. We can consider how our own mother carried us despite her discomfort; how she fed us, cleaned us in our infancy, clothed us, and taught us the rudiments of language and communication that serve as a basis for whatever subsequent learning we have acquired. Or we can consider the dedication and love shown by animals as they tend to their offspring, and we recognize that we have received such care.

Through these practices and contemplations, we allow ourselves to be suffused with a sense of connection, gratitude, and appreciation for what our mothers have done for us. It is then quite natural to develop a desire to repay the kindness of our mothers. At this point, teachers will often talk of how it would be if we were to see our old mother, decrepit and almost blind, approaching a precipice. We would, of course, be moved without hesitation to intercede and assist her. Just so, when we realize that all beings have been our mothers, and that they are blinded by their reactive patterns and about to fall into repeated engagement with pain and suffering, we are moved to intervene on their behalf. It is very common for Tibetan teachers to talk with tenderness of all sentient beings as "our old mothers." We rest with the wish to repay the kindness of all these old mothers. With this wish, we quite naturally feel love and compassion for all these beings who have been our mothers. This is expressed in turn through our wish for them all to be happy and free from suffering.

From within this feeling of love and compassion, we can be stirred to take on the responsibility to establish beings in happiness and freedom from suffering. From the Buddhist perspective, the being most capable of doing this is a buddha, and therefore at this point we naturally, enthusiastically, and in a warm-hearted way create the motivation to become a buddha in order to be able to help beings in a most profound way. We allow our hearts to expand into this feeling, which is the altruistic aspiration to achieve buddhahood, bodhicitta.

I have provided here only a bare outline of the meditation. What makes it powerful is quiet emotional reflection using examples that bring each point vividly to life. There are numerous instances of inspiration available to us to vivify the elements of this meditation if we keep our eyes and ears open to the stories we read or hear from our friends. For example, I was recently moved to tears by an obituary in the *New York Times* for Pepi Deutsch, a 101-year-old Holocaust survivor. The heart of this meditation is spontaneously expressed through an incident that illustrates the relationship of the heroic mother and daughter, Pepi and Clara:

> But that Clara survived told much about the sacrifices her mother was willing to make. In January 1945, after the two women weathered months of hunger, cold, lice and savagery from their guards, Mrs. Deutsch made sure that Clara got to celebrate her 17th birthday. She hoarded three slices of bread, coated them with marmalade and produced a birthday cake.
>
> The daughter repaid her on other occasions, once shaming a young Nazi guard into an apology of sorts after he struck Mrs. Deutsch across the shoulder. Clara simply reminded him to think of his own mother.[27]

Love and compassion are cultivated as part of the path and are taught with some variants in the Theravadin and Mahayana schools. In all instances, such openhearted practice is informed by nonattachment.

For us in the West, understanding the practice of love and compassion from a perspective of nonattachment seems initially problematic, since love seems to be intrinsically linked with positive attachment in our culture. This brings us naturally to consider attachment and nonattachment from a cross-cultural and psychological perspective.

Attachment East and West   11

"ATTACHMENT" is a term central to both Buddhist teachings and the literature on psychological development. However, as is the case with *ego*, with *attachment* we have a word that can have very negative value in the Buddhist English vocabulary, and a very positive one in the psychological domain. The following quotes exemplify the divergent significance of *attachment*. In the quotes from the Theravadin tradition, *thirst, desire, craving,* and *attachment,* used somewhat interchangeably, are seen as the very root of suffering.

> "[T]hirst," desire, greed, craving . . . [give] rise to all forms of suffering.[1]

> Here the term *thirst* includes not only desire for, and attachment to, sense-pleasure, wealth and power, but also desire for, and attachment to, ideas, views, opinions, theories, conceptions and beliefs (*dhamma-tanha*).[2]

> Repeated births are each a torment.
> Seeking but not finding the "House Builder,"
> I wandered through many a Samsaric birth.
> O "House Builder," thou art seen,
> Thou wilt not rebuild the house.
> All thy rafters have been shattered.
> Demolished has thy ridge pole been.

My mind has won the Unconditioned (*Nibbana*),
The extinction of craving is achieved (arhatship).[3]

From craving grief arises,
From craving arises fear,
For him who is craving free
There is no grief, then whence comes fear?[4]

All is burning, all is in flames. And what is the "all" that is in flames, that is burning? The eye is burning. Visible objects are burning. Eye consciousness is burning. Eye contact is burning. Feeling whether pleasant or painful or neither pleasant nor painful that arises with eye-contact as its condition, that too is burning.

With what are they burning? With the fire of craving, with the fire of hate, with the fire of delusion. They are burning with birth, ageing and death, with sorrow, lamentation, pain, grief and woe. . . .

Seeing this the wise become dispassionate towards the eye . . . Through dispassion greed fades away. With the fading away of greed, his mind is liberated. . . .[5]

For those studying the development of human bonding in infancy, *attachment* describes the developmentally appropriate search for closeness by a child. It is a normal and positive quality explained in the following way by John Bowlby, the initiator of psychological study of attachment:

To say of a child that he is attached to, or has an attachment to, someone means that he is strongly disposed to seek proximity to and contact with a specific figure and to do so in certain situations, notably when he is frightened, tired or ill. . . .

Attachment behavior . . . refers to any of the various

forms of behavior that a child commonly engages in to at
tain and/or maintain a desired proximity."⁶

CRAVING, ATTACHMENT, THIRST, AND DESIRE

From the outset we need to clarify the range of meanings for the words
craving, attachment, thirst, and *desire,* when used in Buddhist translations and in Western psychological contexts.

In the Buddhist context, *attachment* is used technically to denote
the state of desire that provokes future rebirth (*upadana*) and as a
gloss for several related terms as well. Just as *anger* is often the term
preferred by translators for hostile intentions, so too *attachment* is
often the word we choose for a variety of technical words in Asian
languages related to a clinging, craving type of connection.⁷

Thirst, attachment, and *craving* are just a few of many words used to
describe unwholesome involvement with things. In Buddhist psychology, all such unwholesome involvements can be understood to be variants of greed (*lobha*) or passionate desire (*raga/kama*). There is a clear
evocative characterization of these attitudes in *The Path of Purification*:

> Of these, *greed* has the characteristic of grasping an object
> like birdlime (lit. "monkey lime")[i.e., bird or monkey
> droppings]. Its function is sticking, like meat put in a hot
> pan. It is manifested as not giving up, like the dye of lamp
> black. Its proximate cause is seeing enjoyment in things that
> lead to bondage. Swelling with the current of craving, it
> should be regarded as taking [beings] with it to states of loss
> as a swift-flowing river does to the great ocean.⁸

Call it what we will—greed, thirst, desire, craving, clinging, attachment—getting stuck on sensuous experience or philosophical positions is seen as a cause for rebirth.⁹ In its most blatant forms, this is
the greed that leads some individuals to restlessly accumulate more
and more money; the craving that leads individuals to engage repeat-

edly in superficial relationships driven primarily by sexual desire and the need for something new and different; the thirst for fame; the attachment to creating a glamorous home for others to admire; or even the intense need to find the perfect outfit to wear to a party. This type of attached longing is clearly described in a process technically known as dependent origination, which delineates how in dependence on specific causes certain conditions inevitably arise.[10] Part of this sequence is that we (1) have experiences that (2) give rise to feelings, which (3) are followed by craving and (4) attachment, and this leads to (5) rebirth and (6) its attendant suffering. This is the heart of the Buddhist understanding of the process of rebirth.

In contrast to the modern Western scientific view, which holds that the mind ceases at death, Buddhists believe that the mind continues after death. Furthermore, the quality of our moment-to-moment reactions and choices influences what our mind continuum will experience in the future. When it is under the influence of attachment, the mind continues to cycle in samsara; when under the influence of liberating wisdom, it can become free from the cycle. For Theravadins, freedom is in the eternal peace of nirvana. For followers of the Mahayana, ultimate freedom is in buddhahood, wherein one can simultaneously dwell in a heavenly pure realm and work to benefit beings in a variety of manifestations.

Westerners are confused when they think that Buddhist translations that counsel giving up attachment, craving, thirst, clinging, and desire mean that we should abandon all motivated activity whatsoever. Although *desire* can refer to a very strong, focused wish to acquire something, it can also mean the simple intention to act: "I desire to present my lecture at four o'clock." The Buddhist teachings do not suggest that we give up intentional activity in general, rather that we give up fixated adhesion to things and ideas, and they offer various strategies for doing so. The difficulty we have in imagining "stick-free" activity shows us how immersed we are in attachment.

I remember visiting Khetsun Sangpo Rinpoche in Dharamsala in 1971. When he went to work in the morning, he just sat down at his desk and started working in a simple, effortless, and unaffected way. He was working, but there was no heaviness to his activity whatsoever. He was modeling unattached activity. This is in contrast to my own experience of sitting down to work. First, I get beset with questions about how I can address what I want to write. Then I have to arrange my desk by fiddling with my papers. This is followed by some sense that I am about to become a "writer" as I sit at my computer. And finally there is the sense of really wishing to say something new and insightful. If I write for three or four hours, a definite tight, sticky feeling arises, and I am tired. If I reflect back, I recognize I have been working under the influence of a variety of attached desires.

Desire, in the sense of intention, is morally neutral; it may be present with either wholesome or unwholesome states of mind.[11] After all, Buddhist teachers throughout history have had the *desire* to act in the sense of intention, although not in the sense of getting preoccupied with things. They have given up driven, fixated, clinging forms of intentionality, not action itself. The key to avoiding misunderstanding is that engagement does not necessarily entail attachment.

Almost every time I give a lecture on Buddhism to a relatively large audience, someone will mistakenly conflate the two meanings of *desire* and ask, "How can I keep a job and take care of myself, my family, and my responsibilities at work if I give up desire?" I explain that all of those activities can continue. The tradition is encouraging us to diminish and ultimately eradicate fixated, stuck forms of wanting, not activity altogether.

The Buddhist context for discussing attachment relates to the origin of cyclic existence and suffering. The various Buddhist systems differ in their practice methods (see chapter 12) and what they emphasize as short-term goals: In working with attachment, some schools emphasize altering behavior; others emphasize developing vision and wisdom to transform or see through attachment; and others emphasize faith as a vehicle for transporting practitioners out of the cycle of suffering that attachment brings.[12] Yet they all agree that diminishing clinging to worldly matters is fundamental. The Buddhist teachings are aimed at people who are presumed to be capable of self-reflection and ethical decision making. The teachings offer a moral narrative that explains that rebirth and suffering are primarily caused by attachment, greed, and fixated clinging.[13] Being able to weaken and abandon these attitudes in turn leads to profound inner freedom.

PSYCHOLOGICAL ATTACHMENT THEORY

Whereas *attachment* has purely negative connotations in Buddhist discourse, the word has a very different meaning in modern psychology. It is worth examining how this word can represent something so negative in one context—that is, the detrimental attitude blamed for leading us into repeated suffering—and so valuable in another—the critical nurturant bond central to human development. Do these two meanings of *attachment* in fact point to the same thing? Or to different things? If they are different, how? I would suggest caution, in light of our cross-cultural consideration of anger, before we conclude that a translated term points to identical usage in two languages. Before jumping to any conclusions, we need to look at the narrative context in which the word is used and how its meaning is shaped by that context.

Psychological attachment theory is a growing branch of developmental psychology that owes its inception to the British psychoanalyst John Bowlby, who in the late 1950s began presenting papers that contested dominant psychoanalytic theory.[14] In "The Nature of the Child's Tie to His Mother," Bowlby countered the analytic view that instinctual-need satisfaction was primary and attachment secondary. He explored infant-mother behavior in terms of the reciprocal bonds between parent and child. Furthermore, he saw attachment as normal rather than a regressive form of dependency. In a second paper, Bowlby articulated reasons for infant attachment and identified their strong responses to separation, including protest, despair, and detachment.[15] Going against the received wisdom of the day, he articulated what we now take as given, that mourning does occur in children,[16] whenever the attachment behaviors of figures to whom they are connected are unavailable. Bowlby suggested that too frequent a change in primary nurturing figures may hamper the child's ability to form relationships.

Unlike Freud, Bowlby saw, in theory, no danger in the overgratification of infants. He also understood, however, that in some instances the mother's pseudoaffection or overprotection are compensation for unconscious maternal hostility and that gratification so motivated may not be in the best interest of the child.[17] For Bowlby, childhood separation anxiety stemmed from threatened or actual rejection and abandonment by parents. Such rejection and abandonment could come in the form of overprotection, underprotection, misattunement, or separation due to death or illness. Children often take the responsibility for these situations.[18]

More recent research indicates that school-age children's sense of security is influenced by consistency, responsiveness, and attunement with parents during infancy, which support the children's sense of connection and attachment.[19] Mary Ainsworth, an American researcher and colleague of Bowlby's, did much to further the empirical study of parent-child attachment. In brief, through careful observation of infants and mothers both in a natural setting and in the laboratory, Ainsworth assessed the effect of the quality of the infant-mother relationship on the child's behavior. She devised a laboratory procedure to examine the balance of attachment and exploratory behavior in the face of high and low stress. Of note in this research were the behavior patterns that toddlers exhibited upon reunion with their mothers during the laboratory procedure. These reactions showed strong similarity to results emerging in naturalistic observations of children separated from their parent in hospitals and to the observations made by Bowlby in his paper on childhood separation.[20] When reunited with mother, the majority of the children sought closeness, interaction, and contact with her and were quickly soothed.[21] These children were understood to have a certain assurance in their relationship, termed *secure attachment*. This is fostered by a parent's capacity to assist children in moderating their feelings.[22] When a child feels upset and is reliably able to go to a parent and be held and soothed, this is a source of deepening attachment.

Other children, however, seemed ambivalent, seeking contact with their mothers yet being angry, not easily soothed, and even kicking or hitting.[23] Others snubbed or avoided their mothers upon return. These two behavior patterns were correlated with a less harmonious home relationship. Such children lacked a certain trust in their mothers. They exhibited what is termed insecure attachment. Here children both were drawn to the parent and wanted to hang back. When upset, they wanted to be held and soothed, but they were frustrated with the inappropriate or incompetent soothing they had received in the past and therefore wanted to stay away.[24] The *avoidant* child, who both tracks her parent and keeps her distance, is balancing the pain of her own loneliness against the ache of parental rejection.[25] The *ambivalent* child, whose parent inconsistently overwhelms and neglects him, is hurt upon separation and has all sorts of conflicted feelings upon re-union because of the fear that his mother will either disappear or in-trude upon his boundaries.[26] In sum, Ainsworth identifies three styles of attachment: *secure, avoidant,* and *ambivalent.* Mary Main, a profes-sor of psychology at Berkeley, has explored attachment patterns in adults, particularly parents, and discovered that patterns from child-hood fairly consistently carry over into adulthood—to parenting, cou-ple relationships, and care of elderly parents.[27] Here secure attachment would be exhibited by those who find comfort in relationships with peers, partners, spouses, children, parents, and colleagues. By way of contrast, avoidant adults would have few friends and even in commit-ted relationships would tend to be unavailable emotionally; the stereo-type here would be of the intellectually gifted but unapproachable scientist. On the other hand, ambivalent adults have relationships marked by intense approach followed by conflictual withdrawal. The characters George and Martha in *Who's Afraid of Virginia Woolf?* ex-emplify this type of rapidly oscillating relationship.

In psychotherapy, our internal working models of who we are in relationship to attachment figures is repeatedly superimposed upon the therapist in the process called *transference*. In addition to being an arena for reenacting the past, therapy also provides a secure base for clients to explore and reorient their internalized expectations.[28] As we shall see, spiritual life is another milieu in which we express our dominant attachment styles.

Attachment thus is considered in very different contexts in Western psychotherapy and in Buddhism. Psychologists start with the development of the human infant and explore its disposition to seek proximity and closeness. This exploration is then used to consider the influence of early child rearing on the quality of an individual's relationships throughout life.[29]

In the following discussion, I will be using a variety of terms and phrases, defined here as follows:

Attachment, in the Buddhist context, refers to those attitudes of mind that involve getting stuck or fixated on ideas or on objects of the senses. For example, it would be present in the obsessive desire to buy a particular new car or the narrow-minded adherence to a political or religious ideology. In the psychological context, attachment is the disposition to seek proximity and contact first seen in infants and then carried into adulthood. In children, it is seen in the child's movement toward his or her parent when feeling afraid. In adults, it is the interest in meeting with friends, lovers, and family to talk about each other's lives.

Nonattachment is a Buddhist value of being not stuck or fixated on things or ideas. As an approach to practice, it refers to reducing clinging to things. As a result of practice, it is an aspect of internal freedom. For example, a monk seeking to deepen his nonattachment might mindfully observe his feelings about his cherished begging bowl; when he is realized, he would be even-minded when his begging bowl is broken. A layperson might become aware of the way she gets lost in pursuing wealth, fame, or popularity and consider whether that is bringing her ultimate satisfaction. In a realized state, she might still be actively involved in her career and family, yet not feel driven or mindless in her moment-to-moment existence.

Avoidant attachment is seen in children when they avoid reuniting with their mothers after separation. We can see this acted out in adults as detachment (which is to be distinguished from nonattachment). Avoidant attachment is a psychological disengagement from relationships, career, and creative pursuits, seen in individuals who in order to avoid the risk of failure or disappointment repetitively avoid challenging jobs or long-term relationships.

Ambivalent attachment is seen in children when they seem to both cling to their mothers and at the same time express anger. We see this acted out in adults as clinging, needy longing toward an unresponsive other.

HEALTHY ATTACHMENT IN ADULTS

Psychotherapist Leigh McCullough Vaillant provides a clear contrast between healthy secure attachment and ambivalent attachment.[30]

In adults, the latter is an attitude of neediness, almost an addiction. It may be angry, clingy, or demanding of closeness. Ambivalently attached individuals are urgent in their moves to closeness, fearful of separateness, and self-absorbed; they may objectify others ("my hunk," "my trophy bride") or ignore their emotional reality. Without a history of appropriate love, it is easy for those with ambivalent attachment to passively accept abuse or neglect and defensively long for that which is unavailable.[31] Such longing is not an attitude that values another but is what Vaillant calls a "grasping need," fueled by an inability to be alone.

This type of defensive attachment is in contrast to appropriate longing for another, which constitutes healthy love. Love, or adaptive attachment, is an attitude marked by care of self and others, exchange of grateful physical holding, experience of gratitude, active desire for closeness, gradual development in closeness, negotiation of needs, respect of others' needs for separateness, empathy, and a sense of fresh, curious communion. It involves enjoyment and a mutual interchange of care, acknowledgment, and validation. In a love of mutual care, there is place for creating a sense of reliability—secure attachment in the Western psychological sense.

Buddhist teachings on nonattachment can be relevant to this type of positive love. Although the idea of losing ourselves in relationship by being glued to an idealized other is a staple of popular songs, romance novels, and movies, a case can be made for avoiding such needy stickiness. When tolerance for the other person's weaknesses or deficiencies is conjoined with warm, engaged affection and effective communication skills, we have the ingredients for a successful relationship.[32] Marital therapist David Schnarch emphasizes that our finest moments in relationship come when we can acknowledge ourselves and others fully for who we are, embracing our differences while continuing our contact.[33] This is connection without fixation—the lifelong process of opening "the space for true togetherness."[34] Here, a quality of Buddhist nonattachment—not being caught up in preconceptions of the other—when integrated into our relationships can contribute to our capacity to acknowledge the other's uniqueness. This process promotes deep intimacy.[35] In this way, we can take the Buddhist value of nonattachment out of its original context and see its relevance to a particular contemporary psychological concern.

ATTACHMENT ISSUES AND ADULT SPIRITUALITY

What are the implications of this for our spiritual lives? Since we develop our style of relating to others in our family of origin, and since it reflects ways in which we may have railed against inconsistency or defended against disappointment, it is fair to expect that some of these patterns will arise in our spiritual relationships.[36]

On the one hand, avoidant individuals, who in early childhood learned how to defend against abandonment by defensively detaching from their relationships with others, may be attracted to Buddhism for specific reasons: They seek a haven in its language of nonattachment because of the support it seems to offer for their avoidant stance toward life. Consequently, they can bring enormous psychological baggage to their fantasies of what Buddhist nonattachment might look like in practice.

On the other hand, Buddhist practitioners with ambivalent styles may have intense emotional reactions to their teachers, their fellow students, or their spiritual involvement altogether. They may be particularly emotionally distraught when they perceive their teacher as abandoning or ignoring them or when some endeavor they have invested in, for example, a particular teaching or event, does not materialize as anticipated.

In *Buddhism and Psychotherapy*, Jeffrey Rubin, a psychoanalyst familiar with mindfulness meditation, wisely uses the word *detachment* when discussing psychological disengagement. I have adopted this usage as well, distinguishing this from the Buddhist usage of *nonattachment*.[37] The former is a disengagement and distancing from life; the latter, a relinquishment of fixation. It is an unfortunate and significant misreading of Buddhist literature to confuse the attitude of a Buddhist practitioner who embodies engaged nonattachment with that of a person who is defensively detached. In terms of optimizing freedom in our lives, we need to understand the differences between healthy nonattached spiritual engagement and defensive detachment. These issues will be addressed in the next chapter.

Traditional Approaches to Nonattachment 12

ONE WAY TO FINE-TUNE our understanding of the Buddhist meaning of nonattachment is to consider the diverse ways it is cultivated. For us in the West, the following questions arise: Do we need to disengage from worldly life like a nun or monk in order to cultivate nonattachment? Did Buddhism traditionally see the cultivation of nonattachment as requiring the monastic restraint of celibacy? What are the different internal ways of working with attachment? Let us explore these questions in turn.

IS THE MONASTERY THE ONLY WAY?

Traditionally, nuns and monks live communally and devote their lives to religious vocation, having abandoned worldly occupations such as farming, business, trading, or being a soldier. This particular form of religious life still is valued and revered in traditional Buddhist cultures. Monasteries and convents have been the physical support for the development, preservation, and spread of Buddhism. The monastic lifestyle is conducive to nonattachment because it limits the possibilities for clinging. Monks and nuns reduce the number of their possessions and give up intimate sexual relationships altogether to minimize the opportunity for attachment. Here, control of the external environment is used to alter the practitioner's internal attitudes.

Without contact with Asian monastics, Westerners may easily confuse nonattachment with disengagement—that is, emotional distance

and absence of commitment to activity. Westerners seeking psychological refuge in a disengaged lifestyle often find Buddhist language particularly attractive.[1]

The reality is that while the monks I have met and read about are
disengaged from worldly activity, they remain deeply committed to
religious endeavor, whether it is study, teaching, ministry, or contemplation. Nonattachment in the Buddhist sense is a description of a way
of acting, not a blanket abstention. In terms of how they relate with
others, the majority of monks and nuns I have met have been person-
able and warm. In traditional contexts, instructions on nonattachment
are counterbalanced by the "moistening" effect of teachings on sympathy, love, and compassion. Practitioners are seeking to be engaged
while not being fixated.

Most Buddhist practitioners in the West today are lay men and
women, and one question of deep concern to them is the attitude of
Buddhism toward sexual desire, one of the most common and easily
identifiable forms of attachment. Attached desire is one of the root
causes for getting caught in the cycle of existence. All Buddhist traditions agree that with progress on the path, attached desire is ultimately
abandoned or transmuted. Traditionally, the subjective sense of freedom this creates, coupled with the understanding that abandoning or
transforming desire leads to an end of the cycle of rebirth, was seen as
sufficient motivation for applying some spiritual discipline to sexual
desire.

Some Westerners readily accept the notion of abandoning sexual
desire; others are more ambivalent. Our culture, which extols the pleasures associated with desire, and the ways in which such pleasures
contribute to our individual satisfaction, is not naturally receptive to
such teachings. Thus, many Western practitioners tend to be attracted
to Buddhist approaches that do not advocate renunciation of desire.
There are several such options, and they have to do with how individuals orient themselves toward sexual desire. We first decide whether we
wish to practice as a monastic or a layperson. The monastic clearly
renounces the behavioral aspect of desire. For both monastics and

laypersons, however, there are a variety of ways to work with desire once it arises, and those practices that do not require suppressing it have a strong appeal in the West.

THE WAY OF RENUNCIATION

The great Nyingma lama Dudjom Rinpoche gave a set of teachings that outline four major ways to work with attachment and sexual desire. In these discussions, he shows the very means of becoming unstuck, which is to develop nonattachment. Using the analogy of a poisonous plant to represent sexual desire, Dudjom Rinpoche describes how a practitioner oriented toward renunciation—in his example, a heterosexual male—proceeds: "First of all, fear and caution. That is a poison: I shall not touch it, I shall not even look at it; I shall turn away from it. . . . [S]ex is a stone of stumbling, so I have nothing to do with women, I do not even look at them."[2] In another context, Dudjom Rinpoche identifies the approach of renunciates in the following way: "[T]hey try to cut down the plant . . . eradicate . . . the negative emotions."[3]

The attitude of turning away from objects of desire and the feelings they engender informs a life of monastic renunciation. Kalu Rinpoche identified this approach as protecting "ourselves from harmful habits by removing ourselves from their causes."[4] Lay people can temporarily approach practice this way as well. For example, when we do ten-day retreats with Theravadin teachers, we are encouraged to observe silence, maintain mindfulness, be celibate, and not get lost in eye contact. The guidelines are to help support our focus so we do not get absorbed in distraction.

Historically, in the Theravadin tradition, monastic renunciation, including celibacy, was a primary way of working with attachment, though there were householder practitioners in this tradition from the start. For householders outside of retreat, the expectation was that renunciation would be practiced through the limitations of monogamy.

Over the last two hundred years, the lay practice of meditation has become widespread in Theravadin countries, perhaps in response to significant lay practice in Christianity. The Theravadin tradition urges practitioners, whether lay or monastic, to reduce attachment, and this begins with restrained behavior. Control of passion, attachment, and anger is much emphasized. This is facilitated by meditation practices that develop mindfulness, which initially allows a practitioner to know when desire is manifest and take steps toward self-restraint. At deeper levels of practice, mindfulness allows the practitioner to observe the processes of desire without being overtaken by it or identified with it. Ultimately, with subtle insight, the practitioner abandons desire, in stages, from the root.[5]

In the Theravadin context, the ultimate goal of mindfulness is a deep quiescence, the freedom from all attachment that occurs with the realization of nirvana. We can understand this is a silence quite apart from the sounds of life. Its nature is clearly illustrated in the excerpt from the discourse that begins with "All is burning . . ." at the beginning of chapter 11, which extols the benefits of wise renunciation. *Nirvana* literally means "extinguishing of fire." The word was initially used to describe the liberation that occurs through the extinction of the fires of sexual desire, attachment, and hatred. In the Theravadin context, the bound life of attachment and the utterly freed silence of nirvana are set in a dualistic tension.

THE WAY OF UNDERSTANDING EMPTINESS

The Mahayana sutra and commentarial tradition supports practice by nuns, monks, and laypeople. In the Tibetan presentation of the Mahayana sutra style of practice, practitioners use the understanding of emptiness—the profound realization that phenomena do not substantially exist in the solid manner in which they appear—to disempower attachment and anger.

Continuing with the metaphor of a poisonous plant to describe attachment, Dudjom Rinpoche describes the second approach, the Mahayana sutra attitude:

> [R]ealizing that the plant is dangerous, but that simply cut-
> ting it down will not be sufficient, since its roots remain to
> sprout anew, they throw hot ash or boiling water over the
> roots to prevent the plant from ever growing again. This is
> the approach of the Mahayana, which applies the realization
> of emptiness as the antidote to ignorance, the root of ego
> and negativity.[6]

> I can approach this poisonous plant, and even eat the fruit
> of it, because I know the antidote. The antidote is the experi-
> ence of unreality, of the Void.[7]

To experience that phenomena are not as substantially established
as they initially appear to be—that they are empty of inherent existence—requires deep realization. With such realization, we don't focus
on eliminating our attachments, as is done with a practice that relies
primarily on renunciation; rather, we understand them as ultimately
void. The second of the two quotes above illustrates the shift that occurs with the Mahayana view, which offers the possibility of being
engaged in the world, knowing its ultimate nature, and yet not being
bound by it. Kalu Rinpoche characterizes this approach as more difficult to understand initially, but easier to practice once it is assimilated,
than the path of renunciation.[8]

From the perspective of the Mahayana, working with attachment is
linked to compassion. Here we "transform afflictions—negative or
self-referent tendencies—into positive and altruistic attitudes based on
love and compassion."[9] The Mahayana mind-training (*blo sbyong*) approaches, such as that taught by Atisha and commented on by Jamgon
Kongtrul as presented earlier, work with negative intentions through
transforming and ultimately defusing them. For example, in this mode
of practice, we link the discomfort of our felt sense of clinging with a
wish to remove that source of suffering from all sentient beings.

THE WAY OF TANTRA

Within the Mahayana, there are also the tantric practices of transmutation and natural liberation. Available to lay people as well as monks

and nuns, the former employs methods that use the passions as a path to profound understanding and freedom. Dudjom Rinpoche says of this approach, "[T]here is a third attitude, that of Tantrayana, founded on the total absence of fear, which consists in deliberately eating the fruit of the poisonous plant, because one knows how to digest it without its doing the slightest harm, because one knows how to transform it, assimilate it, eliminate it."[10]

Here, one does not push aside one's internal attachments, emotions, sexual desire, or anger but uses them as the ingredients for spiritual alchemy. In this approach, poison is turned into medicine.[11] Many teachers of this form of practice have lived as householders and not been celibate. For a tantric householder, grist for the spiritual mill is close at hand. These teachings sound wonderful, but they require a great deal of meditative skill to accomplish.[12] Kalu Rinpoche states that this path is the most difficult to teach and to understand but the quickest and easiest to achieve once it is mastered.[13] Westerners attracted to teachings on the use of sexual desire in tantra often miss the point that this is a practice of transmutation. It entails using the physical and emotional energies of sexuality, harnessing them through the instructions of a teacher, with view, motivation, visualization, and mantra, in the service of deepening one's realization of emptiness and compassion. This practice is reserved for students who have shown themselves capable of undertaking the rigors of such a regimen and received the necessary initiation from their teacher. Tantra is not just a license to party. If snippets of technique are taken out of context without proper guidance and assimilated into our everyday attitudes toward prolonging or enhancing pleasure, they will merely reinforce our inclinations toward hedonism, pragmatism, and peak performance.

We desire sexual pleasure, and we wish to make it work successfully while at the same time hoping for the complete freedom of nonattached realization. The latter, however, comes with a deep change in orientation. Ultimately, freedom from—or within—attachment, through whichever means, is its own distinct form of pleasure and satisfaction. Kalu Rinpoche states that with skill in tantric practice,

"[T]he passions are no longer an obstacle. They even become a help. A traditional image is that they become like wood for the bonfire of wisdom; the more you add, the brighter the flame!"[14]

The Way of Natural Liberation

Open to nuns, monks, and lay people, the approach of self-liberation, or natural liberation, provides the fourth entry into freedom through the guidance and transmission of a teacher.[15] Quite distinct from our book-based model of learning, here it is the relationship between teacher and student that serves as the matrix for transmission of deep nonverbal understanding.

My own practice of this teaching has involved long relationships with several teachers, beginning with Khetsun Sangpo Rinpoche. Immediately after my first retreat in Bombay with Goenka-ji in 1971, I traveled to Dharamsala, the former British hill station in northwest India that is home to the Dalai Lama, to begin a period of study with Khetsun Rinpoche, whom I'd met months before in a tea stall in the village of Sarnath.

The bus ride to Dharamsala was one of the most joyous days of my life. The weather was pleasantly warm, the scenery rich with the yellows and greens of spring flowers. As we wound our way up narrow roads through the majestic, still mountains, I imagined the bright future that this period of study would bring: I was sure it would rapidly lead not only to a Ph.D. but to enlightenment itself.

But this was not to be. Khetsun Rinpoche was gracious with his time in teaching me the foundational meditations of his tradition, but I had difficulties with the language and often could not understand what he was saying. We both realized that we could not continue to work together at that time, although as it happened I encountered Rinpoche again at the University of Virginia in 1974. I was teaching Sanskrit there that year, and Khetsun Sangpo Rinpoche had been invited to teach. I attended a series of his lectures that later formed the basis of his book *Tantric Practice in Nyingma*.[16] These teachings detailed the foundational meditative practices of the Nyingma Dzogchen tradition. One night, a small group of us asked Rinpoche to read to us from his auto-biography, and we gathered around on the carpet as he read from his armchair. Though we were all in our mid- to late twenties at the time, the feeling was of a bunch of kids sitting at Daddy's knee for a bedtime story. Rinpoche read to us about his painful departure from Tibet and subsequent arrival in India, where he constructed a patched-together meditation cabin. He shone with enthusiasm as he described how he was able to be completely satisfied in a deeply meaningful meditative state, even though he had almost no material comforts.

Khetsun Rinpoche's tradition is called in Tibetan "the way of per-sonal advice" (*man ngag gyi sde*), and I now understand that we were given teachings of this tradition that night. Rinpoche touched us all personally with his warm presence, his enthusiasm, and his realization. As with my earlier experience hearing Richard Alpert speak, I got a taste of what Rinpoche was talking about merely by being with him in the telling.

Described as the peak of all approaches, the teachings of self-libera-tion are capable, in theory, of bringing a student to full buddhahood instantaneously.[17] If this doesn't happen, there are various preparatory practices to ripen the student to a point where he or she can effectively assimilate the transmission and thereby experience freedom from at-tachment.[18] The key is the teacher's grace and blessing and the trans-mission of the teacher's realization to the student. Though this is simple to describe, it depends on the present and past relationship between the teacher and student and the student's capacity to receive such transmission. In preparation for this to occur, there are a series of practices that serve to purify the mind, empower it toward realiza-tion, and open the student to understanding reality in a new way.

On that evening in the spring of 1974, Rinpoche told us that we could study with him directly and learn to practice in his tradition if we first worked through the preparatory practices and had a sufficient grasp of Tibetan to understand him. My return to serious Tibetan

Buddhist practice began that evening with Rinpoche's personal introduction to natural liberation.

Ultimately, the focus of practice in this path is becoming aware of
our own pure nature, within which there are no attachments and there
is no bondage.[19] Our freedom, currently obscured, is our natural condition, and this orientation is described as natural liberation, or self-
liberation (rang 'grol). Our buddha nature seems so far away, yet it is
ever so close. This is illustrated by a wonderful tale about the Indian
teacher Atisha seeing an old woman alternately crying and laughing.
Atisha asks her about her behavior and she responds: "[O]ne's own
mind has been a Buddha from beginningless time. By not knowing
this, great complications follow from such a small base of error for
hundreds of thousands of sentient beings. . . . Not being able to bear
the suffering for so many beings, I cry. And then, I laugh because
when this small basis of error is known—when one knows one's own
mind—one is freed."[20]

Dudjom Rinpoche continues with the metaphor of the poisonous
plant to characterize the approach of natural or self-liberation: "[A]
peacock lands, and dances with joy when it sees the poison. It immediately consumes the poisonous plant and turns it into beauty. It is a
Tibetan belief that the peacock owes its beauty to the fact that it eats a
particular species of poisonous plant. . . . thrives on it. The peacock
represents . . . the path of self-liberation. . . ."[21]

With the realization of the nature of the mind, there is no need to
seek a peaceful state in opposition to our ordinary life of attachments.[22]
With this approach, some may understand the deep teachings quickly.
Others may require periods of focused practice to prepare for transmission and to ripen it once it has been received. Ultimately, realization can be expressed in both monastic and householder settings.[23]

In practice, our own personal inclination as well as the type of
teacher we are attracted to play a significant role in determining which
avenue of practice we follow. The way in which we work with our
emotions of anger, desire, or attachment will influence the way in

which we approach our own subjective experience, much in accord with the metaphors of Dudjom Rinpoche.

CHOICES

Q. How come Buddhists don't like vacuum cleaners?

A. They can't handle all the attachments.[24]

Unfortunately, the oft-repeated refrain about the need to "give up attachments" is easily confused by Westerners with giving up the *objects* of our desires—significant others and possessions. Because this seems so difficult, many individuals resist taking this teaching to heart. Lamentably, this manner of understanding the teachings does not reflect the diverse, nuanced ways in which we can work with attachment. Within relationship, while living as a householder and having possessions, there are opportunities for working with the challenges of attachment. True, some paths entail giving up contact with the objects of attachment—nonattachment in the active sense of renunciation—and continue to use mindfulness to monitor any attachment that might arise. Other paths, however, entail working with attachment through understanding, transformation, transmutation, or self-liberation. These paths are supported philosophically by Mahayana nondualism, which sees ultimate truth in the conventional. This position is epitomized by the famous lines of the Mahayana *Heart Sutra*: "Form is emptiness, emptiness is form."[25] With proper understanding, we can be involved and engaged in the world without being ensnared by it. Ultimately, the sounds of life and the sound of silence are not in tension.

It is important to understand that there are different modes of working with attachment, desire, and anger and to consider which makes the most sense for us. Today, one's choice of approaches is not determined by whether one practices as a monastic or a layperson. While the tradition of monasticism has led to widespread beliefs about Buddhist renunciation, models also exist, though they are less well known, of householders with family who are also profoundly spiritually engaged. At the same time, while the practices of Tantra and natural liberation provide rich opportunities for practice as a layperson, today there are numerous Tibetan Buddhist monks and nuns who undertake these practices (some in modified form) while maintaining vows of celibacy.

The diverse paths of practice, when successful, all result in ever greater freedom—nonattachment in a qualitative sense, which is a mode of being rather than a particular act of renunciation; an effect of practice and an expression of realization.

Making Nonattachment Real 13

THE MAJORITY OF WESTERN STUDENTS of Buddhism are lay people, and the most significant question for us is how to find time to practice—both on a daily basis and on an occasional retreat. Whether for a few days, a month, or years, going on retreat has traditionally been how both monastic and lay practitioners intensify their practice and deepen their realization.

Daily practice, with an occasional boost from a more intensive retreat, makes an enormous difference in what we internalize from the teachings. Unfortunately, one of the patterns I see as a teacher is that students would like to keep virtually all of their time commitments the same and yet experience life completely differently—which is impossible, of course. This is attachment (in the Buddhist sense) at its finest! Behavioral psychologists would call it habituation; family therapists, homeostasis; psychodynamic therapists, resistance. In all cases, it is an entrenched form of holding on to old ways, which becomes palpably present when we begin to want to change.

Aside from spiritual prodigies and those few who are touched, or graced, with unexpected insight, the most observable changes in practitioners seem to be directly correlated to how much time they devote to meditation, regularly and cumulatively. Therefore, being able to create more space for practice, to work on attachment in whatever way we have been taught—mindfulness, understanding, transmutation, or natural liberation—is a significant issue for all practitioners. Over the years, friends—and more recently, students—have discussed with me ways to enhance their motivation and time for practice. While there is no sure-fire approach to fit every individual's situation, I have found the following activities and considerations to be helpful, and have seen them to be of similar effect for others who end up devoting significant time in their lives to practice.

- Having contact with realized teachers who serve as inspiration for us to do more practice.

- Deepening rewarding experience by attending extended retreats—for a weekend, a week, or ten days. This then serves as positive reinforcement to encourage daily practice.

- Using reflections and meditations on death to heighten awareness of the limited opportunity we have for practice. Can we make best use of our time today? Tomorrow might not be an option.[1] This particular contemplation grows in force as we connect it to the changes, losses, and deaths of friends, colleagues, and loved ones and those we read about in the news.[2]

- Considering how practice today can affect our capacity to die well and thereby affect our future.[3]

- Using cognitive exercises such as those developed by Stephen Covey to get clear about personal values and how to actualize them in our lives.[4]

- Using psychotherapy as a means for becoming clearer about priorities and creating opportunities to effectively embody them.

The subtle psychospiritual issue in making changes in our behavioral and emotional patterns is whether we can become unstuck, or unattached to our old way of doing things.

Some individuals will channel all of their tight fixation into practice. This has a particular and recognizable flavor to it—one Tibetan text

refers to it as "being rigid in mind like a tree."[5] Here the disease con-
taminates the medicine. It occurs, for example, when a practitioner
feels that her meditation never goes right if she starts after 9:30 PM
sharp or if she has run out of her favorite brand of Tibetan incense.
Practice becomes one more thing to control in a life pervaded by fear.

Another student, when confronted with difficulty with his girlfriend, states in a therapy session with me, "I need to give up my
attachment." In the context of our ongoing work, I recognize that this
is not an actual spiritual reflection on getting stuck or fixated, but
rather a way he is using to avoid looking at his feelings and reflecting
on them, and a way of saying that being engaged in life leads to pain
and it would be safer to live life at the margins as he has tended to
do. Here, good medicine is used in the wrong way, with no positive
change.

Aside from these coarse obstacles, in which the teachings are assimilated to prior patterns, most of us find ourselves tied up in subtle and
pervasive habits that are difficult to challenge. In these situations, the
disease prevents us from using the medicine. John just finds he gets
lost in reading the newspaper after dinner. Deborah says she just
doesn't feel comfortable closing the door to her bedroom and telling
her children they can't come in after ten PM. Robert likes to watch his
favorite show every night, and then there are three chat rooms that he
just has to keep up with. Jennifer is involved with four not-for-profit
organizations with meetings every night, and she also needs to work
every other weekend.

We all know the struggle of feeling that we could be doing something more worthwhile with our time and the tug of the familiar. We
are stuck. The force of doing things in the same way is powerful. It is a
formidable opponent. Creating time for practice is itself an immediate
experience of facing attachment and seeing what it feels like to become
free from it.

From what I have seen, the most effective means for becoming unstuck is starting small with some regular, brief ongoing practice that
we naturally expand following retreats at which we have had deeper

experiences of the rewards of meditation. With that in place, we have a solid experiential base from which to slowly reconsider and alter other commitments in our lives. This process unfolds over months and years. I have seen people come to really determined positions about the significance of practice in their lives and effectively part the Red Sea once their priorities were clear. Where money, time, or child care were obstacles, they no longer are. Practitioners find family baby-sitters, start their day later, become clear with their bosses, take jobs more consonant with their quality of life concerns, or learn how to close the door to their meditation area and not answer the phone.

If we are honest, in most instances, the issue is not that we cannot find time to practice but that we do not wish to give up our habitual behavior. Intensive practice gives us glimpses of light at the end of the tunnel. Teachers and friends can inspire us and support us. Therapists can help us clear out our psychological underbrush. Ultimately, even amid all these supports, only we ourselves can change our behavior. It takes our deliberate consideration. In more mysterious ways, the blessings of our teachers and the compassionate buddhas and bodhisattvas may help open the way for us in a manner difficult to describe or understand.

Some might object that the very cures I suggest entail getting stuck in new habits. Indeed, there is always the possibility that our practice will become assimilated into prior psychological patterns.

In the initial stages of practice, in trying to set up new boundaries around our activities, it is almost inevitable that we will get bogged down in some way. There is a willfulness to our practice.[6] With our hard-won determination to practice, we may feel more distant from others in their ordinary activities.

There is the tale of the Western student engaged in meditating on love and compassion in the north Indian foothills who was constantly being disturbed by visitors who wanted to see someone so devoted to meditation. He said with some impatience, "When will all these people just leave me alone and let me meditate on compassion!" He missed a wonderful chance to become aware of his own fixations (and to reconsider where he set up his retreat). In another way, we may feel spiritually superior and project our own shadow attachments onto others, seeing them as morally suspect.

In response to the pressure, haughtiness, or guilt that we generate in ourselves when initially struggling to set aside time and space to practice, we may feel it wiser just to give it all up. Here the symptom of the disease is moving us to give up the medicine we've begun to take. However, we relieve this pressure not by giving up practice but rather by being mindful of our reactions and gradually relaxing our inner constrictions. In Buddhist psychology, interestingly enough, habits in and of themselves are not necessarily permeated with attachment or fixation. Virtuous habits, as opposed to fixated or pressured reaction patterns, are characterized by a balance-of-mind, mindfulness, and an absence of greed or clinging.[7] That is to say, we assess our behavior only by examining its inner quality. When obstructions are present, we can use awareness and emotional exploration to work with them.[8]

Experientially, over the long term, cultivating love, developing the altruistic aspiration to enlightenment, or following the practice of Jamgon Kongtrul to imagine absorbing others' mental afflictions into our own helps soften the edges of who we think we are and deepen our hearts toward others. Through mindfulness and care, we move away from some of the brittleness that can characterize early practice.

If we find that fixation on practice is creating problems for us, it is wise to consult with our teachers for feedback about the content and quality of our practice. Sometimes practice naturally corrects itself.

THE NONATTACHMENT CONUNDRUM: BAITING THE PRESENT WITH THE FUTURE

Goenka-ji was fond of telling the story of Ananda, Buddha's cousin. The Buddha recruited Ananda to be his secretary, which meant that Ananda would be responsible for mentally retaining all of the teachings the Buddha gave, since it was not then the custom to write things down. Ananda agreed only on the condition that he would either be present at all the teachings or be told those that he might miss. This condition was accepted, and Ananda became the one person who knew all the Buddha's teachings. After Gautama died, the senior disciples met and decided to have a conclave to settle the canon of instructions. They felt that only fully enlightened individuals, those free of all attachment, called arhats in Theravadin Buddhism, should attend. Since he held all the teachings, they wanted Ananda to attend, but they also knew he was not an arhat. They told him to go off and meditate and become one, giving him three months to accomplish this.

Ananda earnestly pursued his task, meditating night and day, sleeping little, and constantly thinking, "I must become an arhat." He got lost in attachment to his goal. During the very early morning hours on his last day in retreat, still unrealized, Ananda became despondent, thinking over and over, "I must become an arhat." At the end, he was exhausted and preparing to take a quick nap before the close of his retreat. He was about to put his head down to rest when he relinquished his fixation on the goal, clearly recognized the reality of the present, and with full mindfulness acknowledged and accepted, "I am *not* an arhat." He then became one.

What Goenka-ji emphasized in telling this story is how important it is to be with the reality that we are experiencing, whatever it is, without attachment to something else. This is a critical piece of spiritual advice.[9] We need to monitor our practice constantly to see if it is getting subordinated to our ordinary agenda of seeking something beyond the moment that is more, quicker, or better. At the same time, I think it is important to look at the larger spiritual framework of practice. It appears that traditions of spiritual development intentionally create a conundrum that engages our attachment. By using language of stages and path, they create goals that appear to be in the future. We feel attracted to goals of mindfulness, clarity, and freedom and then mistakenly become attached to an idea about some imagined future state—for example, becoming an arhat or a buddha. The challenge is to become clearly mindful of our present circumstances without letting attachment to our idea of the future affect our awareness of the present.

Our practice on the spiritual path involves the paradox of knowing about something that is not yet present while understanding that it can only be achieved when we are fully present. Making spiritual progress requires engaging in two aspects of a process—orienting ourselves toward actualizing our full potential and becoming fully present to our actuality—and doing both over an extended period. If we had no goal to experience things differently, we would have no motivation to practice. If we remain in a goal-seeking stance—"I must become an arhat"—we get ensnared in a perpetual chase for our idea of the future and cannot fully experience the present. We see in a direct, personal way how our attachment blinds us from viewing present reality as it really is. If the nature of cyclic existence is to chase carrots dangling in front of us, ever seeking something more, the idea of enlightenment becomes yet another carrot. As Chögyam Trungpa Rinpoche put it so eloquently, "Ego is always trying to achieve spirituality. It is rather like wanting to witness your own funeral."[10]

It is definitely a challenge when we have always been chasing the carrot—or in this case, spiritual understanding that we could never have anticipated—to learn that the carrot drops into our hand when we mindfully stop chasing while continuing our practice. In the context of practice the bait of attachment to dreams of progress inevitably brings us to the hook of letting go of those very same dreams.

The approach advocated by Ram Dass, to "be here now," describes only half the picture.[11] The instruction "be here now" has force because when we are initially engaged with the vision of spiritual development, we mistakenly imagine we can only "get there later." Our spiritual engagement is fueled by a forward-looking hope that is in tension with an ever-deepening clarity about the present. If the idea of a gradual path creates an obstacle to practice, it naturally resolves itself through the course of one's practice, as in the Ananda tale.

The knowledge that there is an identifiable goal and that we have not yet achieved it can create great difficulty for those with an overactive inner critic. However, in the translation of Buddhism into English, the traditional "stages of the path" presentation has been deemphasized, and this has helped to alleviate that pressure. In its place, teachers and authors substitute more immediate and realizable goals in mindfulness practice, such as reduced blood pressure, improved overall physical and emotional functioning, or a general sense of ease. They do this under the sway of psychological pragmatism and wishing to alleviate pressures of perfectionism in their students.

However, without the original "stages of the path" presentation, it is not clear that practitioners can confront and resolve the challenges related to feeling "I want to accomplish that future spiritual state within which I can finally feel fulfilled." By eliminating path talk, teachers may create valuable temporary comfort in their audiences, but they may also preclude the deep liberation that can occur only through struggling to hold both horns—the future and present—of the spiritual dilemma.

Through the story of Ananda, we realize that the traditional presentation of the Buddhist teachings, with its future-oriented language of paths and realization, is like a homeopathic remedy that fights poison with a diluted solution of the very same poison. Our lives are lived in pursuit of evanescent future satisfactions. While the present is potentially rich with all we need, we always scan the future for what will make us feel better. The descriptions of meditation—with ever more beneficial stages of progress—exactly replicate this future-oriented dynamic. With mindfulness, we have an opportunity to witness the operation of this vicious and seemingly implacable orientation. As A. H. Almaas says, "Many spiritual disciplines use the ego activity intentionally, with a great deal of energy and effort, to gain as much as possible from it; but at the same time, they use it in a way that tends to expose its nature. For such disciplines to be successful, the activity must be such that in time its nature and function are revealed."[12] In time, within the framework of the traditional stages of the path, we can either gradually or suddenly come to the dissolution of this future orientation by perceiving its insubstantiality, leaving us in a new and profound ease.

CONTACT WITHOUT ADHESION

In day-to-day life, we can best understand nonattachment as the process of learning how to be involved with others without becoming rigidly fixated. Without skill in nonattachment, we might go to a dance and either doggedly stay with one partner, defensively attached to him or her, or fearfully maintain a detached position on the sidelines, or mentally contrive a detached position by dancing briefly with a number of people. For those who have firmly positioned themselves on the sidelines of life, it may first be necessary to fixate on the difficult, clumsy process of unsticking from the wall and learning how to dance—the fundamentals of movement and the subtleties of grace. Ultimately, nonattachment might be seen as the capacity to stay with one partner, the ability to accept an occasional cut-in, perhaps to visit with another, or to take an occasional rest on the sidelines—in all instances being fully engaged in the process but not stuck in any situation. Nonattachment is not defined by whether we are dancing or standing on the sidelines but by how we do these things. Subjectively, nonattachment is not feeling an internal pressure to get, hold, avoid, or alternate. It is instead moving through life with balanced presence and a deep sense of spacious freedom.

Without reflection, most of us would think of the intense focus of meditation as an attached state. This confuses focus or engagement with getting stuck. They are different. As we saw at the beginning of our discussion of attachment, the Buddhist teachings compare the unwholesomeness of attachment to raw meat on a hot frying pan. On the other hand, wholesome concentration, free from attachment, arises with the capacity to place and sustain the mind on its object, for example, the breath, in a balanced, easily flowing way.

There is a traditional metaphor, derived from the ancient practice of medicine in India, that is used to describe the nonattached activity of concentration. Because there was no refrigeration, doctors had no cadavers for training in surgery. Basic surgical skills were developed through achieving mastery in cutting floating lotus leaves. Surgeons could not be so hesitant that they didn't cut at all, yet if they were so heavy-handed as to break or sink the leaf, they failed. Training was complete when they could engage the leaf and cut it afloat.[13] If the Ananda tale pointed out how mindfulness of the present is necessary for nonattachment, this metaphor indicates its quality of balanced engagement.

Having considered the teachings on nonattachment in the traditional context, we will now look at these instructions from the perspective of Western psychology.

Presence and Absence in Life and Practice 14

THERE IS A SUBTLE DELICACY to Buddhist teachings on nonattachment that emerges as we consider the metaphor of cutting lotus leaves. We see this quality in the relationships of our fully realized teachers. They have warmth and caring that is not sticky. Their involvement with others, described traditionally with words such as love, compassion, and sympathy, is informed by nonattachment cultivated in the ways described here. This is the spiritual context for considering nonattachment.

In the West, we have a psychological context within which we value attachment. When we bring practice into our daily lives, our relationships are affected by our capacity to be psychologically attached in a flexible way. This in turn is related to the way we learned to be together and apart when we were younger. On the subject of parenting, His Holiness the Dalai Lama notes:

> Bonding is very important. Mentally, the method of bonding is not very clear, but physically, it is simple: babies receive bodily touching from their mothers. Physical touch is a very crucial factor for healthy development, including the development of brain cells in the first few weeks. In that moment of bodily touch, if something is negative, it is very harmful and damaging to the development of the brain. It has nothing to do with religion. It is simply that, as human beings, our physical condition requires touch to develop fully.[1]

Even His Holiness the Dalai Lama is clear about the importance of infantile attachment, although it is noteworthy that his discussion is couched primarily in physical versus emotional terms.

As a psychotherapist, I am deeply aware of the significance of healthy attachment for childhood development—the capacity to seek and receive a sense of security through closeness. Given that this is the context in which we in the West often consider attachment, Buddhist teachings on attachment and nonattachment can be confusing if we lack an understanding of the different meaning those terms have in the Buddhist context.

Traditional teachings assume the cultural practice of their times, which largely continues today in many Buddhist cultures—intense care of children by their parents. I have noted this myself in observing Indian and Tibetan families with infants. With secure attachment between child and parent as a background, individuals come into adulthood comfortable with participating in a community of practitioners and able to receive guidance from a teacher.

It is in our childhood relationships that seeds are planted for how we will relate to others as adults. With the cultural shifts of recent decades—the disappearance of the extended family, the rise in single-parent homes, the demands faced by working parents, and the pervasive distraction of television and other electronic media, children in the modern West are receiving less and less attention from their parents. As a consequence, their sense of attachment is being injured. In the worst situations of abuse and neglect, the tears in the bonds of attachment are severe. Harmed thus, as adults they may be beset by depression and anxiety or become loners. In worse situations, they may turn into child abusers, substance abusers, or violent criminals.[2]

Poorly attached teenage sex offenders that I worked with showed, at least on the surface, as much concern about the violence in their own pasts as most people would have about the weather on the other side of the planet. Empathy and genuine feeling were absent. In less severe situations, individuals have difficulty trusting others, remaining in relationships, or following through on commitments, including those related to spiritual practice.

THE DELICACY OF BONDING WITHOUT BONDAGE

We have seen how the contexts of Buddhist nonattachment and psychological attachment differ. Strictly speaking, the modes of being associated with these two terms are not contradictory. One way to clarify this is to consider the psychological presentation of how the capacity to be alone evolves. As we will see, this capacity depends upon a parent-child relationship characterized by psychological attachment and an absence of fixation or rigidity. This is of particular interest to those of us cultivating nonattachment in the Buddhist context, since this spiritual quality is often enhanced by meditation practiced alone in silence, though it is ultimately expressed in relationship with others.

We in the West are not without an appreciation of solitude; we understand its place in the history of the Catholic Church, for example, and in the lives of religious exemplars and creative geniuses.[3] But those of us who have tried to explain our interest in taking time for spiritual practice know that seeking solitude for such purposes is outside the cultural mainstream. In addition to such cultural issues, what are the psychological issues at play in being able to sustain the solitude necessary for intense spiritual practice?

Donald Winnicott, the British psychoanalyst who loved to use paradox in his writings, explores the development of the capacity to be alone, and in the process he offers a significant insight into psychological attachment and Buddhist nonattachment. It is clear from Winnicott's perspective that healthy, adaptive psychological attachment supports our capacity to be alone: "Although many types of experience go to the establishment of the capacity to be alone, there is one that is basic, and without a sufficiency of it the capacity to be alone does not come about; *this experience is that of being alone, as an infant and small child, in the presence of mother.* The basis of the capacity to be alone is a paradox; it is the experience of being alone while someone else is present."[4] According to Winnicott, it is this unusual context of being alone in the presence of another that creates the context for the emergence of the creative True Self. It is in the presence of the parent that the child can relax, become confused, become disoriented, not react to external impingement, or become an actor with a particular interest.[5] Within this context, genuine sensations and impulses can arise, some of which may relate to the mother, which then can get satisfied. These experiences, according to Winnicott, "form the basis for a life that has reality in it instead of futility."[6] Over time, children are able to regularly be in touch with their inner impulses, and with this comes the sense that there is someone there with them. They have adaptively bonded. With maturation, the actual parent need not be present because the child has achieved an internal environment.[7] The child, at the appropriate time, has had "ties that free."[8]

When accomplished successfully, this is a critical developmental process of adaptive psychological attachment to a secure, nurturant, nonengulfing, nonwithdrawing internalized parent, which allows the child to be alone. When parents cannot provide this environment for the child, but instead anxiously impose their agendas, or withdraw and are inattentive, the child begins to attend primarily to others, creating the bondage of the False Self, the constant search for others' approval.

There is something remarkably similar to the quality of attention that the parent provides here and the earlier description of nonattached mental focus. It is a light engagement that neither shrinks away nor is heavy-handed. Based on a warm, caring attachment between parent and child, this is nonfixation at its best. It is clear that a capacity for nonattachment, in this Buddhist sense, is exhibited by parents when they are attentively present while their children grow into being themselves. This optimal psychological space leaves young children neither fixedly clinging to their parents nor avoiding them. Furthermore, with such optimal experiences, children do not get stuck in either exhibitionism or inhibition with respect to their own creative impulses. They find their authentic voice, through the presence of the parent's unintrusive silence.

Winnicott's observations open a window of mutual understanding between modern Western psychotherapy and classical Buddhist practice. The source support for the True Self is the parent who is non-attached (in the Buddhist sense of not being fixated to a particular goal) yet present and attentive, allowing for the child to feel securely attached (in the psychological sense).

With such internalization in place, we as adults can welcome the solitary work of spiritual development and pursue the task of nonattachment with balance. If our parent was overly intrusive, needy, sarcastic, or inattentive, then when we engage in spiritual practice, we may be bedeviled by the fixated and often unconscious psychological need to escape from others or hold on to them. This may look like a student who avoids conferring with teachers, or stays away from sangha events, or one who, on the other hand, insistently seeks to volunteer for all sangha tasks.

We are not aware of such deeply ingrained dynamics; they are not easily accessible during early stages of meditation, nor are they resolvable by such practice alone. Even if we do experience the soothing rewards of meditation, we might face difficulty in retreats or afterward in our relationships if problematic patterns are not addressed appropriately.

REACTIVE DETACHMENT

"Not to get what one wants is suffering," the Buddha noted in his first sermon.[9] He pointed out that we suffer due to the pains of birth, old age, sickness, and death, as well as the discomforts of being separated from those whom we love and being conjoined with those whom we do not love.[10] We in the West initially resonate to the psychological meaning of these teachings, which may hark back to memories of the slights and disappointments we suffered from underinvolved or, overinvolved parents.

The cross-cultural soup gets even thicker when a Westerner with attachment injuries hears that the Buddha identifies the fuel for continued suffering to be attachment. When people who adopt distance as a refuge from pain hear that Buddhism counsels nonattachment in response to suffering, the attraction is immediate.[11] However, the *detachment* we are familiar with is *reactive defensive detachment*, which is cultivated in the face of a slight, injury, or affront. This is not what is being discussed in the Buddhist presentation.

Tom and Miriam, whom I knew from the Buddhist community, were having relationship difficulties. Miriam liked to spend time away from Tom, finding him needy and clingy when they were together for extended periods. She attended a weekend retreat, during which her teacher encouraged students to decrease their attachment and to meditate as much as they could. After the retreat, Miriam told Tom that she was going to spend more time alone meditating in the evening, using the authority of her teacher to justify this. Whenever Tom tried to talk with Miriam about his desire for more contact, she invoked the seriousness of her teacher's instructions and would not discuss it further. She insisted on spending a great deal of time alone in her study, engaged in a variety of activities. After six months, Tom decided to end the relationship.

Like Miriam, some may believe that the teachings suggest that we should minimize contact in our primary intimate relationships. However, in this case, if Miriam had been psychologically sensitive, she would have come to see that because of her reluctance to communicate her interests and need for space, she was inclined to hear the teachings as supporting her wish to distance herself from Tom's neediness. Her reactive isolation, while seeking cover under the umbrella of Buddhist nonattachment, does not reflect the balanced engagement that the teachings intend. She could have been more flexible by talking with Tom and allowing him to respond to her concerns. Her interest in meditation did not preclude being in a successful relationship. Successful, grounded spiritual growth depends on a capacity for engagement that is not hindered by defensive detachment.

If individuals build and strengthen their defensive detachment—either on their own or under the sway of their understanding of Buddhism—as a way of alleviating the psychological suffering stemming from childhood abuse, neglect, or lack of attunement, they may be temporarily successful in avoiding pain through disengagement. Over time, however, they may develop a style of deadening themselves, having few interests and finding difficulty developing deep intimacy.

Others may experience an overall placidity, punctuated by sporadic rage, terror, or hostile withdrawal, and find relationships uninteresting, problematic, or unbearable. Because their emotional sensitivity is shut down, individuals who try to protect themselves through distancing cannot find intimacy with Asian teachers or practitioners, who relate to others on the basis of affective attunement. Lacking the interest and perhaps even the skills to articulate who they are within a relationship, they find themselves without Western intimate relationships as well.[12]

In the early 1980s, I was translating for a Tibetan Buddhist teacher giving a talk on the virtues of living simply and being nonattached. One student, a clearly troubled young man who had difficulty relating to others and a history of marginal employment, hesitantly described his overall withdrawal from life and asked the teacher what direction he should pursue. To my surprise, the teacher enthusiastically approved of his behavior and encouraged him to maintain his "nonattachment." I felt there was something dramatically awry as I translated the teacher's response encouraging this isolated, disempowered young man to continue with his disengaged lifestyle, but at the time I couldn't articulate it. With a little cross-cultural insight, it is easy to understand how a defensively detached Western disciple could describe his disinterest in worldly relationships and pursuits and be encouraged by a psychologically unschooled Asian meditation teacher to remain "nonattached." The teacher means, in general, don't get overly fixated, and in particular don't get stuck in worldly concerns to the exclusion of the spiritual. In this case, the teacher mistakenly presumed that this young man actually had the capacity to *choose* to engage in social and vocational activity or effective spiritual activity, but he did not. For individuals like him, opportunities are restricted and life is muted. They mistakenly hear the teacher's praise of nonattachment as supporting their reactive stance of not being vibrantly engaged in life's activities—worldly or spiritual. When we feel that we have choices with respect to desire and attachment, we can explore the nature of these feelings in a spiritual way if we wish. However, spiritual practice strongly motivated by the defensive need to avoid pain tends to retain an aspect of fear and control. It is not a robust, balanced engagement.

My experience with Asian monastics and lay practitioners engaged in serious spiritual practice has been that they are energetic, dynamic, engaging, and goal-oriented. None of my teachers, whether monastic or lay, has seemed defensively detached in the sense of avoiding relationships or shying away from rigorous activity. My experience with Westerners who are dominated by defensive detachment is that they are distant, lacking energy, and tepid about their life direction. If open, they will talk of a cloudlike malaise that affects their lives.[13]

When Buddhist teachings are used to sustain defensive detachment, the Western disciple has no means to resolve the fears that lead to disengagement, conflict within relationships, and failure to find meaningful vocational expression. Occasionally such practitioners are able to put aside time for retreat for months or years. The retreat experience does not typically resolve the psychological issues.

REACTIVE DETACHMENT AND EMOTIONAL EXPERIENCE

Up to this point we have considered how detachment may affect people's relationships and their engagement in activity. Subjectively, detachment also has a significant effect on an individual's spiritual experience.

Practitioners who attempt to go from defensive detachment to "spiritual nonattachment" without a capacity for healthy adaptive attachment will find that their spiritual lives have a particular tone.[14] Subjectively, mindfulness will be occurring in a field of experience characterized by a sense of neutrality and an experience of distance. For detached individuals, interests will all seem bleached out to the same pale shade. Such individuals may feel heady, disembodied, and ethereal and seem that way to others as well; they are likely to find themselves with few friends. The hyperrational, unemotional Spock on *Star Trek* may be amusing to watch, but would you want to talk with him about your most tender feelings?

For those with a restricted range of affect, practicing mindfulness will allow feelings to become clearer and change more quickly. There may be moments when the clarity of mindfulness ushers in creative flashes or brief eruptions of hard-to-understand emotions. Our rational understanding of ourselves may gain some clarity through psychological insights we generate during sitting. The overall practice of mindful introspection provides some sense of satisfying settledness. However, absent psychotherapy or some dramatic intervention, if we limit ourselves to the practice of mindfulness, what we allow ourselves to feel and our fundamental strategies for facing life's difficulties will typically stay within the general range we are used to. For example, individuals who are uncomfortable feeling anger or expressing it do not typically learn how to feel and effectively express this emotion merely from meditation training. If we take a machine with a restricted range of motion and spray it with lubricant, we will have a smoother-running machine but still one with a limited range of motion.

Some may try to go from defensive detachment to "being spiritual," hoping that if they progress swiftly enough they can ignore their psychological injuries. However, in the process they unwittingly maintain or strengthen their defenses and fears. In their most quiet moments of personal reflection, they may sense that something is not right with their lives—a lurking emptiness, disinterest, pressure to be apart, or lack of social connection haunts them. In extreme cases, individuals who have learned to dissociate as a form of defense against emotional, physical, or sexual abuse may dissociate during meditation and end up in a peaceful, neutral state, but out of their body. One of my students reported to me that her meditation was going well, by which she meant that she always ended up feeling as if she was observing herself from the ceiling, much as she had in childhood when she was being sexually abused. Rather than being able to focus on the immediate reality of her breath, she was reexperiencing the disembodied comfort zone that she had defensively learned to create as a child. One of the things meditators need to be alert to is whether they are moving into defensive dissociative states and away from a grounded clarity associated with mindfulness.

To the extent that we open up to our emotional life and our bodies and develop a flexible approach to the rich range of our experience, we can embody a vibrant nonattachment.[15] Buddhist practice can help to reduce internal pressure, provide more spaciousness, and deepen love and compassion for ourselves and others; in this way, it can contribute to secure attachment. When we have experienced these benefits and remain engaged in meditation practice, yet we continue to experience significant emotional or relational difficulties, it is advisable to consider some other form of intervention.

Buddhist meditation was not devised to deal explicitly with pervasive interpersonal and emotional issues related to attachment difficulties. We have a most humble and forthright illustration of this in Jack Kornfield's brutally honest report that after years in Thailand, some as a monk in retreat, "my meditation had helped me very little with human relationships. I was still tremendously immature, acting out the same painful patterns of blame and fear, acceptance and rejection that I had before my Buddhist training, only the horror now was that I was beginning to see these patterns more clearly."[16] Though meditation does not necessarily deepen our ability to experience and express our feelings or to resolve deep emotional difficulties, it will in some instances clarify or expose emotional issues, sometimes in unpredictable ways. Depending on who we are, where we are in our lives, and even what is currently in the news, sometimes even simple calming exercises such as mindfulness of the breath may make us acutely aware of physical or psychological matters. For example, during the 1980s, when it became culturally acceptable—some would even say people were encouraged—to remember and discuss incest and childhood sexual abuse, there were reports from meditation retreats of men and women recalling these experiences. As with medicine, meditation needs to be used with careful attention to its effects.[17] It is not a universally calming experience.

For Westerners, issues related to relationships, work, and early family dynamics that surface as concerns in meditation are best addressed and resolved outside of traditional meditation practice.[18] It is hard for a teacher from a traditional culture who has no professional training to understand the coarse and subtle injuries that occur during childhood in North America and the pressures associated with self-assertion unique to our culture. Such teachers do not value individual feelings and their expression as we do, and therefore, they do not offer us the opportunity to resolve long-standing issues in the ways Western psychotherapy considers meaningful. Similarly, American meditation teachers who are not therapists also lack the professional skills to address significant emotional issues that may surface, for example, during a retreat.

Noted contemporary authors agree that meditation alone, certainly in its initial stages, in the amount that we typically do in the West, cannot be expected to heal our more intractable psychological problems.[19] At the same time, these same authors agree that the skills of Buddhist meditation, when applied appropriately, can work with therapy synergistically.[20]

When Buddhist meditation is recommended as an adjunct to therapy, if the client is interested, there is much to be gained by learning how to focus, practice mindfulness, visualize, and so forth, as is traditionally taught within the larger vision of Buddhist meditation. Clients can then bring the skills learned in this context to the therapeutic tasks of sensing, reflecting, and freely associating. If practitioners seek to understand the unique vision and qualities of traditional practice, they do need to understand the difference between using the focused awareness of meditation to work with the emotional *content* of their experience and following the traditional meditation instructions to focus on the *process* of their inner experience.

Do We Need to Resolve Our Psychological Issues before Meditating?

Given that psychotherapy can help us when we engage in spiritual practice, should the former precede the latter? Writers on spirituality and psychotherapy have been discussing this issue, stimulated in part by the work of Ken Wilber, who has postulated a theoretical hierarchy of movement from the psychological to the spiritual.[21] Jack Engler has made it clear that his "somebody before nobody" statement should not be read as mandating a sequence for psychological and spiritual work.[22] To date, these discussions have not adequately considered the cultural contexts in which our emotional endeavors are taking place or those in which the spiritual traditions originated.[23]

Whereas the culture and religion of traditional Buddhist societies may have constituted a viable psychospiritual environment, we are not duplicating it here when we remove the practice of meditation from its original setting and adopt it for ourselves. While it is important to recognize the complex web of language, philosophy, social customs, and history that have both informed Buddhism and been informed by it in Asia, there is no way that we can—or should—seek to replicate all segments of that web when we incorporate Buddhist practice into our lives. From what I have seen, it is most effective to craft our own psychospiritual milieu, one that combines both traditional and modern approaches in addressing the broad array of concerns that we currently experience.

There are specific qualities and skills associated with emotional well-being as it is most widely understood in North America—the capacity to form and maintain relationships and the capacity to choose and maintain a vocation—that are thoroughly informed by our culture and unique to our time and place. Some of the cognitive, psychological, and communication skills required in these endeavors do not directly relate to the particular abilities developed in traditional spiritual practice. The skills related to one's capacity to sustain a relationship differ significantly from the capacity to concentrate on the breath or understand the subtle nature of reality. Some functions involved may overlap—for example, the ability to stay focused—but many do not. For example, valuing our feelings and having the interest and capacity to articulate them clearly is thoroughly grounded in our cultural milieu. The ability to do this well has little to do with the skills traditionally cultivated in meditation. This is seen over and over in individuals who meditate yet have trouble communicating or presenting themselves effectively to others.

The converse is also true. Those who are able to negotiate their emotional life well will not necessarily be able right away to sit quietly alone and focus their mind internally; this skill is not generally cultivated in our culture. It is important to recognize that psychological and spiritual skills are distinct and different.

Once we acknowledge this, does one set of skills take precedence over the other? The psychological skills emphasized by our culture, while enormously valuable for negotiating daily life or for a well-rounded spirituality, are not in any way prerequisites for the practice of meditation. Individuals who are struggling with the most basic emotional issues necessary for developing relationships are still capable of having significant spiritual experiences. As a practical matter, however, someone who is interested in meditation must at a minimum have the capacity to structure his or her time and space in order to practice.[24] And from the opposite side, there is no identifiable level of spiritual development necessary before an individual can productively engage in psychotherapy. A basic ability to trust others—a psychological and spiritual value—would be a minimum requirement for engaging in the therapeutic relationship.

Since the skills for psychological functioning and traditional spiritual development reflect diverse tasks as well as different cultural expectations, there is no reason to view the two disciplines of modern psychotherapy and traditional spirituality hierarchically, with the former necessarily preceding the latter.[25] A more nuanced approach is to see that psychotherapy can be of enormous benefit for those negotiating spiritual growth and that spiritual practice offers much to those seeking to enhance their psychological functioning.[26] Theory aside, it is clear from my own and others' experience that spiritual and psychotherapeutic development do not always occur systematically or in a neat progression. Some people come into life with spiritual gifts, and for others, realization occurs without immediate apparent rhyme or reason.[27] For others, some psychological resolution occurs off the couch.[28]

Thus, while Wilber's map of progression creates a neat theory, it does not necessarily cover the multitude of possibilities that we have as human beings. The best we can do is to follow our hearts in what attracts us spiritually and seek psychological help when we need it. In ideal circumstances, we will find spiritual teachers who are sensitive to the possibility that therapy may be necessary and therapists who can appreciate our spiritual engagement.[29] It is important to know that it is possible, and probable for many of us, to be learning how to engage in relationship in an adaptive manner—psychologically attached in a balanced way—while we are training to be spiritually nonattached.

Psychotherapy is not the only resource for effecting internal changes that can facilitate our psychological and spiritual process. People who do not relate to talking about their problems but recognize that they are stuck in a significant way can find avenues for change through physical and energetic interventions such as Reichian energetic work, qi gong, t'ai chi, or Rolfing. Looking at repetitive behavior through the lens of energetic constriction and openness, such methods can bring dramatic change with little or no discussion.

In some cases, maturation and life experience may contribute significantly to a person's expansion and movement from the sidelines. In the 1960s, I was surprised to learn that Geshe Wangyal would tell young adults in their early twenties who wanted to live for free at his Retreat House in Washington, New Jersey, to go get a job before coming to study Buddhism seriously with him. Geshe-la, who grew up at the crossroads of Eastern and Western culture in the Kalmyk country of Russia, was an instinctive psychologist and recognized that spiritual practice based on mature adult capacity would be different from that based on reactive disengagement. Effective psychological or somatic work, or the right kinds of life experience, or both, can facilitate as well as deepen our spiritual endeavor.

Practice, Performance, and Finding Our Voices   15

"**P**RACTICE, PRACTICE, PRACTICE, Buddhists are always talking about practice," Robert Thurman says. "What I want to know is, 'When is the performance?'"[1] His division between practice and performance stimulates us to reflect on how we ultimately bring our practice to fruition.

Initially, we consciously feel that the values, goals, or results of practice stimulate our interest, and we put forth willful energy toward our spiritual pursuit. Our vision of the future pulls us forward, and we methodically cultivate certain meditations to open our hearts and deepen our understanding. Occasionally, within such ongoing practice, experiences will arise spontaneously; they are related to our practice, but we may be surprised by their quality or intensity and the depth, vibrancy, and aliveness that we feel. The ongoing discipline of meditation serves as the cocoon for such new and startlingly fresh spiritual experiences.

At the same time, psychological issues related to the past can insinuate themselves into our spiritual life and lead us to repeat the past rather than become free from it. Through self-reflection or work with a therapist, we begin a process that can lead to more autonomy. Our issues resolve, or we learn to view our vulnerabilities within a larger vision.[2]

With further psychological and spiritual maturation, through experience of deeper states of mind and through the blessings of the buddhas and bodhisattvas, practitioners arrive at yet another style of embodying spirituality. Their practice is no longer characterized by deliberate effort toward a future ideal, nor are they in thrall to unconscious dynamics of psychological need influenced by the past. Rather, grounded in the present, they experience inner fullness, richness, and creativity. The adept sparkles, drawing upon a well within.[3]

Realized individuals manifest differently in the diverse traditions. In Theravada, Gautama is portrayed as free from all mental discomfort while being energetic, sometimes humorous, openhearted, and kind. Goenka-ji had an air of soft warmth and buoyant liveliness from the compassion he so clearly projected. Though he was not inclined to express himself emotionally as a Westerner would, Goenka-ji presented himself quite differently from individuals who are defensively shut down. I hold in my heart his joyous melodious chanting and his tender love.

In Tibetan Buddhism, it is understood that a teacher may display any type of emotion as a skillful means to benefit students. The most realized Tibetan Buddhist teachers I've known have exhibited a variety of feelings and characteristics, including love, compassion, strong disagreement, humor, boundless energy, sadness, and fear, while conveying that their experience is in the context of a spacious mind that is very different from the ordinary. I remember talking with teachers and feeling that their voices had a sweetness I could almost taste. Some teachers have been notable for the way their warmth of heart seemed to permeate and open my own heart; others for the spacelike quality of their presence or the diamondlike clarity of mind they communicate. Thousands of people have witnessed such fullness and ease, warmth, and clarity in His Holiness the Dalai Lama.

It is a relief for those of us still in the foothills to recognize that at some point, the spiritual journey has its own momentum and is self-fueling. We may have to exert ourselves for a long way up, but at a certain point we can hang-glide in our practice and then ride the thermals of our natural experience. This stage of spirituality is clearly different from when we had to make an effort to create time and space *to practice* or felt pressured by internal dynamics. The Tibetans have a helpful punning instruction: "Don't *practice* meditation, *habituate*."[4] Within habituation, heavy-handed willfulness can eventually evaporate, and spontaneity arises.[5]

The answer to Robert Thurman's question is that the rehearsals are over and the actual performance begins when realization spontaneously permeates more and more of our activities. Here spiritual value has been woven into the fabric of our daily life—it no longer needs to be embroidered as a decoration. Habituation takes over from willful endeavor and mutates into uncontrived spiritual expression. Effort gives way to spontaneity; practice to performance.

Buddhist masters live within the precepts of their practice. For example, Tibetan practitioners usually do a large number of recitations each morning and evening. Those who are realized continue to do recitations. Spontaneity here does not mean arbitrary rule breaking, though there are sometimes instances of that in stories of unusual great masters. The spontaneous energy, clarity, and engaging presence of the realized shine forth through the repetitive ordinary activities of their lives, just as the meticulously arranged patterns of stained glass take on a new cast when the sun shines through them.

SECURELY ENGAGED WITHOUT FIXATION

> First tighten with tightness,
> Then loosen with looseness.
> The view's essence is here.[6]

Following the initial effortful stages of tightly exerting energy in practice comes a time of loosening, when wisdom, nonattachment, and compassion are united and flow easily and naturally.

These qualities tend to manifest in subtle ways in everyday life. For example, during the four months of Khetsun Rinpoche's stay in 1974, my job was to bring him home at the end of his class, offer him hot chocolate, and teach him English. At the time, my practice of mindfulness meditation had caused my kinesthetic sensitivity to the energy of people around me to be greatly enhanced. Sitting with Khetsun Rinpoche, I appreciated his emotional engagement, and I typically also felt a cool, calming presence.

When Khetsun Rinpoche was in the United States in 1996, he often talked of a point along the path where a new, intense, "inconceivable" compassion dawns naturally in our hearts. As he was not one to speak about his own practice directly, my wife and I intuited that he was not describing mere theory, and this was confirmed in small but significant ways.

My wife and I would occasionally need to talk with Rinpoche late at night. He tended to go to bed early, so we often ended up rousing him from sleep. We both noticed that he would go from sleeping to waking and immediately beam at us beneficently in an absolutely touching way, saying, "Yes, what is it, Harvey-la?" "Do you need something, Annie-la?"[7] I realized that if someone were to wake me in the middle of the evening, I would wake up grumpy, perhaps struggle to put on an acceptable persona, and then say something like "Wajawant?" What a difference! We were witnessing uncontrived care—light, spontaneous, engaged, yet nonattached. Hearing about this and then seeing it played out in reality revealed new possibilities.

CHALLENGING TRADITIONAL PSYCHOLOGICAL MODELS

Shantideva wrote: " 'If I give, what shall I enjoy?' Such concern for one's own welfare is fiendish. 'If I enjoy, what shall I give?' Such concern for the welfare of others is divine."[8] Such spontaneous spiritual fullness is not readily accounted for in traditional models of psychology, which based their approach on the biological sciences, with a bias toward considering developmental issues related to infancy and childhood. From such sources have come need-based models of human behavior, with Freud emphasizing instinctual drive and its gratification as the primary engine of human bonding.[9] John Bowlby, the ethologist and psychoanalyst, based many of his understandings on observing and considering behavior in animals and their biological needs.[10] The British psychoanalysts moved from Freud's emphasis on sexuality to the human need for connection as the driving force of human relationship.[11] In all cases, these are deficit models: They see action as a response to some deep inner biological or human need, and their formulation owes much to what we see in the world of animals and neonates.

When applied appropriately, such models can help us discern psychological agendas that tend to derail our spiritual pursuits. The models work with respect to symptoms and problems. However, to date, mainstream psychologists do not have a model of graceful, spontaneous spiritual fullness that is not driven by deficit or sublimation. In this our situation is somewhat akin to one that faces physical scientists. Newtonian physics works well in terms of the everyday world but breaks down in the extremely subtle sphere of quantum reality. Similarly, the theories of mainstream psychology offer much for understanding and resolving everyday problems. A different set of principles seem to be operative, however, in the deeply realized.

Contact with those who are realized challenges us to consider the farther reaches of human development. Buddhist teachings on psychology—whether it is the pure mind of Theravada or the buddha nature of Mahayana—indicate that the mind has capacities for wisdom, love, and compassion that our Western theories do not acknowledge.[12] I saw this in Khetsun Sangpo Rinpoche's way of acting. It is clear that deeply realized individuals are secure and connected in their relationships with others, and in this they are psychologically attached in a healthy way. But this takes note of the least of it. Their secure attachment does not stem from having found what they need in the external world. Rather they interact with others out of fullness and inner expansion.

Much of Western psychological literature has been framed around the developmental tasks of attachment, separation, and individuation. These emphases have thus far limited what we include in our consideration of human potential. The caring that emerges from practice can be understood as the spiritual equivalent of such a developmental task. The Buddhist model suggests two other bases upon which to consider relationships with others: engaged concern (compassion and love) and an absence of fixated connection (nonattachment).[13] These are significant aspects of the Buddhist path, and they are not completely foreign to our experience. Winnicott's description of the caring mother creating space for the child to be alone and find her own voice is just such a type of flexible, attentive care. Similarly, a teacher's openhearted inner silence facilitates the emergence of the student's spiritual voice.

The mothering metaphor is extremely apt for the teacher's attitude toward all sentient beings. Khetsun Rinpoche has glossed the Tibetan word for teacher, *lama*, as unsurpassed mother (*ama*)—indicating that our spiritual guide is concerned with nurturing us in a most profound manner so that we are borne from the pains of cyclic existence into the joy of realization. When exposed to the genuine, heartfelt love of a teacher, we experience the touching quality of his or her presence, even as we know there is no clinging in it.

Khetsun Sangpo Rinpoche has stressed the importance of compassionate care for others and nonattachment from worldly matters as central to spiritual engagement. When he visited the United States in 1996, he taught extensively about cultivating love for others, but his teaching on not clinging was pointed and powerful: "With attachment, there is no path." This was a reminder about the internal attitude that leads to and characterizes realization. As he moved about and engaged in our world ever so skillfully, he was like the proverbial lotus, growing out of the mud but completely unsullied by it.

In his embodied spirituality, with his deep realization and warm compassion, he was not split off from others but spontaneously delighted with everyone. He did not place himself above anyone else, nor did he denigrate those not engaged in practice. He was inclusive. His lightness, humor, love, and spacious openness conveyed a vision of an entirely different order of human possibility. The vision that I bring to my practice from this encounter is of the possibility of moving from the effortful, sometimes overly gripping intentionality of the beginner to the effortless engaged spontaneity of the mature practitioner.

MAKING IT HAPPEN, HERE AND NOW

Traditionally, Buddhist meditators would arrive at the level of spontaneous practice through weeks, months, and years of solitary retreat or practice in small, silent, hermetic communities. Many of us are trying to emulate such practice however we can, though doing so as householders in the West is a challenge. How do we integrate a model that mandated weeks, months, or years of retreat into our forty-hour workweek, our family-oriented lifestyle, and our two weeks of vacation per year? If the truth be told, all of us interested in Buddhist practice are experimenting with a variety of ways to mix contemplative practice into our lives.

We are of necessity coming up with intermediate practice arrangements that were never seen in Asia. Weekly meditation sessions on Saturday or Sunday morning are already common. Groups such as Shambhala International offer child care during meditation retreats, and others are sure to follow.[14] Most teachers advise setting aside daily periods for meditation to sustain the continuity of practice, and many practitioners do this. We are seeing the evolution of an entirely new style of Buddhism in the West, influenced by cultural forces not prevalent in traditional Asia. This new Buddhism includes study groups, Western-style universities, retreat sites for ten-day or thirty-day retreats, and a decided shift toward lay practice, with lay teachers and lay scholastics transmitting the traditions.

This exciting and complex process is being considered from diverse perspectives.[15] Many of the issues being debated—whether to use native language recitation, the respective roles of Asian and American teachers, whether to use the traditional texts or new material in the liturgy, the place of meditation in weekly services, and the issue of financial support for practice communities—are beyond the scope of this book. Our uniquely Western contributions to Buddhism will emerge as we grapple with these and other questions.

FINDING OUR VOICES IN SILENCE

"If you asked me what I came into this world to do," Emile Zola wrote, "I will tell you: I came to live out loud."[16]

During my three decades of involvement with Buddhist groups in Asia and in the West, I have become aware of the social isolation of practitioners here. In general, social and monastic structures in Asia ensure that practitioners are sustained within a supportive web of interconnection. In the West, most practitioners do not join monastic communities, and the disconnectedness that marks our society goes unrelieved in Dharma centers that simply host programs of meditation, visualization, or chanting. In recent decades, some Western Buddhist communities have begun to consider ways to lessen this isolation.[17] As I became more and more aware of this, I developed an inchoate but continuing yearning to address this situation, which played out in the following way.

During the early 1980s, I had the good fortune to become familiar with structured twelve-step meetings modeled on Alcoholics Anonymous. In such meetings, people share their experience, strength, and hope; they talk about where they have come from, how they are working with their personal issues, and their aspiration for a different life. When I share my story in such a group, my sharing may be inspired by the vision of others who have successfully made use of the group. Through seeing them, I have consciously decided that participating in a group is a way of moving beyond my prior limitations. My participation may be fueled by both unconscious and conscious dynamics. Much like my Buddhist practice, my sharing will be initially influenced by issues from the past and visions of the future.

As I share my story, my truth, my clarity, there is a quickening in the room; others' minds and bodies are responding to what I am saying. Lights are going on for them. They are recognizing that they are not alone. They may see hope in the way I negotiated my life. They may see success in the mere fact that I could get to a meeting amid the personal difficulties I describe.

As I speak, I recognize that I am drawing on the group's support, yet at the same time I am presenting a gift. The meeting itself has taken what might have been merely my own need and permeated it with a spontaneous, creative sense of offering.

The sharing is transformed by the setting in which it occurs. This experience of twelve-step groups has given me some taste of moving from incompleteness and will to spontaneity, release, and fullness—a telescoped experience of moving from deficit to flow, from effort to ease. This experience is available to any participant in such a group; it does not require a lengthy history of spiritual practice. In a one-hour meeting, *practice* becomes *performance*.

Because our cultural heritage constitutes intimacy through sharing feelings, many of us have realized spiritual expansion through participation in twelve-step groups, self-help groups, psychoeducational meetings, psychotherapy groups, or intimate relationships.[18] At their best, these experiences allow us to deepen our awareness, connection, and sense of meaning. For example, the unique practices of the twelve-step approach, in which speakers do not respond to one another, is extremely powerful for creating an environment in which we can be attentively mindful of what others say and, in the process, of our own reactions. Some marital therapists use a slightly different method, whereby each partner mindfully mirrors, validates, and empathizes with the other.[19] Again, the particulars in a way are not as important as creating the space and opportunity where normal reactive expression is restrained and resonant receptivity to oneself and the other is cultivated.

To the extent that we formally or informally structure our interactions to provide space so that we are not merely reacting unthinkingly, we create space for mindful accepting awareness of others and ourselves. And this spacious awareness, because of the depth and meaning associated with it, can open us to a spiritual dimension, hinted at by Martin Buber's evocative phrase "I and Thou."[20] The contribution that we in the West make to the articulation of mindfulness is that we have realized that there are productive ways of developing awareness among one another.

In North America, the predominant social dynamic in many Buddhist groups is the vertical relationship between teacher and disciples, with less emphasis placed on the social relationships among the members of the sangha. Having been on many retreats where we in the sangha did not speak to one another but only to the teacher, because this was the rule, I find it easy to understand how this vertical dynamic develops. The traditional Asian model of social support, which is vertical as well as horizontal, is grounded in social and religious structures that we lack here, and traditional teachers are not familiar with the intricate ways in which we in the West create social support for one another verbally. Without consciously addressing this issue, we remain in our isolated worlds.

I am not prescribing a structure, and I frankly oppose any sort of imposed sharing. I am, however, suggesting that open, honest communication by members of a sangha about heartfelt matters provides an important opportunity for emerging from aloneness. Since we in the West today are more relationally adrift than our traditional Asian counterparts, we need to pay explicit attention to fellowship in order to create healthy, nurturing communities.

For years I remained puzzled about how to bring these insights into reality within a Buddhist community. I didn't want to ape a twelve-step meeting. For a while, I toyed with the idea of doing mindful communication exercises, in which people mindfully report what others tell them about arbitrary topics, but that seemed forced. I also did not want to impose any kind of therapeutic intervention, such as group therapy, on our spiritual community. I was stumped.

In the winter of 1999, my wife and I were visiting our friends Tsultrim Allione and David Petit at their retreat center, Tara Mandala, in Pagosa Springs, Colorado. On a cold walk to an ancient Indian kiva atop Chimney Rock, we shared with Tsultrim how just lecturing and holding discussions left us feeling out of touch with our community.

She recommended that we do a circle with them, a practice described in the book *The Way of Council*.[21]

We walked for about an hour and a half up the mountain, talking of these matters. It was very cold. We hadn't brought any water or snacks. We had not slept much the night before. When we got to the top of Chimney Rock, Tsultrim suggested that the eight of us do a circle. If the truth be told, I was so cold, hungry, and tired that it was very difficult to get grounded and focus. I was too busy trying to figure out how to close all the zippers and buttons on my winter coat to stay warm. However, a seed had been planted.

Other conversations I had around the same time, on the subject of dialogue based on the work of David Bohm, led me to realize that we should incorporate elements of the circle and dialogue at Dawn Mountain, our Buddhist center in Houston. These approaches have allowed us to know our students better, allowed them to know one another, and provided the social context for the experience of mindfulness that I had been considering for a number of years. Around the same time, we came across a very thoughtful book by Gregory Kramer that synthesizes several of the ideas presented here with respect to the usefulness of mindfulness to enhance self-awareness into a practice he calls "Insight Dialogue."[22] Nowadays, at Dawn Mountain, following a period of inner silence, we may do a circle following the guidelines in *The Way of Council* or engage in mindful exercises of communication, exploring issues related to incorporating Buddhist practice into our daily lives.[23] We ask participants to share from the heart, listen from the heart, and speak from a sense of presence.[24] No one is pressured to participate. This has become a rich and meaningful part of our community life. What begins as a need to say something, or a desire for attention, or a shy reticence becomes transformed in the crucible of awareness into an opportunity for self-understanding and open-handed offering.

Throughout this work, we have been showing that traditional Buddhism has unique tools for bringing us to a love for others that is grounded in silence, gratitude, and presence. Silence is the context in which people can know themselves deeply and freshly and out of which they can express themselves while remaining present. We are continually touched and privileged to participate and bear witness to individuals giving voice to what is born of silence. We collectively honor with silence, and our community is graced with palpable love.

Epilogue: Life as Pilgrimage

IN DECEMBER 1999, my wife and I were invited to join our teacher, Khetsun Sangpo Rinpoche, on pilgrimage to the major Buddhist sites of India. The opportunity to meet Rinpoche in Sarnath, the place of the Buddha's initial teaching, twenty-eight years after my first meeting with him there was extremely touching.

Khetsun Sangpo Rinpoche offered us advice on what to contemplate during the course of our pilgrimage. I have since come to see that our whole life is a pilgrimage and that the specific advice he gave is useful under all circumstances:

Rinpoche suggested that we always have love and compassion in our hearts. With this, when we have suffering or discomfort of any sort, we should imagine the ripening of all others' suffering in our own.

We should draw inspiration from those who came before and emulate them in our practice. They left their blessings where they practiced, and we should be receptive to these when we visit holy places.

As we proceed through life, it is helpful to realize there exists not one iota of "self" or "I."

When we observe the physical remains of what has come before, we see that nothing remains intact. It is all subject to decay and impermanence. All conditioned phenomena are insubstantial in this way. They are all like a dream, an illusion, changeable and evanescent. We now have a precious opportunity to practice and should use it.

Mangalam. (Good auspices to all.)

Notes

CHAPTER 1

1. Victor Sogen Hori, "Sweet-and-Sour Buddhism," *Tricycle* 4, no. 1 (Fall 1994): 48–52.

CHAPTER 2

1. Bhadantacariya Buddhaghosa, *The Path of Purification (Visuddhimagga)*, 2d ed., trans. Bhikkhu Nyanamoli (Colombo, Ceylon: A. Semage, 1964), 798–800.
2. Walpola Rahula, *History of Buddhism in Ceylon* (Colombo, Ceylon: M. D. Gunasena, 1956).
3. Steve Goodman and Nina Egert have pointed this out in personal communications.
4. Shinobu Kitayama and Hazel Rose Markus, eds., *Emotion and Culture: Empirical Studies of Mutual Influence* (Washington, D.C.: American Psychological Association, 1994), 110.
5. Franklin Edgerton, *The Bhagavad Gita* (Cambridge, Mass.: Harvard University Press, 1972).
6. "Advice to Sigala," in Walpola Rahula, *What the Buddha Taught* (New York: Random House, 1959), 119–25.
7. Confucius, *The Analects of Confucius*, trans. Arthur Waley (New York: Vintage Books, 1989).
8. Richard A. Shweder and Edmund J. Bourne, "Does the Concept of the Person Vary Cross-Culturally?" in *Thinking Through Cultures: Expeditions in Cultural Psychology*, ed. Richard A. Shweder (Cambridge, Mass.: Harvard University Press, 1991), 149.
9. Ibid., 148–52. In Buddhist Asia, the social "self" is interdependent. Shinobu Kitayama and Hazel Rose Markus define the social self from the perspective of social scientists: "The self, then, is an organized locus of the various,

sometimes competing, understandings of how to be a person, and it functions as an individualized orienting, mediating, interpretive framework giving shape to what people notice and think about, to what they are motivated to do, and . . . to how they feel and their ways of feeling." Hazel Rose Markus and Shinobu Kitayama, eds., "The Cultural Construction of Self and Emotion: Implications for Social Behavior," in Kitayama and Markus, *Emotion and Culture*, 92. This social "self" is quite different from the Buddhist concept of the "self" discussed in chapter 7.

10. Karma Lekshe Tsomo, ed., *Sakyadhita: Daughters of the Buddha* (Ithaca, N.Y.: Snow Lion Publications, 1988), 87–88, 95.

11. Ibid., 96.

12. Richard A. Shweder and Joan G. Miller, "The Social Construction of the Person: How Is It Possible?" in Shweder, ed., *Thinking Through Cultures*, 167–70.

13. Ibid., 168.

14. Ibid., 156.

CHAPTER 3

1. Anne C. Klein, *Meeting the Great Bliss Queen: Buddhists, Feminists and the Art of the Self* (Boston: Beacon Press, 1995), 25–37.

2. Ibid., 31–37, 89–122.

3. Ibid.

4. Hazel Rose Markus and Shinobu Kitayama, "The Cultural Construction of Self and Emotion: Implications for Social Behavior," in *Emotion and Culture: Empirical Studies in Mutual Influence*, ed. Shinobu Kitayama and Hazel Rose Markus (Washington, D.C.: American Psychological Association, 1994), 96.

5. David Schnarch, *Passionate Marriage* (New York: W. W. Norton, 1997), 56.

6. William Safire, "The Bush Comeback," *New York Times*, February 7, 2000.

7. Cited in Richard A. Shweder and Edmund J. Bourne, "Does the Concept of the Person Vary Cross-Culturally?" in *Thinking Through Cultures: Expeditions in Cultural Psychology*, ed. Richard A. Shweder (Cambridge, Mass.: Harvard University Press, 1991), 122.

8. Richard A. Shweder and Joan G. Miller, "The Social Construction of the Person: How Is It Possible?" in Shweder, ed., *Thinking Through Cultures*, 168–69.

9. Margaret Mahler, *The Psychological Birth of the Human Infant* (New York: Basic Books, 1975).

10. Joseph Campbell, *The Power of Myth with Bill Moyers* (New York: Doubleday, 1988), 151.

11. Ibid., 117.

12. "From an independent view of the self, the most important features of the self are the internal and private ones, and thus the corresponding individual, subjective experience will receive an elaborated and privileged place in the behavioral process (Levy, 1984). Key features of this subjectivity are a heightened awareness of one's inner attributes and the tendency to organize one's reactions and actions according to these attributes. The goal is to realize and express these internal attributes. Subjective experience is a result of these efforts that, in turn, foster these efforts." Markus and Kitayama, "Cultural Construction," 101. The citation is to R. I. Levy, "Emotions in Comparative Perspective," in *Approaches to Emotion*, ed. K. R. Scherer and P. Ekman (Hillsdale, N.J.: Erlbaum, 1984), 397–412.

13. Markus and Kitayama, "Cultural Construction," 110–11; E. Richard Sorenson, "Preconquest Consciousness," in *Tribal Epistemologies*, ed. Helmut Wautischer (Aldershot, England: Ashgate, 1998), 79–115. I am indebted to Christian deQuincey of John F. Kennedy University for the latter citation.

14. Richard A. Shweder, "To Speak of the Unspeakable," review of *After the Silence: Rape and My Journey Back,* by Nancy Venable Raine, (New York: Crown Publishers, 1998), *New York Times Book Review,* September 20, 1998.

15. Markus and Kitayama, "Cultural Construction," 89–130.

16. Herbert Benson, *The Relaxation Response* (New York: William Morrow, 1975); Jon Kabat-Zinn, *Full Catastrophe Living: Using the Wisdom of Your Body and Mind to Face Stress, Pain and Illness* (New York: Delta, 1990).

17. Bhadantacariya Buddhaghosa, *The Path of Purification (Visuddhimagga),* 2d ed., trans. Bhikkhu Nyanamoli (Colombo, Ceylon: A. Semage, 1964), 145–53.

18. "Happiness indeed means 'I feel good' and it plays a central role in American discourse and is the basis of psychological well being. . . . The American practice of smiling and being generally friendly is important because it is an indication that one has good self-feelings and such feelings reflect that one has the culturally required good inner self. That is, they indicate that the observed behavior is being directed by an autonomous self replete with positive attributes." Markus and Kitayama, "Cultural Construction," 109.

19. Mark Epstein, M.D., *Thoughts Without a Thinker: Psychotherapy from a Buddhist Perspective* (New York: Basic Books, 1995), 105–222; Jeffrey B. Rubin, *Psychotherapy and Buddhism: Toward an Integration* (New York: Plenum Press, 1996), 57–77, 155–88; John Welwood, *Toward a Psychology of Awakening: Buddhism, Psychotherapy, and the Path of Personal and Spiritual Transformation* (Boston: Shambhala Publications, 2000), 58–129; Tara Bennett-Goleman, *Emotional Alchemy: How the Mind Can Heal the Heart* (New York: Harmony Books, 2001).

20. Epstein, *Thoughts Without a Thinker,* 219–22.

21. Edmund J. Bourne, *The Anxiety and Phobia Workbook* (Oakland, Calif.: New Harbinger Publications, 1995), 78–82; Mary Ellen Copeland, *The Depression Workbook* (Oakland, Calif.: New Harbinger Publications, 1992), 232–40.

22. Jeffrey M. Schwartz, M.D., with Beverly Beyette, *Brain Lock: Free Yourself from Obsessive-Compulsive Behavior* (New York: Regan Books, 1997), xxxv–xxxvi, 1–12; Marsha M. Linehan, *Cognitive-Behavioral Treatment of Borderline Personality Disorder* (New York: Guilford Press, 1993), 144–47; Matthew McKay, Peter D. Rogers, and Judith McKay, *When Anger Hurts: Quieting the Storm Within* (Oakland, Calif.: New Harbinger Publications, 1989), 109–10; Matthew McKay and Patrick Fanning, *Self-Esteem* (New York: St. Martin's, 1987), 239–49; John Gottman, *Why Marriages Succeed or Fail . . . And How You Can Make Yours Last* (New York: Fireside, 1994),180.

23. Rubin, *Psychotherapy and Buddhism,* 77.

24. Hazel Markus and Shinobu Kitayama identify our individualistic pattern of striving for unique positive experiences: "Those with independent selves will develop self-evaluative schemas that are especially sensitive or 'tuned in' to positive information. These people will be motivated to feel unique in a positive manner and, when they are able to construct or locate such information, they will feel good. Discussing and expressing positive, internal attributes of the self is the 'right' thing to do." Markus and Kitayama, "Cultural Construction," 114.

25. Advertisement, *PC,* November 16, 1999, 65.

26. In Theravadin Buddhism as well, over and over the reasons given for practice illustrate a sense of relatedness, indebtedness, and duty. "Monks, you should carefully assume those practices which I have taught you for the sake of direct knowledge. You should practice them, cultivate them, and make much of them, so that this religious practice will last for a long time, will be long-standing. This is for the welfare of the multitudes, the happiness of the multitudes, the benefit, welfare, and happiness of gods and humans. This is out of sympathy with the world." Harvey B. Aronson, *Love and Sympathy in Theravada Buddhism* (Delhi: Motilal Banarsidass, 1980), 17.

27. Markus and Kitayama, "Cultural Construction," 109.

CHAPTER 4

1. Richard A. Shweder, ed., *Thinking Through Cultures: Expeditions in Cultural Psychology* (Cambridge, Mass.: Harvard University Press, 1991); Jeffrey J. Kripal, "Afterword: Psychoanalysis and Hinduism: Thinking Through Each Other," in *Vishnu on Freud's Desk: A Reader in Psychoanalysis and Hinduism,* ed. T. G. Vaidyanathan and Jeffrey J. Kripal (New York: Oxford University Press, 1999).

2. Shweder, ed., *Thinking Through Cultures,* 108–10.

3. Ibid., 108.

4. Ibid.

5. Ibid., 109.

6. Michele Martin, personal communication, Woodstock, N.Y., April 1998.

7. Shweder, ed., *Thinking Through Cultures*, 108–10.

8. As Shweder says, the "process of representing the other goes hand in hand with a process of portraying one's own self as part of the process of representing the other." (Ibid.) For a wonderful instance of such cross-cultural reflections with respect to Zen Buddhism in the United States, see Victor Sogen Hori, "Japanese Zen in America," in *The Faces of Buddhism in America*, ed. Charles S. Prebish and Kenneth K. Tanaka (Berkeley: University of California Press, 1998), 50–77.

9. I am indebted to mindfulness instructor Mary Rees for identifying this issue in a conversation with me in Houston in 1999.

10. Sandy Boucher, *Turning the Wheel: American Women Creating the New Buddhism* (Boston: Beacon Press, 1988); Rita Gross, *Buddhism After Patriarchy: A Feminist History, Analysis, and Reconstruction of Buddhism* (Albany: State University of New York Press, 1993); Marianne Dresser, ed., *Buddhist Women on the Edge: Contemporary Perspectives from the Western Frontier* (Berkeley: North Atlantic Books, 1996); Anne C. Klein, *Meeting the Great Bliss Queen: Buddhists, Feminists and the Art of the Self* (Boston: Beacon Press, 1995); Karma Lekshe Tsomo, ed., *Sakyadhita: Daughters of the Buddha* (Ithaca, N.Y.: Snow Lion Publications, 1988); Karma Lekshe Tsomo, ed., *Innovative Buddhist Women: Swimming Against the Stream* (Richmond, Surrey, U.K.: Curzon Press, 2000).

11. Sandy Boucher, "Bending the Gender Lines," *Turning Wheel* (Spring 1999), 24–25; Roger Corless, "Coming Out in the Sangha: Queer Community in American Buddhism," in *The Faces of Buddhism in America*, ed. Charles S. Prebish and Kenneth K. Tanaka (Berkeley: University of California Press, 1998), 253–65; "Dalai Lama Meets with Lesbian and Gay Leaders," *Turning Wheel* (Fall 1997), 25–29.

12. Poet-author Mushim Ikeda-Nash reports that attention to race and ethnicity became focused in the San Francisco Bay Area following a one-day workshop in Berkeley in 1998, called Healing Racism in Our Sanghas, and organized by individual Buddhists in the Ad Hoc Working Group on Buddhism and Racism. From personal communication, December 2003.

13. See Shweder's defense of "astonishment" in *Thinking Through Cultures*, 1–23.

14. Kripal, "Psychoanalysis and Hinduism," 438–39.

CHAPTER 5

1. Jack Engler, "Therapeutic Aims in Psychotherapy and Meditation: Developmental Stages in the Representation of Self," in *Transformations of Con-*

sciousness: Conventional and Contemplative Perspectives on Development, ed. Ken Wilber, et al. (Boston: Shambhala Publications, 1986), 28, citing Philip Rieff, *The Triumph of the Therapeutic* (New York: Harper and Row, 1966).

2. Mark Epstein, M.D., *Thoughts Without a Thinker: Psychotherapy from a Buddhist Perspective* (New York: Basic Books, 1995), 147; Jeffrey B. Rubin, *Psychotherapy and Buddhism: Toward an Integration* (New York: Plenum Press, 1996), 121–25.

3. Epstein himself notes this distinction in "Beyond the Oceanic Feeling: Psychoanalytic Study of Buddhist Meditation," in *The Couch and the Tree*, ed. Anthony Molino (New York: North Point Press, 1998), 124–25.

4. Daniel Brown and Jack Engler, "The Stages of Mindfulness Meditation: A Validation Study, Part II," in Wilber et al., eds., *Transformations of Consciousness*, 195–96.

5. Ibid.

6. Hazel Rose Markus and Shinobu Kitayama, "The Cultural Construction of Self and Emotion: Implications for Social Behavior," in *Emotion and Culture: Empirical Studies in Mutual Influence*, ed. Shinobu Kitayama and Hazel Rose Markus (Washington, D.C.: American Psychological Association, 1994), 101.

7. Mark Epstein, *Going to Pieces Without Falling Apart: A Buddhist Perspective on Wholeness* (New York: Broadway Books, 1998), 36, citing Donald W. Winnicott, *The Motivational Processes and the Facilitating Environment* (New York: International Universities Press, 1965), 185–86.

8. Brown and Engler, "Stages of Mindfulness Meditation."

9. For an excellent introduction to Buddhist mindfulness meditation, see Joseph Goldstein and Jack Kornfield, *Seeking the Heart of Wisdom: The Path of Insight Meditation* (Boston: Shambhala Publications, 1987), 25–30, 46–58, 138–49.

10. Both A. H. Almaas and Ira Progoff use exploration of psychological material in their paths.

11. Almaas points out that, as a matter of course, when students deepen their realization, layers of psychological issues emerge in overt and covert ways. This makes it difficult for many to traverse traditional spiritual paths effectively without some attention to these issues. In his system, he assists people through contemplative inquiry to clarify and then disidentify from obstructive identifications. See A. H. Almaas, *The Point of Existence: Transformations of Narcissism in Self-Realization* (Berkeley: Diamond Books, 1996), 107–8, 183–86; Almaas, *Diamond Heart Book Three: Being and the Meaning of Life* (Berkeley: Diamond Books, 1990), 72–87; Almaas, "Sacred Psychology on Essence" (Tapes 1&2), *Talks on Tape: A. H. Almaas* (Berkeley: Almaas Publications, 1993); Almaas, *Spacecruiser Inquiry: True Guidance for the Inner Journey*, Diamond Body Series I (Boston: Shambhala Publications, 2002). For

an overview of Almaas's work, see John Davis, *The Diamond Approach: An Introduction to the Teachings of A. H. Almaas* (Boston: Shambhala Publications, 1999).

12. Adapted from Ira Progoff, *At a Journal Workshop* (Los Angeles: Jeremy Tarcher, 1992), 328–49.

13. Ibid., 300–11.

14. Jamgon Kongtrul, *The Great Path of Awakening: A Commentary on the Mahayana Teaching of the Seven Points of Mind Training*, trans. Ken McLeod (Boston: Shambhala Publications, 1987), 14–15; Chögyam Trungpa, *Training the Mind and Cultivating Loving-Kindness,* (Boston: Shambhala Publications, 1993), 64–67; Pema Chödrön, *Start Where You Are: A Guide to Compassionate Living* (Boston: Shambhala Publications, 1994), 33–43.

15. Kongtrul, *Great Path of Awakening*, 15.

16. For more on doing this meditation as a visualization, see Kongtrul, *Great Path of Awakening*, 14. At a retreat in Houston at Dawn Mountain in October 1999, Tulku Thubten of California taught that if we do this as a visualization we take in our own and others' suffering in the form of darkness and direct it at the fear and self-cherishing in our heart with the motivation to dissolve these. When we send out light for others, he suggested we simultaneously let go of all self-oriented hope.

CHAPTER 6

1. Hugh Rosen, *Piagetian Dimensions of Clinical Relevance* (New York: Columbia University Press, 1985), 6.

2. Ibid., 59–60.

3. William B. Parsons, *The Enigma of the Oceanic Feeling* (New York: Oxford University Press, 1999), chapter 6, especially 124ff.

4. Erich Fromm, D. T. Suzuki, and Richard De Martino, *Zen Buddhism and Psychoanalysis* (New York: Harper Colophon, 1960); A. Watts, *Psychotherapy East and West* (New York: Pantheon, 1961).

5. Mark Epstein, M.D., *Thoughts Without a Thinker: Psychotherapy from a Buddhist Perspective* (New York: Basic Books, 1995); Jeffrey B. Rubin, *Psychotherapy and Buddhism: Toward an Integration* (New York: Plenum Press, 1996).

6. Psychologist John Welwood makes a brief exploration of some of these issues in his essay "Embodying Your Realization," in *Toward a Psychology of Awakening* (Boston: Shambhala Publications, 2000), 200–207.

7. Robert Bosnak, *Tracks in the Wilderness of Dreaming: Exploring Interior Landscape Through Practical Dreamwork* (New York: Delacorte Press, 1986), 70.

8. John Davis, *The Diamond Approach: An Introduction to the Teachings of A. H. Almaas* (Boston: Shambhala Publications, 1999), 51–52; A. H. Almaas, *Diamond Heart Book Three: Being and the Meaning of Life* (Berkeley: Diamond

Books, 1990), 73. In psychodynamic psychotherapy, *resistance* and *defense* are used somewhat interchangeably, and there is a significant body of literature on dealing with defenses in the context of therapy, for example, Leigh Mc-Cullough Vaillant, *Changing Character: Short-Term Anxiety-Regulating Psychotherapy for Restructuring Defenses, Affects and Attachment* (New York: Basic Books, 1997), 113–89. The first step in working with resistance is clarifying and recognizing our actual present experience, and then we can explore whether there is anything to be done about it.

CHAPTER 7

1. Peter Harvey, *The Selfless Mind* (Richmond, Surrey, U.K.: Curzon Press, 1995), 51.
2. My paraphrase of Henry Clarke Warren's translation of the Maha Vagga, *Buddhism in Translations* (New York: Atheneum, 1963), 146.
3. Harvey, *The Selfless Mind*, 32–33, 43–44.
4. Pali translation, ibid., 17; quotation, Walpola Rahula, *What the Buddha Taught*, 2d ed. (Bedford, England: Gordon Fraser, 1967), 57.
5. Rahula, *What the Buddha Taught*, 53–54, 40.
6. Harvey, *The Selfless Mind*, 32; Piyadassi Thera, *The Buddha's Ancient Path* (Kandy, Sri Lanka: Buddhist Publication Society, 1974), 95.
7. Rahula, *What the Buddha Taught*, 45.
8. This distinction between objective and subjective discourse is based on comments made by A. H. Almaas at a ten-day retreat in San Francisco, August 1999, and on teachings given by Chogyal Namkhai Norbu Rinpoche, Houston, Texas, September 1999.
9. Harvey, *The Selfless Mind*, 28–30.
10. Ibid., 29.
11. Annie Gottlieb, "Crisis of Consciousness," *Utne Reader* (January–February 1997), 45–109.
12. Warren, *Buddhism in Translations*, 129–33. This is also in W. M. Theodore de Bary, *The Buddhist Tradition in India, China and Japan* (New York: Modern Library, 1969), 21–23.
13. Ibid.
14. Lama Anagarika Govinda, *The Psychological Attitude of Early Buddhist Philosophy* (London: Rider, 1969), 115.
15. Jack Kornfield, *Buddhist Meditation and Consciousness Research* (Sausalito, Calif.: Institute of Noetic Sciences, 1990), 17, citing Jack Engler's observation that Buddhist meditation is a grieving process. For a groundbreaking exploration of self-representation during the course of spiritual work, see A. H. Almaas, *The Point of Existence: Transformations of Narcissism in Self-Realization* (Berkeley: Diamond Books, 1996). While Almaas couches his observa-

tion in his particular framework of understanding Being—our fundamental nature—and its essential aspects, most of what he says will ring true to individuals traversing any spiritual path. In particular, see pages 314–15 on the dread and terror associated with giving up the *concept* of self.

16. Jack Engler, "Therapeutic Aims in Psychotherapy and Meditation: Developmental Stages in the Representation of Self," *Journal of Transpersonal Psychology* 16, no. 1 (1984): 26.

17. James Masterson, *The Real Self* (New York: Bruner/Mazel, 1985), 10–11, citing Bruno Bettelheim, *Freud and Man's Soul* (New York: Alfred A. Knopf, 1982).

18. Engler, "Therapeutic Aims," 51.

19. Jack Engler, "Being Somebody and Being Nobody: A Reexamination of the Understanding of Self in Psychoanalysis and Buddhism," in *Psychoanalysis and Buddhism*, ed. Jeremy D. Safran (Boston: Wisdom Publications, 2003), 35–79.

20. Engler, "Therapeutic Aims," 28–33.

21. Ibid., 51–53, and note his more recent "Being Somebody," 50–52.

22. Engler, "Therapeutic Aims," 34–39.

23. Harvey, *The Selfless Mind*, 20.

24. Warren, *Buddhism in Translations*, 165–66.

25. Engler, "Therapeutic Aims," 14.

26. Arnold Goldberg, *Advances in Self Psychology* (New York: International Universities Press, 1980), 4, citing Heinz Kohut and Ernest S. Wolf, "The Disorders of the Self and Their Treatment: An Outline," *International Journal of Psycho-Analysis* 59 (1978): 413–26.

27. Heinz Kohut, *The Analysis of the Self* (New York: International Universities Press, 1971), xv.

28. Ralph Klein, M.D., "Introduction to the Disorders of the Self," in *Psychotherapy of the Disorders of the Self: The Masterson Approach*, ed. James F. Masterson and Ralph Klein (New York: Bruner/Mazel, 1989), 30–35.

29. Donald W. Winnicott, *The Maturational Process and the Facilitating Environment: Studies in the Theory of Emotional Development* (New York: International Universities Press, 1965), 140–52.

30. Govinda, *The Psychological Attitude*, 115–35.

31. Ibid.

32. *American Heritage Dictionary of the English Language* (Boston: Houghton Mifflin, 1973), 417.

33. Bhadantacariya Buddhaghosa, *The Path of Purification (Visuddhimagga)*, 2d ed., trans. Bhikkhu Nyanamoli (Colombo, Ceylon: A. Semage, 1964), 798–803.

34. T. W. Rhys Davids and William Stede, *The Pali Text Society's Pali English Dictionary* (London: Pali Text Society, 1972), 528.

35. Harvey, *The Selfless Mind*, 32, 40.

36. Ibid.

37. Buddhaghosa, *Path of Purification*, 103, n.18.

38. Narada Maha Thera, *A Manual of Abhidhamma: Abhidhammattha Sangaha* (Kandy, Ceylon: Buddhist Publication Society, 1968), 380–81.

39. See in particular, Mark Epstein, M.D., *Thoughts Without a Thinker: Psychotherapy from a Buddhist Perspective* (New York: Basic Books, 1995), 157–222, and A. H. Almaas, *The Point of Existence: Transformations of Narcissism in Self-Realization* (Berkeley: Diamond Books, 1996).

40. Harry Guntrip, *Schizoid Phenomena, Object Relations and the Self* (New York: International Universities Press, 1969), 177, italics in original; for a full discussion of ego weakness, see 167–271. For a more extended discussion of ego deficiency and spiritual life, see A. H. Almaas, *The Pearl Beyond Price: Integration of Personality into Being: An Object Relations Approach* (Berkeley: Diamond Books, 1988), 358–87.

41. Guntrip, *Schizoid Phenomena*, 183–213.

42. See Epstein, *Thoughts Without a Thinker*, 177, for a discussion of His Holiness the Dalai Lama's difficulty understanding "low self-esteem." See also His Holiness the Dalai Lama and Howard C. Cutler, *The Art of Happiness* (New York: Riverhead, 1998), 283–89. Cutler suggests that self-hatred may not be as common in the West as assumed; he cites research on the prevalence of feelings of social superiority in our culture. In note 77, I cite the research on social superiority and offer a possible answer to the question of whether we in the West hold ourselves to be better than or less than others. I would suggest that because this conversation on self-hatred spans two cultures, in reflecting on why low self-esteem seems more prevalent here than, for example, among Tibetans, we have to take account of differences in early childhood discussed in chapter 14. Furthermore, the difference in how often low self-esteem is articulated in the two settings may relate to the significance of psychological experience and the value on discussing *personal* emotion in our culture. Finally, we have to consider how our experience is shaped by our cultural appreciation of a psychological narrative of vulnerability—"owning" our weaknesses—whereas the traditional Tibetan Buddhist narrative is largely oriented toward conscious moral efficacy and liberation. See Harvey B. Aronson, "The Buddhist Practice of Vajrasattva Meditation: Healing Through Cross-cultural Perspectives," presented at the conference *Psyche, Soma and Spirit,* under the auspices of the Ford Foundation at Rice University, March 30–April 1, 2001.

43. Govinda, *The Psychological Attitude*, 108; Harvey, *The Selfless Mind*, 32.

44. Govinda, *The Psychological Attitude*, 120–24, 148.

45. Ibid.

46. Ibid.

47. Bhikkhu Bodhi, Buddhist Publication Society, personal communication, May 1998.

48. Almaas, *The Point of Existence*, 86.
49. Ibid.
50. Almaas points out that hope, fear, and resentment, which he labels "ego activity," always pull us out of presence. See *The Point of Existence*, 86.
51. Thera, *The Buddha's Ancient Path*, 95.
52. Ibid.
53. Harvey, *The Selfless Mind*, 63.
54. Almaas, *The Point of Existence*, 86.
55. Buddhaghosa, *The Path of Purification*, 323.
56. Ibid., 322.
57. Santideva, *The Bodhicaryavatara*, trans. Kate Crosby and Andrew Skilton (Oxford: Oxford University Press, 1995), 96.
58. Jamgon Kongtrul, *The Great Path of Awakening: A Commentary on the Mahayana Teaching of the Seven Points of Mind Training*, trans. Ken McLeod (Boston: Shambhala Publications, 1987), 16.
59. After writing this, I became aware that Mark Epstein clarifies other significant Buddhist meanings of *ego* through identifying four types of egolessness. He adds two additional meanings of *egolessness* (his third and fourth are similar to the first two misunderstandings I enumerated above): (1) absence of personal constraint, (2) trance states of union, (3) subjugation or masochism, and (4) an ultimate transpersonal state. While he identifies the first three as misunderstandings of the Buddhist concept, he sees the fourth as a mistaken idea that the psychodynamic ego can be transcended. Mark Epstein, "The Varieties of Egolessness," in *Paths Beyond Ego: The Transpersonal Vision*, ed. Roger Walsh and Frances Vaughan (Los Angeles: Jeremy Tarcher, 1993), 121–23.
60. A. H. Almaas, *The Elixir of Enlightenment* (New York: Samuel Weiser, 1984), 14–15. See also Byron Brown, *Soul Without Shame: A Guide to Liberating Yourself from the Judge Within* (Boston: Shambhala Publications, 1999).
61. On disidentification, see A. H. Almaas, *Diamond Heart Book Three: Being and the Meaning of Life* (Berkeley: Diamond Heart Books, 1990), 72–87. On mindfulness and low self-esteem, see Tara Bennett-Goleman, *Emotional Alchemy: How the Mind Can Heal the Heart* (New York: Harmony Books, 2001), 119–206, and Brown, *Soul Without Shame*.
62. Samuel Bercholz and Sherab Chodzin Kohn, eds., *An Introduction to the Buddha and His Teachings* (New York: Barnes and Noble, 1993), 154–55.
63. Klein, "Disorders of the Self." See also James F. Masterson, M.D., *The Emerging Self: A Developmental, Self and Object Relations Approach to the Treatment of the Closet Narcissistic Disorder of the Self* (New York: Bruner/Mazel, 1993).
64. Author's translation of "Aggi-Vacchagottasuttam," in *Majjhima Nikaya*, ed. V. Trenckner (London: Oxford University Press, 1948), 486.

65. In Buddhism, in order to be liberated, one must give up pride, measuring oneself, holding to oneself in a certain status. A. H. Almaas, using slightly different language, sheds some light on this. See Almaas, *The Point of Existence*, 108 particularly. In his psychospiritual system, Almaas identifies all self-representations as obstacles to realizing presence.

66. Ibid., 58–59.

67. Ibid.

68. For traditional teachings on the way this type of disidentification occurs through understanding a lack of self and emptiness in Mahayana, see Kalu Rinpoche, *Luminous Mind: The Way of the Buddha* (Boston: Wisdom Publications, 1997), 137–39; Kongtrul, *The Great Path*, 10–12; Jeffrey Hopkins, *Emptiness Yoga: The Tibetan Middle Way*, ed. Joe B. Wilson (Ithaca, N.Y.: Snow Lion Publications, 1995). I am indebted to A. H. Almaas for language that bridges modern American experience and the spiritual insights of Buddhism in an accessible metaphor. Almaas, *The Point of Existence*, 108; Almaas, "Who Am I?" and "Disidentification and Involvement," in *Diamond Heart Book Three*, 17–35, 72–88. Jack Engler, whose work is based in Theravadin practice, states that subsequent to having some internal psychological structure—the most basic level of development—the next issue in psychospiritual realization is to explore self and object constancy, and then one ultimately moves even beyond that. See Engler, "Therapeutic Aims," 34–51, especially 47.

69. See Daniel P. Brown and Jack Engler, "The Stages of Mindfulness Meditation: A Validation Study," in *Transformations of Consciousness: Conventional and Contemplative Perspectives on Development*, ed. Ken Wilber, et al. (Boston: Shambhala Publications, 1986), 211–12; Almaas, *The Point of Existence*, 128.

70. I have found the following material particularly helpful in sorting out how therapy contributes to flexibility of image, whereas certain spiritual disciplines are oriented to liberation from the mediating effects of self-images altogether: Almaas, *The Point of Existence*, 102–8, 128–31; Almaas, *Sacred Psychology on Essence: Talks on Tape by A. H. Almaas* (Berkeley: Almaas Publications, 1993).

71. Jeffrey Rubin also finds it useful to distinguish analysts' "particulate" view of self from what he sees as a "wave" view of self in Buddhism. See Jeffrey B. Rubin, *Psychotherapy and Buddhism: Toward an Integration* (New York: Plenum Press, 1996), 76, citing Shinzen Young in C. Tartt, "Adapting Eastern Spiritual Teachings to Western Culture: A Discussion with Shinzen Young," *Journal of Transpersonal Psychology* 22, no. 2 (1990): 149–55. Here, I am not using the metaphor of particle and wave with respect to the self per se but to the specific experience of pain. For a similar report of experience during vow sittings with Goenka-ji, see Bennett-Goleman, *Emotional Alchemy*, 36–

37. I see the metaphor as useful in terms of distinguishing the narrative of psychotherapy, with its goal of flexibility with respect to the sense of self, from that of Buddhist insight meditation, which leads to freedom from static identification with any particular self-representation.

72. Almaas, *The Pearl*, 358–87; Almaas, *The Point of Existence*.

73. Epstein, *Thoughts Without a Thinker*, 159–222. Epstein backs up this very interesting point with poignant testimony from his own experience. Insofar as pride is completely abandoned only in the final stage of insight, I hold as an open question, How will insight meditation, with or without psychotherapy, affect the broad range of practitioners' narcissistic injuries and symptoms at earlier stages of practice?

74. Khetsun Sangpo Rinbochay, *Tantric Practice in Nying-ma*, trans. and ed. Jeffrey Hopkins, co-ed. Anne C. Klein (Ithaca, N.Y.: Gabriel/Snow Lion, 1982), 190.

75. This observation came out of conversations during a workshop in Palo Alto, California, organized by the Sati Institute in Santa Cruz, April 7, 2001.

76. Masterson, *The Real Self*, 3–9, 21–29; Masterson and Klein, eds., *Disorders of the Self*, 30–46.

77. Hazel Rose Markus and Shinobu Kitayama, "The Cultural Construction of Self and Emotion: Implications for Social Behavior," in *Emotion and Culture: Empirical Studies of Mutual Influence*, ed. Shinobu Kitayama and Hazel Rose Markus (Washington, D.C.: American Psychological Association, 1994), 105, citing D. Myers, *Social Psychology*, 3d ed. (New York: McGraw-Hill, 1989). This material on positivity in our culture seems to contradict Guntrip's observations on ego weakness, but only on the surface. Guntrip himself points out that in order to avoid the experience of ego weakness, we will often hide this feeling behind detachment, conformity, aggressiveness, bodily illness, self-mastery, addiction to duty, or service to others. (Guntrip, *Schizoid Phenomena*, 184.) Self-mastery and even grandiosity are ways in which we often cover over deeper feelings of weakness and deficiency. See also Almaas, *The Pearl*, 364–65.

78. Markus and Kitayama, "Cultural Construction," 105.

79. For thoughtful reflections on psychodynamic and Buddhist views of narcissism and approaches to its resolution, see Epstein, *Thoughts Without a Thinker*, 157–222, and Almaas, *The Point of Existence*.

80. Markus and Kitayama, "Cultural Construction," 89–93.

81. Ibid., 106.

82. Rahula, *What the Buddha Taught*, 2–3.

83. See Buddhaghosa, *The Path of Purification*, 679–835. In the Theravadin path, the first stage of practice is ever more clearly discriminating mental and physical phenomena. This is followed by examining the nature of these experiences with mindfulness and wisdom, which becomes increasingly subtle

and profound. For a summary of this material, see Jack Kornfield, *A Path with Heart: A Guide Through the Perils and Promises of Spiritual Life* (New York: Bantam, 1993), 135–56. For approaches to wisdom in the Mahayana, see Kalu Rinpoche, *Luminous Mind*, 15–44, and Kongtrul, *The Great Path*, 10–12. For the value of having full experience and mindful observation in unifying both psychological and spiritual development, see Almaas, "Disidentifying and Involvement," in *Diamond Heart Book Three*, 72–76, and John Davis, *The Diamond Approach: An Introduction to the Teachings of A. H. Almaas* (Boston: Shambhala Publications, 1999), 51–52. Using technical distinctions clarified in a conversation with Jack Engler in 1983, we may say that working in the manner described by Almaas leads to a balance between observing and experiencing ego that grounds and embodies our psychospiritual development.

84. A metaphor that keeps occurring to me is of trapeze artists, letting go of one trapeze before grasping another. With deeper realization, practitioners are living more and more in that state of suspension. As they make that leap, the quality, momentum, and grace of their movement will be affected by all of their training and experience. Similarly, the character and tenor of our spirituality, the quality of our letting go of the trapeze of worldly concerns, will be greatly affected by the psychological experiences that we create for ourselves and allow ourselves to have. The flavor and style of our spiritual expression is dependent on our prior emotional development.

85. Karma Lekshe Tsomo, ed., *Sakyadhita: Daughters of the Buddha* (Ithaca, N.Y.: Snow Lion Publications, 1988), 103–59.

86. Sandy Boucher, *Turning the Wheel: American Women Creating the New Buddhism* (Boston: Beacon Press, 1993); Anne C. Klein, *Meeting the Great Bliss Queen: Buddhists, Feminists, and the Art of the Self* (Boston: Beacon Press, 1995); Kate Wheeler, "Bowing, Not Scraping," in *Buddhist Women on the Edge: Contemporary Perspectives from the Western Frontier*, ed. Marianne Dresser (Berkeley: North Atlantic Books, 1996), 57–79.

87. In Theravadin psychology, activity motivated by love, compassion, generosity, or wisdom will naturally be free from any unwholesome traits such as pride. Govinda, *The Psychological Attitude*, 115–24.

CHAPTER 8

1. Daniel Goleman, *Emotional Intelligence: Why It Can Matter More Than IQ* (New York: Bantam, 1995), ix.

2. Bhadantacariya Buddhaghosa, *The Path of Purification (Visuddhimagga)*, 2d ed., trans. Bhikkhu Nyanamoli (Colombo, Ceylon: A. Semage, 1964), 324.

3. Ibid.

4. Leigh McCullough Vaillant, *Changing Character: Short-Term Anxiety-Regulating Psychotherapy for Restructuring Defenses, Affects, and Attachment* (New York: Basic Books, 1997), 239.

5. For example, in the Theravadin tradition, the following words are synonyms for *hate*: "hurtfulness, warding off, repulsion, ill temper, anger (*kodha*), harmfulness of mind." T. W. Rhys Davids and William Stede, *The Pali Text Society's Pali English Dictionary* (London: Pali Text Society, 1972), 332, citing the *Cullaniddesa*. Author's translation of this passage. In the Tibetan Gelukpa monastic curriculum, the definition of *anger* is simply "an intent to harm." Personal communication, Anne C. Klein, Rice University, 1998.

6. Richard A. Shweder, "'You're Not Sick, You're Just in Love': Emotion as an Interpretive System," in *The Nature of Emotions: Fundamental Questions*, ed. Paul Ekman and Richard J. Davidson (New York: Oxford University Press, 1994), 32–44.

7. Buddhaghosa, *Path of Purification*, pp. 325–26.

8. Daniel Cozort, "Cutting the Roots of Virtue: Tsongkhapa on the Results of Anger," *Journal of Buddhist Ethics* 2 (1995): 83.

9. Henry Clarke Warren, *Buddhism in Translations: Passages from the Buddhist Sacred Books and Translated from the Original Pali into English* (New York: Atheneum, 1963), 126, a translation from the *Majjhima Nikaya*, Sutta 72.

10. Gustav Niebuhr, "A Monk in Exile Dreams of Return to Vietnam," *New York Times*, October 16, 1999.

11. "'[E]motion' terms are names for particular interpretive schemes (e.g., 'remorse,' 'guilt,' 'anger,' 'shame') of a particular story-like, script-like, or narrative kind that any people in the world might (or might not) make use of to give meaning and shape to their somatic and affective 'feelings.' More specifically, 'feelings' (both somatic and affective) have the shape and meaning of an 'emotion' when they are experienced as a perception of some self-relevant condition of the world and as a plan of action for the protection of dignity, honor, and self-esteem." Shweder, "You're Not Sick," 32–33. For further information on Shweder's discussion, upon which my discussion is based, see also ibid., 37–38.

12. Shinobu Kitayama and Hazel Rose Markus, "Introduction to Cultural Psychology and Emotion Research," in *Emotion and Culture: Empirical Studies of Mutual Influence*, ed. Shinobu Kitayama and Hazel Rose Markus (Washington, D.C.: American Psychological Association, 1994), 7.

13. Ibid., 8.

14. Jacob Neusner, "A Rabbi Argues with Jesus," *Newsweek*, March 27, 2000, 57.

15. Peter de Jonge, "Man's Best Friend," *New York Times Magazine*, July 21, 2002, 29.

16. Kitayama and Markus, "Introduction to Cultural Psychology," 8.

17. Hazel Rose Markus and Shinobu Kitayama, "The Cultural Construction of Self and Emotion: Implications for Social Behavior," in *Emotion and Culture: Empirical Studies of Mutual Influence*, ed. Shinobu Kitayama and Hazel Rose Markus (Washington, D.C.: American Psychological Association, 1994), 102.

18. Ibid.
19. Shweder, "You're Not Sick," 41.
20. Ibid., 40–41.
21. Arthur Kleinman, *Social Origins of Distress and Disease* (New Haven: Yale University Press, 1986), cited in Richard A. Shweder, "Suffering in Style: On Arthur Kleinman," in *Thinking Through Cultures,* ed. Richard A. Shweder (Cambridge, Mass.: Harvard University Press, 1991), 313–31.
22. Ibid., 316–17.
23. Ibid., 317.
24. Ibid., 317–19.
25. Ibid.
26. Kitayama and Markus, "Introduction to Cultural Psychology," 9, citing Shweder, "You're Not Sick."
27. Ibid.
28. Anna Fels, M.D., "Mending of Hearts and Minds," *New York Times,* May 21, 2002, D5.
29. Shweder, "Suffering in Style," 321–22.
30. This holds true for Pali, Sanskrit, and Tibetan—the languages of traditional Buddhist teachings in India and the Himalayan region.
31. This differentiation emerged during the course of a conversation with Morton Letofsky, teacher of A. H. Almaas's Diamond Approach, Houston, April 2000.
32. Shweder, "You're Not Sick," 40–41.
33. Ibid.
34. Jane G. Goldberg, *The Dark Side of Love: The Positive Role of Our Negative Feelings—Anger, Jealousy and Hate* (New York: Jeremy Tarcher, 1992); H. G. Lerner, *The Dance of Anger* (New York: Harper and Row, 1985).
35. Matthew McKay, Peter D. Rogers, and Judith McKay, *When Anger Hurts: Quieting the Storm Within* (Oakland, Calif.: New Harbinger Publications, 1989); Michele Martin, personal communication (regarding women's self-confidence).
36. Jay R. Greenberg and Stephen A. Mitchell, *Object Relations in Psychoanalytic Theory* (Cambridge, Mass.: Harvard University Press, 1983), 32.
37. George Lakoff, *Women, Fire, and Dangerous Things: What Categories Reveal About the Mind* (Chicago: University of Chicago Press, 1987), 380–415.
38. Greenberg and Mitchell, *Object Relations,* 62.
39. Ibid., 79–187.
40. Harry Guntrip, *Psychoanalytic Theory, Therapy and the Self: A Basic Guide to the Human Personality in Freud, Erikson, Klein, Sullivan, Fairbairn, Hartmann, Jacobson, and Winnicott* (New York: Basic Books, 1971), 37–38.
41. Newton Hightower, *Anger Busting 101* (Houston: Bayou Publishing, 2002), 21–24, 77–78.

42. Vaillant, *Changing Character*, 27–32.

43. Ibid., 239–44.

44. Ibid.

45. Ibid.

46. Linda Johnson, "Compassion Born of Rage," *Yoga Journal* (November/December 1998): 69–138. See also China Galland, *The Bond Between Women: A Journey of Fierce Compassion* (New York: Riverhead, 1998). In a similar vein see Anita Barrows, "The Light of Outrage: Women, Anger and Buddhist Practice," in *Buddhist Women on the Edge: Contemporary Perspectives from the Western Frontier*, ed. Marianne Dresser (Berkeley: North Atlantic Books, 1996), 51–56.

47. This observation comes out of an exchange of e-mail with author Mushim Ikeda-Nash, March 2000.

48. Judith Hooper, "Prozac and Enlightened Mind," *Tricycle* 8, no. 4 (Summer 1999): 38. See also Letters, *Tricycle* 9, no. 1 (Fall 1999): 5–7.
Interestingly, I have not encountered this particular constellation of issues to be a major concern among the older generation of Tibetans I have known—whether they are teachers, monks or nuns, or laypersons.

49. Lama Anagarika Govinda, *The Psychological Attitude of Early Buddhist Philosophy* (London: Rider, 1969), 102; Buddhaghosa, *The Path of Purification*, 324–32.

50. Buddhaghosa, *The Path of Purification*, 800.

51. Govinda, *The Psychological Attitude*, 107–11.

52. Vaillant, *Changing Character*, 239–46.

53. The way that psychotherapy differs from Buddhist mindfulness practice in encouraging "staying" with this emotion was highlighted for me by psychotherapist Dennis Portnoy during the course of e-mail correspondence, April 2001.

54. See also Goldberg, *The Dark Side of Love*, for another psychodynamic therapist's similar understanding.

55. See also Burrows, *Light of Outrage*, 51–56, on the place of anger in therapy with women and the abused and in addressing injustice.

56. Vaillant, *Changing Character*, 241.

57. Goldberg, *The Dark Side of Love*, 65.

58. Daphne Merkin, "The Literary Freud," *New York Times Magazine* (July 13, 2003): 40–44.

CHAPTER 9

1. John Gottman, who is the leading figure in the empirical study of relationships, distinguishes complaint from criticism. The former is fine in relationships, the latter adds an element of blame. Criticism is the first of the four

horsemen of the apocalypse—along with contempt, defensiveness, and stonewalling—that lead to the destruction of relationships. See John Gottman, *The Marriage Clinic: A Scientifically Based Marital Therapy* (New York: W. W. Norton, 1999), 41–48. Here Gottman reports that a certain number of instances of contempt by one spouse were predictive of infectious disease in the other spouse. See also Gottman, *Why Marriages Succeed or Fail . . . and How You Can Make Yours Last* (New York: Fireside, 1995), 68–102.

2. Gottman, *The Marriage Clinic*, 45.
3. Bhadantacariya Buddhaghosa, *The Path of Purification (Visuddhimagga)*, trans. Bhikkhu Nyanamoli (Colombo, Ceylon: A. Semage, 1964), 684.
4. Jon Kabat-Zinn, *Full Catastrophe Living: Using the Wisdom of Your Body and Mind to Face Stress, Pain, and Illness* (New York: Delta, 1990), 59–74, 120–46; Jack Kornfield, *A Path with Heart: A Guide Through the Perils and Promises of Spiritual Life* (New York: Bantam, 1993), 56–68, 287–96; Mark Epstein, M.D., *Thoughts Without a Thinker: Psychotherapy from a Buddhist Perspective* (New York: Basic Books, 1995), 105–28; Tara Bennett-Goleman, *Emotional Alchemy: How the Mind Can Heal the Heart* (New York: Harmony Books, 2001), 119–88.
5. Piyadassi Thera, *The Buddha's Ancient Path* (Kandy, Sri Lanka: Buddhist Publication Society, 1974), 85.
6. Gay Hendricks, Ph.D., and Kathlyn Hendricks, Ph.D., *At the Speed of Life: A New Approach to Personal Change Through Body-Centered Therapy* (New York: Bantam, 1993), 151–19; Susan Thesenga, *The Undefended Self: Living the Pathwork of Spiritual Wholeness* (Madison, Va.: Pathwork Press, 1994), 233–53.
7. Leigh McCullough Vaillant, *Changing Character: Short-Term Anxiety-Regulating Psychotherapy for Restructuring Defenses, Affects and Attachment* (New York: Basic Books, 1997), 240–44.
8. See also Epstein, *Thoughts Without a Thinker*, 206–9, on the significance of owning anger.
9. The contrasted approaches of mindfulness practice and psychotherapy discussed in this section were clarified during the course of e-mail correspondence with psychotherapist Dennis Portnoy in April 2001.
10. Walpola Rahula, *What the Buddha Taught* (Bedford, England: Gordon Fraser, 1967), 109–19.
11. The distinctions made here between knowing and experiencing arose during a conversation in the early 1980s with Jack Engler, who mentioned that he thought Theravadin practice emphasized the observing ego as opposed to the experiencing ego. See also Vaillant, *Changing Character*.
12. For a thoroughgoing Western model that embodies these values and is based on time-tested interventions with overexpressers, see Newton Hightower, *Anger Busting 101* (Houston: Bayou Publishing, 2002).

13. Vaillant, *Changing Character*, 238–48.
14. Henry Clarke Warren, *Buddhism in Translations* (New York: Atheneum, 1963), 353–77; Mahasi Sayadaw, *Practical Insight Meditation* (San Francisco: Unity Press, 1972), 23–28.
15. Harvey B. Aronson, *Love and Sympathy in Theravada Buddhism* (Delhi: Motilal Banarsidass, 1980), 40–48.
16. Ibid.; Tsong-ka-pa, Kensur Lekden and Jeffrey Hopkins, *Compassion in Tibetan Buddhism* (Valois, N.Y.: Gabriel/Snow Lion, 1980), 36–49; Khetsun Sangpo Rinbochay, *Tantric Practice in Nying-ma*, trans. and ed. Jeffrey Hopkins (Ithaca, N.Y.: Gabriel/Snow Lion, 1982), 125–40; Kalu Rinpoche, *Luminous Mind: The Way of the Buddha* (Boston: Wisdom Publications, 1997), 125–56; Gampopa, *The Jewel Ornament of Liberation*, trans. Herbert V. Guenther (London: Rider, 1959), 173–79; His Holiness the Dalai Lama and Howard Cutler, M.D., *The Art of Happiness* (New York: Riverhead, 1998), 113–29.
17. Buddhaghosa, *The Path of Purification*, 324–32.
18. Jamgon Kongtrul, *The Great Path of Awakening: A Commentary on the Mahayana Teachings of the Seven Points of Mind Training*, trans. Ken McLeod (Boston: Shambhala Publications, 1987), 15.
19. Alcoholics Anonymous, *Alcoholics Anonymous: The Story of How Many Thousands of Men and Women Have Recovered from Alcoholism* (New York: Alcoholics Anonymous World Services, 1976), 65–71; Hightower, *Anger Busting*, 78–79.
20. Steven Stosny, Ph.D., *The Powerful Self: A Workbook of Therapeutic Self-Empowerment* (Silver Spring, Md.: Community Outreach Service, 1995), 47–68; Stosny, *Anger Regulation* (Council for Marriage, Family, and Couple Education Conference, 1997), The Resource Link, cassette 757-37 (1-800-241-7785); Stosny, *Regulating the Many Forms of Anger and Resentment Before They Regulate You* (Silver Spring, Md.: Community Outreach Service, n.d.).
21. Stosny, *Regulating*, 14–35.
22. Stosny, *The Powerful Self*, 55; Stosny, *Anger Regulation*.
23. Dalai Lama and Cutler, *The Art of Happiness*, 277–78.
24. Stosny, *Regulating*, 18–35.
25. Ibid. For ways of using mindfulness in conjunction with cognitive therapeutic insights to defuse inner reactivity, see Bennett-Goleman, *Emotional Alchemy*, 119–88.
26. Ibid. See also David Schnarch, Ph.D., *Passionate Marriage: Sex, Love and Intimacy in Emotionally Committed Relationships* (New York: W. W. Norton, 1997), 100–126; Gottman, *Why Marriages Succeed*, 176–81.
27. Santideva, *The Bodhicaryavatara*, trans. Kate Crosby and Andrew Skilton (Oxford: Oxford University Press, 1995), 96.
28. Robert E. Alberti, Ph.D., and Michael L. Emmons, Ph.D., *Your Perfect Right: A Guide to Assertive Behavior*, 3d ed. (San Luis Obispo: Impact Publishers,

1981); Matthew McKay, Peter D. Rogers, and Judith McKay, *When Anger Hurts* (Oakland: New Harbinger, 1989), 184–91; Vaillant, *Changing Character*, 239–43.

29. See also Gregory Kramer, *Meditating Together, Speaking from Silence: Experiencing the Dharma in Dialogue* (Portland, Ore.: Metta Foundation, 1999).
30. Newton Hightower, *The New ABC's for Angry Men* (Houston: Center for Anger Resolution, n.d.), cassette; Gottman, *Why Marriages Succeed*, 176–81; McKay, Rogers, and McKay, *When Anger Hurts*, 127–79.

CHAPTER 10

1. Harvey Aronson, *Love and Sympathy in Theravada Buddhism* (Delhi: Motilal Banarsidass, 1980).
2. For other discussions of love and compassion in Buddhism, see Tsong-ka-pa, Khensur Lekden, and Jeffrey Hopkins, *Compassion in Tibetan Buddhism* (Valois, N.Y.: Gabriel/Snow Lion, 1980); Jeffrey Hopkins, *Cultivating Compassion: A Buddhist Perspective* (New York: Broadway Books, 2001); Sharon Salzberg, *Lovingkindness: The Revolutionary Art of Happiness* (Boston: Shambhala Publications, 1997); Robert A. F. Thurman, *Inner Revolution: Life, Liberty, and the Pursuit of Real Happiness* (New York: Penguin, 1999); Natalie Maxwell, "Great Compassion: The Chief Cause of Bodhisattvas" (Ph.D. diss., University of Wisconsin, 1975); Martin Lowenthal et al., *Opening the Heart of Compassion: Transform Suffering Through Buddhist Psychology and Practice* (New York: Charles Tuttle, 1993).
3. Paul Edward, ed., *The Encyclopedia of Philosophy* (New York: Macmillan, 1967), 8:105–15.
4. Tsong-ka-pa et al., *Compassion*, 89.
5. Santideva, *The Bodhicaryavatara*, trans. Kate Crosby and Andrew Skilton (Oxford: Oxford University Press, 1995), 99.
6. Gampopa, *The Jewel Ornament of Liberation*, trans. Herbert V. Guenther (London: Rider, 1959), 153.
7. Timmen L. Cermak, M.D., *Diagnosing and Treating Co-dependence* (Minneapolis: Johnson Institute Books, 1986), 17.
8. For a discussion of "willfulness" and "willingness," see Gerald G. May, M.D., *Will and Spirit: A Contemplative Psychology* (San Francisco: HarperSanFrancisco, 1982), 5–21.
9. Sigmund Freud, *Civilization and Its Discontents*, trans. Joan Riviere (London: The Hogarth Press Ltd., 1955), 68–93; William B. Parsons, *The Enigma of the Oceanic Feeling: Revisioning the Psychoanalytic Theory of Mysticism* (New York: Oxford University Press, 1999), 39–42; Franz Alexander, "Buddhistic Training as an Artificial Catatonia," in *The Couch and the Tree*, Anthony Molino, ed. (New York: North Point Press, 1998), 12–25.

10. Donald W. Winnicott, *The Maturational Process and the Facilitating Environ-ment: Studies in the Theory of Emotional Development* (New York: Interna-tional Universities Press, 1965), 140–52.

11. Patricia McKinsey Crittenden, "Attachment and Psychopathology," in *At-tachment Theory: Social, Developmental, and Clinical Perspectives,* ed. Susan Goldberg, Roy Muir, and John Kerr (Hillsdale, N.J.: The Analytic Press, 1995), 378. This assessment of affect is drawn from careful examination of how the children smile and the duration of their feelings as well as the observation that their exchange of feelings is atypical, being brief and out of context.

12. Ibid.

13. Ibid.

14. Winnicott, *The Maturational Process,* 145–48.

15. Harry Guntrip, Ph.D., *Schizoid Phenomena, Object Relations and the Self* (New York: International Universities Press, 1969), 243–71; John Bradshaw, *Bradshaw on: Healing the Shame That Binds You* (Deerfield, Fla.: Health Communications, 1998), 86–88.

16. Since the mid-1990s, when I first wrote this chapter, other teachers and ther-apists considering the psychological issues facing meditators have also noted this issue. See, for example, Jack Kornfield, *A Path with a Heart: A Guide Through the Perils and Promises of Spiritual Life* (New York: Bantam, 1993), 215–26; Mark Epstein, M.D., *Thoughts Without a Thinker: Psychotherapy from a Buddhist Perspective* (New York: Basic Books, 1995), 174–78; Jeffrey B. Rubin, *Psychotherapy and Buddhism: Toward an Integration* (New York: Ple-num Press, 1996), 169–86; John Welwood, *Toward a Psychology of Awaken-ing: Buddhism, Psychotherapy, and the Path of Personal and Spiritual Transformation* (Boston: Shambhala Publications, 2000), 209.

17. Ralph Klein, M.D., *Closet Narcissistic Disorder: The Masterson Approach* (New York: Newbridge Communication, 1995), 16.

18. See A. H. Almaas, *The Point of Existence: Transformations of Narcissism in Self-Realization* (Berkeley: Diamond Books, 1996), 151–55, and in particular 296–301.

19. Santideva, *The Bodhicaryavatara,* 97.

20. Gampopa, *The Jewel Ornament,* 154–56.

21. Jamgon Kongtrul, *The Great Path of Awakening: A Commentary on the Ma-hayana Teachings of the Seven Points of Mind Training,* trans. Ken McLeod (Boston: Shambhala Publications, 1987), 14–15.

22. Based on Michael J. Sweet and Craig G. Johnson, "Enhancing Empathy: The Interpersonal Implications of a Buddhist Meditation Technique," *Psycho-therapy* 27, no. 1 (Spring 1990): 19–29. I added "May I be free from all abuse, internal and external" to explicitly address self-hatred, which is so prevalent here. I added "May I be blessed to see the challenge of my adversity" to

provide an alternative perspective for reflecting on trauma, neglect, and other misfortunes. I added "May my life be rich in meaning and centered in purpose," as this seems to explicitly address a core spiritual concern that Westerners bring to their meditation practice.

23. Bhadantacariya Buddhaghosa, *The Path of Purification (Visuddhimagga),* trans. Bhikkhu Nyanamoli (Colombo, Ceylon: A. Semage, 1964), 323.

24. Ibid., 321–40.

25. These include Geshe Sopa, Kensur Ngawang Lekden, Geshe Wangyal, Joshua Cutler, Diana Cutler, Natalie Maxwell, S. N. Goenka, Robert Hover, Geshe Rabten, Jeffrey Hopkins, Khetsun Sangpo Rinpoche, Dudjom Rinpoche, Ga Rinpoche, Lati Rinpoche, Denma Locho Rinpoche, Khensur Yeshe Thubten, Sharon Salzberg, Jacqueline Mandell, Joseph Goldstein, Jack Kornfield, Namkhai Norbu Rinpoche, Tenzin Wangyal Rinpoche, Lama Gonpo Tseden Rinpoche, Lama Tharchin Rinpoche, Geshe Lobzang Tseden, Geshe Thubten, Khenpo Orgyen Trinley, Tulku Thubten, Adzom Paylo Rinpoche, Jetsunma Sherab Chontso, and His Holiness the Dalai Lama.

26. "An Interview with Tibetan scholar Jeffrey Hopkins and an Excerpt from His New Book," *Tricycle* 11, no. 4 (Summer 2001):115.

27. Joseph Berger, "Pepi Deutsch, 101, Holocaust Survivor with Remarkable Tale," *New York Times,* November 8, 1999, A29.

CHAPTER 11

1. Walpola Rahula, *What the Buddha Taught,* 2d ed. (Bedford, England: Gordon Frazer, 1967), 29.

2. Ibid., 30.

3. Piyadassi Thera, *The Buddha's Ancient Path* (Kandy, Ceylon: Buddhist Publication Society, 1974), 66.

4. Ibid., 61.

5. Ibid., 164.

6. John Bowlby, *Attachment and Loss,* volume 1 of *Attachment,* 2d ed. (New York: Basic Books, 1982), 371.

7. The Theravadin author Piyadassi Thera uses *attachment, craving,* and *desire* interchangeably for the technical term *thirst (tanha),* which is the initial condition enumerated when discussing the processes leading to rebirth. Thera, *The Buddha's Ancient Path,* 60. The Theravadin author Walpola Rahula similarly glosses *tanha* as desire and attachment, as seen in the quote at the beginning of this chapter.

8. Bhadantacariya Buddhaghosa, *The Path of Purification (Visuddhimagga),* 2d ed., trans. Bhikkhu Nyanamoli (Colombo, Ceylon: A. Semage, 1964), 529.

9. Rahula, *What the Buddha Taught,* 29–44; Thera, *The Buddha's Ancient Path,* 54–66.

10. Rahula, *What the Buddha Taught,* 51–55.

11. Lama Anagarika Govinda, *The Psychological Attitude of Early Buddhist Philosophy* (London: Rider, 1969), 115–25.

12. On Pure Land Buddhism in China and Japan, see William Theodore de Bary, ed., *The Buddhist Tradition in India, China and Japan* (New York: Modern Library, 1969), 197–204, 314–44. On Nichiren Shoshu and faith in *The Lotus Sutra,* see 345–54.

13. Richard A. Shweder, " 'You're Not Sick, You're Just in Love': Emotion as an Interpretive System," in *The Nature of Emotions: Fundamental Questions,* ed. Paul Ekman and Richard J. Davidson (New York: Oxford University Press, 1994), 41. Shweder identifies three different modes of explanation, or narratives, that people tend to use around the world seemingly to explain inexplicable alterations of mood or fate: ascribing experience to bewitchment, biology or psychology, or karma (i.e., moral or immoral activity).

14. Inge Bretherton, "The Origins of Attachment Theory: John Bowlby and Mary Ainsworth," in *Attachment Theory: Social, Developmental and Clinical Perspectives,* ed. Susan Goldberg, Roy Muir, and John Kerr (Hillsdale, N.J.: Analytic Press, 1995), 53, citing John Bowlby, "The Nature of the Child's Tie to His Mother," *International Journal of Psycho-Analysis* 39 (1958): 1–23.

15. Bretherton, "The Origins," 54–55, citing Bowlby, "Separation Anxiety," *International Journal of Psycho-Analysis* 41 (1959): 1–25.

16. Bretherton, "The Origins," 55–56, citing Bowlby, "Grief and Mourning in Infancy and Early Childhood," *The Psychoanalytic Study of the Child,* volume 15 (New York: International Universities Press, 1960), 3–39.

17. Bretherton, "The Origins," 55.

18. Ibid., 68.

19. Jeremy Holmes, "Something There Is That Doesn't Love a Wall: John Bowlby, Attachment Theory, and Psychoanalysis," in *Attachment Theory,* ed. Goldberg, et al., 19–43.

20. Bretherton, "The Origins," 61.

21. Ibid.

22. Holmes, "Something There Is," 33–34.

23. E. Lynn Schneider, "Attachment Theory and Research: Review of the Literature," *Clinical Social Work Journal* 19, no. 3 (Fall 1991): 256.

24. Holmes, "Something There Is," 35.

25. Ibid.

26. Ibid.

27. Susan Goldberg, "Introduction," in *Attachment Theory,* ed. Goldberg et al., 4–6; Bretherton, "The Origins," 70–71.

28. Bretherton, "The Origins," 69–70.

29. This is a *psycho*-somatic interpretation of how feelings arise that sees emotional and physical causes as influencing later psychological experience, as

opposed to morality or bewitchment. The Buddhist discussion attributes *moral* quality to fixed adhesive states of mind and sees these as bringing forth various feelings in the future. See Richard A. Shweder, "You're Not Sick," 41.

30. Leigh McCullough Vaillant, *Changing Character: Short-Term Anxiety-Regulating Psychotherapy for Restructuring Defenses, Affects, and Attachment* (New York: Basic Books, 1997), 248–50. Vaillant uses the phrase *defensive attachment* for what others have called the ambivalent type.

31. Ibid.

32. On the significance of acceptance, see N. S. Jacobson and A. Christensen, *Integrative Couple Therapy: Promoting Acceptance and Change* (New York: W. W. Norton, 1996).

33. David Schnarch, *Passionate Marriage: Sex, Love, and Intimacy in Emotionally Committed Relationships* (New York: W.W. Norton, 1997), 51–74.

34. Ibid., 74

35. Ibid., 55–74.

36. Ana-Maria Rizzuto, M.D., *The Birth of the Living God: A Psychoanalytic Study* (Chicago: University of Chicago Press, 1979), 54–84.

37. Jeffrey B. Rubin, *Psychotherapy and Buddhism: Toward an Integration* (New York: Plenum Press, 1996), 167.

CHAPTER 12

1. For an extended case study, see Jeffrey B. Rubin, *Psychotherapy and Buddhism: Toward an Integration* (New York: Plenum Press, 1996), 169–86.

2. Arnaud Desjardins, *The Message of the Tibetans* (London: Stuart and Watkins, 1969), 73.

3. Sogyal Rinpoche, *Dzogchen and Padmasambhava* (Berkeley: Rigpa Fellowship, 1989), 81.

4. Kalu Rinpoche, *Luminous Mind: The Way of the Buddha* (Boston: Wisdom Publications, 1997), 97.

5. Lama Anagarika Govinda, *The Psychological Attitude of Early Buddhist Philosophy* (London: Rider, 1961), 107–11.

6. Sogyal Rinpoche, *Dzogchen*, 81.

7. Desjardins, *The Message*, 73.

8. Kalu Rinpoche, *Luminous Mind*, 173.

9. Ibid., 97.

10. Desjardins, *The Message*, 73–74.

11. Sogyal Rinpoche, *Dzogchen*, 81.

12. Namkhai Norbu, *Dzogchen: The Self-Perfected State*, ed. Adriano Clemente, trans. John Shane (London: Arkana, 1989), 23.

13. Kalu Rinpoche, *Luminous Mind*, 173–74.
14. Ibid., 237.
15. Norbu, *Dzogchen*, 32–41; Sogyal Rinpoche, *The Tibetan Book of Living and Dying* (San Francisco: HarperSanFrancisco), 152–53.
16. Khetsun Sangpo Rinbochay, *Tantric Practice in Nying-ma*, trans. and ed. Jeffrey Hopkins, co-ed. Anne C. Klein (Ithaca, N.Y.: Gabriel/Snow Lion, 1982).
17. Ibid., 187.
18. Ibid.
19. Ibid., 190.
20. Ibid.
21. Sogyal Rinpoche, *Dzogchen*, 81.
22. Ibid.; Khetsun Sangpo Rinbochay, *Tantric Practice*, 192–93.
23. Both Tantra and natural liberation teachings have traditionally been kept closely between teacher and student, as they are easily misunderstood. This also prevents the distortion and ultimate devaluation of these special teachings that would almost inevitably result from their overexposure in today's mass media.
24. Personal communication from author-poet Mushim Ikeda-Nash, who heard the joke from "Dangerous" Dan Brewer.
25. Samuel Bercholz and Sherab Chodzin Kohn, eds., *An Introduction to the Buddha and His Teachings* (New York: Barnes and Noble, 1993), 153–56.

CHAPTER 13

1. Khetsun Sangpo Rinbochay, *Tantric Practice in Nying-ma*, trans. and ed. Jeffrey Hopkins, co-ed. Anne C. Klein (Ithaca, N.Y.: Gabriel/Snow Lion, 1982, 1996), 57–63.
2. Sogyal Rinpoche, *The Tibetan Book of Living and Dying* (San Francisco: HarperSanFrancisco, 1992), 21–35.
3. Ibid., 223–43; Khetsun Sangpo Rinbochay, *Tantric Practice*, 57–63.
4. Stephen R. Covey, *The Seven Habits of Highly Effective People: Powerful Lessons in Personal Change* (New York: Simon and Schuster, 1989), 96–182.
5. Khetsun Sangpo Rinbochay, *Tantric Practice*, 204.
6. See a very stimulating distinction of willfulness and willingness in Gerald G. May, M.D. *Will and Spirit: A Contemplative Psychology* (New York: HarperSanFrancisco, 1982), 5–21.
7. Lama Anagarika Govinda, *The Psychological Attitude of Early Buddhism* (London: Rider, 1969), 120–24.
8. In Asia, practitioners will make use of the *moral* authority of the tradition to inspire their practice and suppress pride or haughtiness. In the West, some element of *emotional* understanding brought to bear on obstacles to practice will often be of significant benefit.

9. A. H. Almaas points out that hope, fear, and resentment, which he labels "ego activity," always pull us out of presence. See Almaas, *The Point of Existence* (Berkeley: Diamond Books, 1996), 86.

10. Chögyam Trungpa, *Cutting Through Spiritual Materialism* (Boston: Shambhala Publications, 1987), 64.

11. Ram Dass, *Be Here Now* (New York: Crown, 1971).

12. Almaas, *The Point of Existence*, 258, 564n35.

13. Bhadantacariya Buddhaghosa, *The Path of Purification (Visuddhimagga)*, trans. Bhikkhu Nyanamoli (Colombo, Ceylon: A. Semage, 1964), 141.

CHAPTER 14

1. Anne Hubbell Maiden and Edie Farwell, *The Tibetan Art of Parenting: From Before Conception Through Early Childhood* (Boston: Wisdom Publications, 1997), 109.

2. Richard Rhodes, "A Personal View: What Causes Brutality? The People Nurturing It," *New York Times*, October 16, 1999, A17.

3. Helen Waddell, trans. and ed., *The Desert Fathers* (New York: Vintage, 1998); Anthony Storr, *Solitude: A Return to the Self* (New York: Free Press, 1988).

4. Donald W. Winnicott, *The Maturational Processes and the Facilitating Environment* (New York: International Universities Press, 1965), 29–36, italics in original.

5. Ibid., 34.

6. Ibid.

7. Ibid.

8. Robert D. Stolorow, Bernard Brandchaft, and George Atwood, "Bonds That Shackle, Ties That Free," in *Psychoanalytic Treatment: An Intersubjective Approach*, ed. Robert D. Stolorow, Bernard Brandchaft, and George Atwood (Hillsdale, N.J.: Analytic Press, 1987), 47–65.

9. Walpola Rahula, *What the Buddha Taught*, 2d ed. (Bedford, England: Gordon Fraser, 1967), 92–94.

10. Ibid.

11. Jack Engler, "Therapeutic Aims in Psychotherapy and Meditation: Developmental Stages in the Presentation of Self," *Journal of Transpersonal Psychology* 16, no. 1 (1984): 37; Jeffrey B. Rubin, *Psychotherapy and Buddhism: Toward an Integration* (New York: Plenum Press, 1996), 167, 181.

12. Hazel Rose Markus and Shinobu Kitayama, "The Cultural Construction of Self and Emotion: Implications for Social Behavior," in *Emotion and Culture: Empirical Studies of Mutual Influence*, ed. Shinobu Kitayama and Hazel Rose Markus (Washington, D.C.: American Psychological Association, 1994), 110–11.

13. For two vignettes illustrating some of these issues, see Rubin, *Psychotherapy and Buddhism*, 97–111, 169–86.

14. Both Lama Surya Das and John Welwood identify this type of attempt as "spiritual bypass." Lama Surya Das, *Eight Steps to Enlightenment: Awakening the Buddha Within* (New York: Broadway Books, 1998), 283; John Welwood, *Toward a Psychology of Awakening: Buddhism, Psychotherapy, and the Path of Personal and Spiritual Transformation* (Boston: Shambhala Publications, 2000), 207–13. Jack Engler calls this attempt an " 'end run' around normal tasks of human development." Andrew Cohen, "The 1001 Forms of Self-Grasping: An Interview with Jack Engler," *What Is Enlightenment* 17 (Spring/Summer 2000): 98.

15. Gay Hendricks and Kathlyn Hendricks, *At the Speed of Life: A New Approach to Personal Change Through Body-Centered Therapy* (New York: Bantam, 1993), 150–54.

16. Jack Kornfield, *A Path with Heart: A Guide Through the Perils and Promises of Spiritual Life* (New York: Bantam, 1993), 7.

17. Ferris B. Urbanowski and John J. Miller, "Trauma, Psychotherapy and Meditation," *Journal of Transpersonal Psychology* 28, no. 1 (1996): 31–48.

18. Mark Epstein, M.D., *Thoughts Without a Thinker* (New York: Basic Books, 1995), 159–222; Kornfield, *A Path with Heart*, 244–53; Jack Kornfield, "Even the Best Meditators Have Old Wounds to Heal: Combining Meditation and Psychotherapy," in *Paths Beyond Ego*, ed. Roger Walsh and Francis Vaughan (Los Angeles: Jeremy Tarcher, 1993), 67–69; Rubin, *Psychotherapy and Buddhism*, 97–111, 169–86; Das, *Eight Steps to Enlightenment*, 283; Welwood, *Toward a Psychology*, 192–226.

19. See Kornfield, *A Path with Heart*; Judith Hooper, "Prozac and Enlightened Mind," *Tricycle* 8, no. 4 (Summer 1999): 38.

20. See also Tara Bennett-Goleman, *Emotional Alchemy: How the Mind Can Heal the Heart* (New York: Harmony Books, 2001), 119–257, for how these can be synthesized into "a mindful therapy."

21. Ken Wilber, *Sex, Ecology, Spirituality: The Spirit of Evolution* (Boston: Shambhala Publications, 1995); Donald Rothberg, "Ken Wilber and Contemporary Transpersonal Inquiry: An Introduction to the *ReVision* Conversation," *ReVision* 18, no. 4 (Spring 1996): 2–8; Roger Walsh, "Developmental and Evolutionary Synthesis in the Recent Writings of Ken Wilber," *ReVision* 18, no. 4 (Spring 1996): 9–18; Michael Washburn, "The Pre/Trans Fallacy Reconsidered," *ReVision* 19, no. 1 (Summer 1996): 2–10; Stanislav Grof, "Ken Wilber's Spectrum Psychology. Observations from Clinical Consciousness Research," *ReVision* 19, no. 1 (Summer 1996): 11–24; Donald Rothberg, "How Straight Is the Spiritual Path? Conversations with Buddhist Teachers Joseph Goldstein, Jack Kornfield, and Michele McDonald-Smith," *ReVision* 19, no. 1 (Summer 1996): 25–40.

22. Jack Engler, "Being Somebody and Being Nobody: A Reexamination of the Understanding of Self in Psychoanalysis and Buddhism," in *Psychoanalysis*

and Buddhism: An Unfolding Dialogue, ed. Jeremy D. Safran (Boston: Wisdom Publications, 2003), 35–100.

23. Welwood's *Toward a Psychology of Awakening,* which came out in the final stages of my writing, does not explicitly address Wilber's map and does mention culture as a factor that differentiates Western practitioners from their Asian counterparts. See 202–7.

24. See Engler, "Therapeutic Aims," 42–44, for ways in which the unstructured experiences of meditation may be contraindicated for individuals with weak internal psychological structure. See also Cohen, "The 1001 Forms of Self-Grasping," in which Engler states that in the absence of acute psychological distress, *basic* meditation can be helpful for anyone. In this interview, Engler makes clear that he is concerned that those with weak internal structure might find the *deeper* reaches of insight meditation hard to tolerate. In support of Engler's position on the usefulness of basic meditation skills, see Marsha M. Linehan, *Cognitive-Behavioral Treatment of Borderline Personality Disorder* (New York: Guilford Press, 1993), 144–47, where basic mindfulness is used in conjunction with a variety of cognitive-behavioral techniques in psychoeducational group work with individuals developing more internal psychological structure.

25. Without resorting to cross-cultural consideration, Dan Brown and Jack Engler come to the same conclusion based on the empirical psychological study of meditators. See Daniel P. Brown and Jack Engler, "The Stages of Mindfulness Meditation: A Validation Study," in *Transformations of Consciousness: Conventional and Contemplative Perspectives on Development,* ed. Ken Wilber, et al. (Boston: Shambhala Publications, 1986), 211–12.

26. For examples of such integration, see A. H. Almaas, *The Pearl Beyond Price: Integration of Personality into Being: An Object Relations Approach* (Berkeley: Diamond Books, 1990); Almaas, *The Point of Existence: Transformations of Narcissism in Self-Realization* (Berkeley: Diamond Books, 1996); Epstein, *Thoughts Without a Thinker*; Rubin, *Psychotherapy and Buddhism*; Welwood, *Toward a Psychology of Awakening*; Bennett-Goleman, *Emotional Alchemy*.

27. Suzanne Segal, *Collision with the Infinite* (San Diego: Blue Dove Press, 1996).

28. James Masterson, M.D., *The Real Self: A Developmental, Self, and Object Relations Approach* (New York: Bruner/Mazel, 1985), 115–66.

29. Kornfield, *A Path with Heart,* 244–53; Das, *Eight Steps to Enlightenment,* 283; Pythia Peay, "Interview: At the Cutting Edge of Using Psychological Concepts in Soul Work Is Spiritual Teacher Hameed Ali," *Common Boundary* (November/December 1999): 18–25.

CHAPTER 15

1. Robert A. F. Thurman, *Inquiring Mind* 13, no. 1 (Fall 1996), cover.

2. Harry J. Aponte, "Clinical Applications of Spirituality: Questions and Answers," Texas Association of Marriage and Family Therapy, 2000 Annual Conference, January 29, 2000.

3. I wrote this chapter several years before becoming familiar with the work of A. H. Almaas, who articulates something very similar in his highly developed notion of the Personal Essence, the profound fullness that can emerge during the course of spiritual maturation. A. H. Almaas, *The Pearl Beyond Price: Integration of Personality into Being: An Object Relations Approach* (Berkeley: Diamond Books, 1990), 70–80, 94–98.

4. *Sgom pa ma yin; goms pa yin.*

5. I am indebted to my friend and colleague Mike Mauldin, Ph.D., for alerting me to the distinction between willfulness and willingness as developed in the writing of Gerald G. May, *Will and Spirit* (San Francisco: HarperSan Francisco, 1982), 35–37.

6. Khetsun Sangpo Rinbochay, *Tantric Practice in Nying-ma*, trans. and ed. by Jeffrey Hopkins, co-ed. Anne C. Klein (Ithaca, N.Y.: Gabriel/Snow Lion, 1982), 40.

7. *La* placed after a person's name in Tibetan is a common mark of respect and endearment.

8. Santideva, *The Bodhicaryavatara*, trans. Kate Crosby and Andrew Skilton (Oxford: Oxford University Press, 1995), 99.

9. Jay R. Greenberg and Stephen A. Mitchell, *Object Relations in Psychoanalytic Theory* (Cambridge, Mass.: Harvard University Press, 1983), 21–49.

10. John Bowlby, *Attachment and Loss*, volume 1 of *Attachment*, 2d ed. (New York: Basic Books, 1982).

11. Greenberg and Mitchell, *Object Relations*, 119–230.

12. Lama Anagarika Govinda, *The Psychological Attitude of Early Buddhism* (London: Rider, 1969), 99–111; Harvey Aronson, *Love and Sympathy in Theravada Buddhism* (Delhi: Motilal Banarsidass, 1980), 39–59; Kalu Rinpoche, *Luminous Mind: The Way of the Buddha* (Boston: Wisdom Publications, 1997), 19, 27, 67, 209. For a spiritual psychology that is nonsectarian and grounded in ego psychology and object relations, yet accounts for spiritual realization through the manifestation of Being—the fundamental nature of reality—rather than some derivative of need or instinct, see Almaas, *The Pearl*, 91–161, 348–53, and *Spacecruiser Inquiry: True Guidance for the Inner Journey* (Boston: Shambhala Publications, 2002), 249–429.

13. Anne C. Klein, *Meeting the Great Bliss Queen: Buddhists, Feminists and the Art of the Self* (Boston: Beacon Press, 1994), 89–102, suggests that Buddhist teachings on caring may add to the feminist reconsideration of autonomy-oriented psychology. Therapists Elizabeth Young Bruehl and Faith Bethelard use Japanese material on *amae*, the child's relationship to the mother, to similarly try to expand the developmental foci of psychoanalytic thought. See Stephen Wilson, "Talking About Wu Wei," review of *Cherishment: A Psychology of the Heart*, by Elizabeth Young Bruehl and Faith Bethelard, *New York Times*, March 26, 2000. On *amae*, see also David C. Bell and Allen J. Richard, "Caregiving: The Forgotten Element in Attachment," *Psychological Inquiry* 11, no. 2 (2000): 69–83.

14. Michele Martin, personal communication, April 1998.

15. For a discussion of the issues surrounding the transmission and practice of the various forms of Asian Buddhism in the United States, see Charles S. Prebish and Kenneth K. Tanaka, eds., *The Faces of Buddhism in America* (Berkeley: University of California Press, 1998). Another valuable resource is Don Morreale, *The Complete Guide to Buddhist America* (Boston: Shambhala Publications, 1998).

16. Émile Zola, *My Hatreds/Mes Haines,* trans. Palomba Paves-Yashinsky and Jack Yashinsky, (1866; trans., Lewiston, N.Y.: The Edwin Mellen Press, 1991). Quoted in Norbert Guterman, *A Book of French Quotations,* 1st ed. (Garden City, N.Y.: Doubleday, 1963). The U.S. Library of Congress assisted in finding the source of this quote.

17. For a fine discussion of integrating small group relationship building, meditation, and social activism, see Jeanne Achterberg and Donald Rothberg, "Relationship as Spiritual Practice," *ReVision* 19, no. 2 (Fall 1996): 8–9.

18. On the enhancement of meaning through relationship, see Kathy Weingarten, "The Discourses of Intimacy: Adding a Social Constructionist and Feminist View," *Family Process* 30, no. 3 (September 1991): 285–305.

19. Harville Hendrix, Ph.D, *Getting the Love You Want: A Guide for Couples* (New York: Harper and Row, 1990); Wade Luquet, *Short-Term Couples Therapy: The Imago Model in Action* (New York: Bruner/Mazel, 1996).

20. Martin Buber, *I and Thou,* 2d ed., trans. Ronald G. Smith (New York: Scribner, 1958).

21. Jack Zimmerman in collaboration with Virginia Coyle, *The Way of Council* (Las Vegas: Bramble Books, 1996).

22. Gregory Kramer, *Meditating Together, Speaking from Silence: Experiencing the Dharma in Dialogue* (Portland, Ore.: Metta Foundation, 1999).

23. We also make use of repeating questions and modes of inquiry inspired by the work of A. H. Almaas. See Tony Schwartz, "Uncovering the Essential Self," *New Age Journal* (May/June 1995): 67–134; Byron Brown, *Soul Without Shame: A Guide to Liberating Yourself from the Judge Within* (Boston: Shambhala Publications, 1999); Almaas, *Spacecruiser Inquiry.*

24. Zimmerman, *The Way of Council,* 28–37. The four guidelines for a circle are to talk and listen from the heart, to be brief, and to speak from within the moment.

Index